CONTENTS

FROM THE EDITOR

The title of the 2007 Presidential Forum, "The Humanities at Work in the World," would be equally apt for *Profession 2008*. Many of the contributions gathered here demonstrate how the study of language and literature intersects with the larger social and cultural spheres in which we live. The structures and practices of the academy, such as the organization of departments or the procedures for tenure and promotion, may also be profitably viewed by going beyond the inside/outside dichotomy and recognizing that the humanities always function in relation to the world and not, despite the myth of the ivory tower, in isolation from it. In choosing the theme for his Presidential Forum, Michael Holquist endeavored to show how the humanities can be put to work on topics relevant to the lives of all kinds of people in all kinds of situations. As you will see from his introduction to the various essays presented at his forum, he brought together a range of humanities theorist-practitioners whose work changes our understanding of what the humanities are good for. Holquist's eloquent summary of the new learning that took place as a result of his forum needs no supplement from me: I encourage you to follow his invitation and read for yourselves the compelling narratives written by Marjorie Garber, David Marshall, Wendy Steiner, Peter Brooks, Robert F. Barsky, and James V. Wertsch.

Readers will encounter a wide variety of engaging issues in the essays gathered under the rubric "Reports from the Field." Nancy K. Miller reflects on having come across a fictionalized composite of herself and Carolyn Heilbrun in the story of a former student published in the *New Yorker.* Her experience reads like, well, a great story. Analyzing her response to Tama Janowitz's piece allows Miller to trace the genealogies of academic feminism, to comment on how that community handles differences and disagreements, and finally to face the loneliness and discover the potential of what she calls the "liminal classroom." In writing about her experiences, Miller deals courageously with disturbing conflicts and resists being defensive—not an easy thing to do under the circumstances.

1

The next two articles provide an interesting contrast to the feminist classroom. Peter Kerry Powers addresses religion in the classroom and examines academic discomfort where faith is concerned. He argues that religious beliefs should be understood in terms of "cultural formations out of which students think and act and through which they form a sense of themselves as human agents." Geoffrey Galt Harpham describes his experience teaching *Heart of Darkness* at the Air Force Academy to look at the classroom dynamics involved in "reading Conrad with America's soldiers." He argues that the hard training required in the military of those whose service is, in Marlow's words, "a choice of nightmares" can be complemented by the humanistic cultivation of a habit of reflection and a consideration of the ethical and historical contexts in which literary characters function.

All teachers have heard—if not said—how underprepared first-year students are at everything having to do with composition and reasoning, including grammar, spelling, and punctuation. In his article on the rhetoric of complaint against student writing, David Gold traces this tradition and concludes that we do ourselves a disservice as a profession when we make public negative views on student writing. What is worse, we do our students harm when we fail to meet them where they are in terms of academic development and to teach them what they need to know.

"Cultural studies was a hitchhiker's dream," William B. Warner and Clifford Siskin write about the fellow travelers who tried to escape academic literary studies several decades ago. Warner and Siskin give a "brief and selective account" of how cultural studies emerged and articulate the problems that have befallen the field that promised liberation. They ask about the relation of cultural studies to the disciplines from which it emerged and explore a paradox: *culture* understood capaciously takes us away from our disciplinary home, but it returns us there when understood in its specialized meaning. The challenge for English departments now, they assert, is to retool so that both established means of mediation and new approaches can take hold. To save what is good about cultural studies may mean stopping to reclaim the value that emerged in the first place.

Rita Felski discusses courses in critical method in her contribution to *Profession 2008*. She explains why they not only give graduate students a contemporary perspective on intellectual debates but also make them aware of the interpretive choices they will face in their own critical projects. By stressing method over theory, Felski gives her students a knowledge of how "the tacit protocols and defining assumptions of literary studies" play themselves out in the work we scholars and teachers do. Her article is also a rich guide for those who seek to develop or refine courses in critical method.

"Do we teach disciplines or do we teach students?" is Marshall Gregory's framing question in an exploration of how teaching works. Knowing a discipline well does not necessarily mean that one knows how to teach it, and Gregory stresses that we must think about communicating knowledge in such a way that it is absorbed. That is, students who are taught well profit from the disciplinary practices we impart even when they forget the information or content. Beginning professors, however, get caught up in the need to demonstrate mastery over content and therefore have difficulty focusing on student ethos. Gregory mounts a vigorous argument for teaching students so they can "acquire such capacities of mind and heart as will assist them in living lives that are autonomous, personally enriched, socially responsible, intellectually perspicuous, and morally defensible." I find this challenge humbling and inspiring, and I also wonder how many professors of languages and literatures can see themselves in that role.

Linguistic human rights generate a great deal of discussion in the world today, and Lucinda Martin gives her view on the topic in an examination of the German-only rule that was instituted at the Hoover School in Berlin. The controversy surrounding the Hoover School fits into the debate in Germany about the role of minorities. Martin contrasts *Multikultur* and *Leitkultur*, the models for understanding culture in Germany, and she situates them in the tradition of language policy in Old Europe. She shows how "Germany has used language as a tool to keep foreigners from competing" and, at the same time, "condemn[s] itself to the burden of parallel societies." Whether or not the particular circumstances of Germany interest you, this article can shed light on similar conflicts with which you may be familiar—starting, of course, with questions of immigration and language in North America.

Doug Steward looks at academic freedom in the humanities in "Taking Liberties." He begins by examining the specious argument that the faculty has surrendered its right to academic freedom because of its engagement in politics in the classroom, its adoption of low standards, and its moral relativism. He analyzes the contemporary consumerist view of higher education and confronts the activism of groups such as the American Council of Trustees and Alumni who attempt to diminish academic freedom and to discredit teachers as authorities in the classroom. Steward contemplates the paradoxes, contradictions, and ironies involved in the history and present of academic freedom, and he rightly stresses that current conditions (overuse of adjunct labor, privatization of higher education, post-9/11 surveillance) have made the academy vulnerable to attacks on it. His conclusion is worth quoting in full: "If academic freedom protects the right to the pursuit of truth and knowledge, it is in the humanities that we learn what we are pursuing. And to the extent that language is the ground of the human figure, the field of language and literature is the epicenter of the humanities." In other words, if we in the fields of English and other languages don't think, write, and teach about academic freedom, who will?

Profession 2007 contained the report of the MLA Task Force on Evaluating Scholarship for Tenure and Promotion, along with nine articles that either commented on the report or presented material adjunctive to it. The task force report continues to generate much discussion in the scholarly community, and I am pleased to present four more responses in *Profession 2008*. Michael Bernard-Donals argues in "It's Not about the Book" that the primary issue the task force sought to address is "the nature of faculty scholarly work and the obstacles to evaluating that work fairly." From the perspective of one who has chaired a large English department and who has been a writing program administrator, he discusses issues that the report does not cover adequately, such as evaluating work that does not conform to traditional or rigid notions of scholarship and service—especially in the fields of composition and rhetoric, applied linguistics, and creative writing—and recognizing the role that disciplinary diversity plays in tenure and promotion. Dana Ringuette finds that the task force's recommendation on the optimal balance of publication, teaching, and service is a problematic one. We "put our profession at risk," he says, "by not foregrounding more fully . . . our job as primarily teachers and educators." In sum, the task force report stresses the importance of teaching *as* scholarship, but it is less vocal about the key role of teaching *tout court*. Ringuette offers compelling arguments for a reexamination of our role as educators.

W. B. Carnochan's response to the report contests the crisis rhetoric surrounding "the tyranny of the monograph" (Lindsay Waters's term) in relation to tenure. Citing the lack of hard evidence that the monograph is in decline and speculating on the future of the book as an electronic publication, Carnochan encourages the profession to reexamine the entire system in which the value of the monograph has been established. Another issue that the task force raised is evaluating scholarship produced in collaboration. Lara Lomicka Anderson and Gillian Lord offer guidelines to departments to help them understand the nature of coauthorship and perform appropriate assessments for tenure and promotion. Anderson and Lord tabulate the number of coauthored articles per year in a variety of journals, then explain how jointly produced work can give scholars easier entry into a particular field and help develop the ability to work well with others. They also explore the potential pitfalls of collaboration. I hope these four articles on the task force report will stimulate further discussion in our academic community, and I encourage you to think of *Profession* as an outlet for your work on this topic.

Another item from *Profession 2007* that has generated a great deal of attention is the report of the MLA Ad Hoc Committee on Foreign Languages. Since the release of the report, several campuses have staged conferences to discuss its recommendations, and numerous panels have taken place at academic meetings. This year we present four commentaries on the foreign language report, two of which come from colleagues who served on the committee (Karin C. Ryding and Michael E. Geisler). The study of Arabic has risen dramatically in the past six years, as has interest in other less commonly taught languages. Ryding discusses the shortage of trained teachers of Arabic at a time when they are most needed. She also explores the reverse privileging of the written language in traditional Arabic classrooms and reminds us that today's learners need exposure to the spoken Arabic vernaculars. For students to grasp the world of Arab cultural practices, they must have access to a network of signifying practices: "written, drawn, built, chanted, broadcast, spoken, woven, carved, designed, sung."

Nicoletta Pireddu exposes some of the contradictions she finds in the committee report when it comes to the role of literary study in languages other than English. She worries that the foreign language major, by adding a dash of history, politics, geography, and art to some literature, might devolve into a bad copy of an area studies program that sacrifices "coherence and depth in the name of an illusory extensiveness." Pireddu discusses some imaginative ways to preserve the centrality of literary studies while moving in the general directions the report suggests. Geisler, like other members of the committee on foreign languages, has been participating in discussions of the report on campuses and at conferences throughout the United States and Canada. He outlines the arguments against focusing a foreign language curriculum exclusively on texts drawn from high literary culture and provides examples of what an integrated curricular approach might accomplish. He advocates adopting a "dynamic archive of seminal cultural texts" and urges us to teach our students the central cultural metaphors generated by the specific historical and discursive traditions of our fields. Pireddu and Geisler stand in distinct contrast to each other and provide much to think about.

The last article in this section was coauthored by five language program directors, and it offers a much-needed perspective on the role that these professionals should play whenever we speak of changing the way languages are taught in the academy. The authors contest the view of the two-tiered system for language teaching that the report presents and offer evidence of more progressive models in place at many institutions. The central challenge is "how to envision radically diverse curricula that are theoretically and empirically sound and that help learners achieve advanced competencies." The authors conclude with five recommendations designed to help language and literature specialists see how collaboration can result in programs that are stronger and that take advantage of what each of us brings to the table. "The Language Program Director in Curricular and Departmental Reform" can be read as a challenging appendix to "Foreign Languages and Higher Education: New Structures for a Changed World." As all four responses show, we still need to improve how languages are taught at all levels on our campuses today.

Profession 2008 concludes with a forum section that contains two comments on articles published in last year's issue and one author response. I invite you to continue the tradition of addressing issues that concern you by sending letters to the forum and original articles for consideration for *Profession 2009.* The members of the *Profession* Advisory Committee—Stephen A. Fredman, Donald Haase, and Amy Kaminsky—reviewed the submissions we received this year and provided helpful comments, for which I thank them. I am also grateful to my colleagues David Laurence and Nelly Furman for their advice on the final selection, and to Carol Zuses, the managing editor. We hope to receive submissions on the following issues: academic freedom in the twenty-first century, new approaches to the deterioration of full-time faculty positions, and outcomes assessment in language and literature. As I write these words, the world economy is in crisis and the United States presidential election approaches. The educational landscape will look markedly different over the next decades. What do we need to know now so we can face the future? What are the essential questions for this moment in our professional history? Let us think together so we may act in the best interests of our students, ourselves, and our society. These times demand nothing less of us.

Rosemary G. Feal

Traffic in the Humanities

MICHAEL HOLQUIST

Caught up in the swirling ideas and people at an MLA convention, I have sometimes experienced an irresistible sense of carnival in the air, especially when catching a hurried drink between sessions at one of the crowded hotel bars. And of course "the MLA" (as the convention is frequently called, sometimes without even the article) in many ways is a carnival—or at least is carnivalesque. Not only because of its revelry, or the intellectual inversions of authority found in many of the papers, but also because the convention, like carnival, is, underneath its surface chaos, highly structured. I was reminded again of the convention's ritualized aspect while organizing the 2007 Presidential Forum. As part of that preparation, I did a brief review of previous forums. Of course the speakers are different each year, except for their uniform eminence. But the structure of the forum itself has remained pretty much the same for several years now. Even more uniform is the underlying theme pursued each year: since the early 1990s, past presidents, for all their professional and personal differences, have in one way or another almost all organized the forum as a defense of the humanities.

The year 2007 was, in this sense at least, no different. I suspect we are all not only responding to current events but also harking back to 1991. That was the year when the MLA Executive Council raised questions about a particular appointment to the NEH board, arousing a storm of attacks against the MLA in the media that were of a totally unexpected

The author is professor emeritus of Slavic and comparative literature at Yale University, a senior fellow at Columbia University, and a past president of the Modern Language Association.

violence. Some of this storm could be traced to the efforts of Lynne Cheney, the NEH chairman then. But the breadth and harshness of the public response could not all be explained by the machinations of any single individual. A previously unsuspected hostility to our profession came as a shock to many.

I believe that the attack was a traumatic event for the profession, one from which we are still recovering. In any case, something like this explanation helps one understand the dedication of so many subsequent Presidential Forums to the task of defending not just literature and language acquisition but the humanities at large.

The 2007 forum, as I've said, is very much in this tradition. But an attempt was made to complicate the debate by exploring some of the different meanings *the humanities* has at present, within and without the university community. This goal mandated an unusually numerous and heterogeneous panel of participants, some credentialed by the academy and others by the world outside the university. In addition to the usual distinguished cast of professors, an equally eminent contingent of nonacademics—made up of a working journalist, an activist public intellectual from Mexico, and a distinguished representative from the world of high finance—were invited to Chicago.

What such a heteroglot mix makes immediately clear is that the ivory tower is really a co-op: the differences between inside and outside the academy are much less hard-edged than we often assume and—in surprising ways—sometimes nonexistent. Those from outside what we consider the walls of our professional domain made learned (and unexpectedly novel) arguments for the importance of language and literature. And speakers who currently define what is best in the university highlighted the permeability of borders by demonstrating how their academic skills could be put to work on topics "ripped from today's headlines."

Marjorie Garber, David Marshall, Wendy Steiner, and Peter Brooks explicitly address in their essays the interpenetration of academy and world. Garber weaves an avian argument of great subtlety, but her point could not be more blunt: no need to proselytize, the humanities are already in the world—and vice versa. Marshall, from his perspective as a dean of arts and sciences, makes the important point that not all our problems are to be found outside the academy. We must demonstrate our value to our colleagues in other departments, especially in the sciences. Work done in medical schools and in physics and biology departments has always been expensive, of course. However, we have recently witnessed an explosion of new and even more staggering investment in such research. Columbia, Harvard, and Yale—and there are many other examples—are about to open whole new campuses dedicated to the sciences. The staggering cost of such development makes humanist competition for funds more difficult—and more necessary—than ever. The 2007 forum is an attempt to demonstrate from a variety of perspectives the excitement and, yes, the necessity of what we do.

With her animated opera, Steiner provides not only a moment of aesthetic pleasure but also a lively show-and-tell demonstration of how Chaucer (and professors) can leap institutional and disciplinary barriers in a single bound. Brooks demonstrates how multidirectional traffic can be between even so abstruse a technology as deconstruction and such depressingly immediate problems as the Bush administration's policy on torture. Robert Barsky's passionate voice has won its authority from his activity in Canada's immigration courts and on death row in the Tennessee state prison system. James Wertsch's talk makes evident the utility of literary methodology in understanding overtly political strife between nations. His concept of the narrative template as a basis for explaining the primordial power of collective memory in shaping conflict between Russians and Estonians is one of the clearest arguments I know for the real-life significance of methods that have their origin in the study of literature.

Because I sought to acknowledge some ways in which the world finds its place in the academic humanities as well as demonstrate the effect of the work we do in the world, the 2007 forum was larger than usual. Convention attendees also heard the considerable contributions made to our discussions over two days by Alex Beam, Carlos Monsiváis, Bruce Robbins, and Richard Franke (who was the recipient of the 2007 Phyllis Franklin Award for Public Advocacy of the Humanities). Beam, a columnist for the *Boston Globe*, is currently working on a book about great-books courses. He provided historical perspective on past experiments (at the University of Chicago, Columbia, St. John's, and other places) and speculated on the future of such courses. Monsiváis is perhaps Mexico's leading intellectual. Citing Dostoevsky, he reminded the audience that traffic between the world of art and the world of politics has always been in both directions. Robbins challenged his listeners to think of their teaching and publishing as worldly activities undergoing change in a period of radical institutional and political upheaval. And Franke made a moving defense for liberal arts education. He drew on his experience as the founder of the immensely popular Chicago Humanities Festival to make the point that training in the liberal arts is training for life across the boards. His talk made clear why he was so inevitable a choice for the Phyllis Franklin Award.

No single person or organization can speak for the complex of practices, traditions, and enjoyments that in our poverty we lump together as the humanities. But over the years the MLA and its individual members have been among the most eloquent and effective advocates. I'd like to take this opportunity to thank my colleagues who participated in the 2007 forum for so brilliantly manifesting the dignity, fun, and ineluctability of traffic in the humanities.

Good to Think With

MARJORIE GARBER

The topic of the Presidential Forum for 2007, "The Humanities at Work in the World," led me to reflect on a number of moments in my own career, as well as on a set of literary texts that engage—and provoke—thought on this question. Before I turn directly to the implications of my title, "Good to Think With," I will frame my argument with a personal anecdote and then with a fairy tale. It will be clear, I believe, that these two narratives are versions of the same story.

When I was in college, I was seized with the idea that I needed to be doing something more important and meaningful than studying English literature. It was the sixties, after all. So I looked up the address of an agency in New York City that arranged for American students to emigrate and do work in another country. I was full of idealism, optimism, energy. I arrived for my appointment and sat across the desk from a woman who was organizing such arrangements. My idea was to get closer to the soil, perhaps, and to the people. So I burst out with my ideas about farming, building, and clearing the land. "Do you have any experience with these things?" she asked. (At this distance I can't recall whether she asked gently or pointedly—but in any case I began, dimly, to get the point.) "Have you ever worked on a farm or built a house?" No, I confessed. Not yet. But I could learn. "What *do* you know how to do?" she asked. "I study English literature," I said, rather haltingly. Poetry and novels and plays. But I could

The author is William R. Kenan, Jr., Professor of English and of Visual and Environmental Studies and director of the Carpenter Center for the Visual Arts at Harvard University. A version of this paper was presented at the 2007 MLA convention in Chicago.

learn to do useful work, I was sure of it . . . I could contribute to the work of the world. "We need English teachers," she said.

All the way home on the train I thought about this advice, which was surely both gentle *and* pointed. I had assumed that my liberal arts training, my interest in literature, my interest, even, in criticism and scholarship were things to be got past on my way to entering the world.

I wanted to work in the world, to do good in the world, to make the world a better place. My interest in, penchant for, obsession with the humanities and arts seemed to me, at the time, a self-indulgence. What I learned from this experience was that the humanities were my work and that they were already in the world.

That was the anecdote. Here is a fairy tale.

In *The Blue Bird*, a symbolist play by the Belgian writer Maurice Maeterlinck, two children search the world for a special bluebird. The brother and sister, who live in a woodcutter's cottage, have been told that Father Christmas will not come to them this year. On Christmas Eve, as they are peering out the window, watching the rich children next door receive toys, cakes, and fruit, a fairy appears to them in the form of an old woman of the neighborhood and demands that they find the bluebird, which she needs to cure her little girl, who is very ill.

The children set out on their journey. In the space of what they think is a year but what turns out to be a long Christmas night's dream, they travel to the Land of Memory, the Palace of Night, the Graveyard, and the Kingdom of the Future, but although they often glimpse a bluebird, they can never quite capture it. "The one of the Land of Memory turned quite black," laments the young boy, "the one of the Future turned quite pink, the Night's are dead and I could not catch the one in the Forest. . . . Is it my fault if they change color, or die, or escape? . . . Will the Fairy be angry and what will she say?" "We have done what we could," is the answer. "It seems likely that the Blue Bird does not exist or that he changes color when he is caged."

Returning home—or, depending on your reading, awakening from their dream on Christmas morning—they discover that their pet turtledove, a caged bird they have undervalued and overlooked, is in fact colored blue: "Hullo, why it's blue! . . . it's much bluer than when I went away! . . . Why, that's the blue bird we were looking for! . . . We went so far and it was here all the time!"

Our modern cliché about the bluebird of happiness comes from this play, which was first performed in 1908 at Constantin Stanislavsky's Moscow Art Theatre. As you can see, it is a close relation of J. M. Barrie's *Peter*

Pan, written at about the same date. (Barrie's first book about Peter was in fact called *The Little White Bird*.) But what I want to underscore here is that the children of this story needed to travel around the world, and to the worlds of the past and the future, in order to recognize that what they had been seeking was at home with them all along. They had neglected or failed to value it, because it seemed so ordinary.

Their bluebird, when they finally put it to work in the world, giving it to the neighbor's child and curing the child's illness, ultimately escapes. At the end of the play, one of the children addresses the audience, charging them with the task of finding and returning the bluebird: "If any of you should find it, would you be so very kind as to give it back to us? . . . We need it for our happiness, later on. . . ." Curtain.

Whether this play is a parable about empty signifiers, the return of the repressed, the unattainability of desire, or the spirit of Christmas depends on the reader, the context, and the performance. The very phrase "bluebird of happiness," which does not appear in the play, seems to foreclose a decision; the search remains open. But let me draw our attention first to the neglect and then to the escape of the bird. Where has it been all along? Where does it go? Which is the home, and which is the world?

In 1962, the French structural anthropologist Claude Lévi-Strauss coined the phrase "good to think with." It has been so successful that it is now, arguably, almost meaningless, something between a tautology and a cliché. Among the concepts, objects, theories, practices, and organs that have been recently declared by scholars to be "good to think with" are feminism, science, architecture, taxes, the body, food, hypertext, networks, the liberal tradition, capitalism, and the brain.

Scholars and theorists are drawn to this phrase, I think, because it has a certain validating power: it explains, or purports to explain, why we do what we do and why it matters. It seems, that is to say, to explain the work of the humanities to the world. As if the humanities were not in the world, not the same as the world, not the language of the world.

No phrase I know of has been more consistently footnoted to a list of secondary sources. That it's not only attributed to Lévi-Strauss but also often as quoted by someone else is a sign not of its elusive nature but rather of its ubiquity.

The actual citation is in Lévi-Strauss's book *Totemism*, first published in French in 1962 and translated into English the following year. The context is a discussion of what would come to be a central practice of structuralism: "How to make opposition, instead of being an obstacle to integration, serve rather to produce it" (89).

This formulation is the primal scene of the binary opposition. It comes to Lévi-Strauss as he is reading the work of another anthropologist, A. R. Radcliffe-Brown, on the persistently interesting and puzzling question of the totem. The key examples from Radcliffe-Brown are two bird clans, the eagle hawks and the crows. Lévi-Strauss claims that "the animals in totemism" serve an intellectual and speculative function. They are not, or not only, objects of symbolism or identification, much less objects of culinary desire, but part of a structure of thinking. Here is the passage, in Rodney Needham's translation:

> The animals in totemism cease to be solely or principally creatures which are feared, admired, or envied; their perceptible reality permits the embodiment of ideas and relations conceived by speculative thought on the basis of empirical observations. We can understand, too, that natural species are chosen not because they are "good to eat" but because they are "good to think." (*Totemism* 89)[1]

Bonnes à penser. Animals, Lévi-Strauss said, are "good to think [with]." This phrase is not really a maxim about animals (or science, or feminism, or hypertext, or any of the other things critics have said are "good to think with")—it is not about the referent, the thing in the world; it is a celebration and validation of thinking. Thinking may have its initial impetus in "empirical observations," those vital signs of the social sciences, the physical sciences, or the life sciences, but its payoff is in speculation, which is then reattached to, embodied in, or reembodied in the objects, concepts, or beings that gave rise to it. Now the empirical (or edible) facts reemerge as figures of speech or, more precisely, figures of thought: metaphors, metonyms, personifications, allegories, categories, oppositions, analogies—the work product of the humanities.

For Lévi-Strauss, this opposition was central, because it allowed one to categorize and interpret elements of culture. The next move, which has proved equally important to theoretical work in the humanities, is to question the boundary between the terms of the opposition, and to use that questioning as a way of thinking beyond an impasse.

What impasse can Lévi-Strauss's opposition ("not because they are 'good to eat' but because they are 'good to think'") help us think beyond? In our case, it is the demand that the humanities be useful, that they demonstrate their utility either in terms of dollars and cents or of power, be it ethical, moral, religious, therapeutic, or ameliorative. This is one meaning, though not the only meaning, of "the humanities at work in the world."

Are the humanities "good to eat" or "good to think with"? Before we can refuse this opposition, we should at least examine it.

"Some books are to be tasted, others to be swallowed, and some few to be chewed and digested," Francis Bacon famously wrote. His explanation of this aphoristic statement is less often cited, though it follows immediately: "that is, some books are to be read only in parts, others to be read, but not curiously, and some few to be read wholly, and with diligence and attention." Bacon was a courtier, a politician, a diplomat, a philosopher, and a scientist before that word was invented. His notion of a digested book is the opposite, we might suppose, of the excerpted snippets in a modern-day digest—not only the *Readers' Digest*, still the best-selling consumer magazine in the United States, but also the executive summary, talking points, and *PowerPoint* presentations of today. Indeed the most modern sentiment in Bacon's essay ("Of Studies") may be his acknowledgment that "some books also may be read by deputy, and excerpts made of them by others."

For another exploration of whether the humanities are "good to eat" or "good to think with," we might turn to a poem by Ben Jonson—where we will encounter another set of totemic birds.

Jonson's poem "Inviting a Friend to Supper," written in imitation of a poem by Martial, makes it pretty clear that the main focus of the meal will be poetry and conversation. There might be a "short-legged hen / If we can get her," but the enjambment makes it less than certain, and the grand bill of fare is full of ifs:

> . . . though fowl, now, be scarce, yet there are clerks,
> The sky not falling, think we may have larks.
> I'll tell you of more, and lie, so you will come:
> Of partridge, pheasant, woodcock, of which some
> May yet be there, and godwit if we can:
> Knat, rail, and ruff too. Howsoe'er, my man
> Shall read a piece of Vergil, Tacitus,
> Livy, or some better book to us,
> Of which we'll speak our minds, amidst our meat;
> And I'll profess no verses to repeat.

Godwit, knat, rail, and ruff are all birds. Even the wine to be served at this supper is bird-themed—a "pure cup of rich canary" (the sweet wine of the Canary Islands; though the etymology of *canary* refers to dogs, not birds: the Canaries were the "Isle of Dogs"). But notice that these edible birds are all supposititious meals, not real ones ("a hen if we can get her"; "godwit if we can"; "we may have larks"; "some may yet be there"; "I'll . . . lie, so you will come"). The only certain nourishment will come from books: Vergil, Tacitus, Livy. Good to think with. This is a banquet, or symposium, for two (plus a literate servant), but the avian fare is elusive. The godwit of happiness—or the partridge, pheasant, woodcock, or lark—may or may not be captured. (The woodcock was proverbial for its stupidity and easy to catch. The godwit, wrote Sir Thomas Browne, was the "daintiest dish in England" [382].) But what is promised on this occasion is history, poetry, the classics—the humanities. A better kind of sustenance.

That was then; this is now. Are the humanities good to eat or good to think with? The concern today would seem to be that there is not enough of either kind of nourishment in what are sometimes now called, in a kind of back-formation, "the academic humanities," a term presumably coined to distinguish them from the applied humanities, the public humanities, and the national humanities initiatives—all of which are more evidently examples of "the humanities at work in the world." Let me briefly describe each of these, since each in a different way interrogates the relation between the humanities and the world, and each offers an opportunity and a challenge for us to rethink our teaching, scholarship, and training.

1. The concept of the applied humanities already exists in academic institutions, and indeed such fields are flourishing: medical humanities, humanities and justice (or justice studies), law and literature, journalism and media studies, applied ethics. They seem to be both good to eat and good to think with, promising a material payoff: a changed policy, an improved world, or a well-paying and influential job. Universities are scrambling to add such programs, since there is great student demand. But there are problems, as well as opportunities, here—not the least of which is the idea that humanistic works can be reduced to case studies of human decision making and human character. Part of the question is who is applying the humanities to issues of medicine, law, war, ethics, leadership, or management. Often the instructors come from the other or partner discipline—law, business, medicine, public service. Increasingly applied humanities programs are also being established outside universities, in independent leadership institutes and executive training sessions like Carol Adelman and Ken Adelman's Movers and Shakespeares, "based on the insights and wisdom of the Bard" (*Movers*). (Is Falstaff a good decision maker? What makes Henry V an effective corporate leader?) It's one of the more intriguing paradoxes of our time that executives pay big bucks to attend sessions on topics they didn't think relevant in college. And it's simply not the case that college teachers in the humanities are theory heads or stuck-in-the-archives historicists who don't know how to bring texts alive in the classroom. This problem is cultural, not pedagogical.

2. Humanities outreach programs for the public are sometimes run by colleges and universities and feature lectures and symposia as well as arts

festivals, performances, and postperformance conversations—events designed to bring together what was once called, rather quaintly, "town and gown." The intended audiences are not college students but people "in the world" (children, working adults, alumni, retired persons). There are political, public-relations, and even financial benefits to the universities in presenting or partnering with such programs. But the presenters are often tenured faculty members and emeriti. Here is a situation in which younger, emerging scholars, assistant professors and graduate students, might be given an opportunity to address a wider audience. As every writer knows, explaining a current research or writing project to an interested group of nonspecialists can be extraordinarily clarifying, about both the goals and the stakes of such research.

3. The National Endowment for the Arts sponsors initiatives like Shakespeare in American Communities, Poetry Out Loud, and The Big Read—this last is a program that describes itself as "designed to revitalize the role of literature in American popular culture and bring the transformative power of literature into the lives of its citizens" (*National Initiatives*). I would like to know how many MLA members, and indeed how many college and university teachers of literature, have been asked to contribute to these projects and aid in their design. "American communities," "American popular culture," and American "citizens" are all located inside as well as outside universities and colleges. What we do, what we have chosen to do, what we train ourselves and our graduate students to do is precisely to revitalize the role of literature in our classes and our writing and to address—or question—ideas like "the transformative power of literature." (I can't resist pointing out here that one of the first books showcased in The Big Read is Harper Lee's *To Kill a Mockingbird*. Good to eat or good to think with?)

National prescriptions for the humanities and the arts do not always, I believe, take into serious-enough consideration the commitment of college and university teachers, scholars, and critics. They tend to work around us rather than with us, as if they thought (or thought that we thought) that the humanities in the world was not our business, that educators are not the same as college professors.

So here is my real question: Why should we accept the dichotomy between academia and the world? between our workplace and the world? Isn't the university part of the world? not only in its outreach capacity but in its everyday life? Isn't the classroom part of the world? If we draw a line between our work in the world and our work as college professors, or if we allow others to draw it for us, we encourage students to think that such a line inevitably exists.

I began with the personal and return to it now, because there are ways in which my career as a scholar has always had this binocular, stereoscopic view.

I am a peripatetic writer. Many of the topics on which I've chosen to write seem to be in the world and to be in it in a timely way: cross-dressing, sexuality, dogs, houses, the relation of the humanities to academic culture. I've just finished a project on the arts and the ambivalent relation that contested category has to the university and to the world (including the so-called art world). As a result of the restlessness in my work, which is always moving sideways, associatively and metonymically, I've had a chance to speak to a wide range of audiences, from the Fantasia Fair in Provincetown to high-end realtors in New York City to dog breeders, Shakespeareans, literary theorists, actors, artists, Oprah, and Geraldo. But my books are not principally about the referent (golden retrievers, say, or real estate) but about the argument. They are books about ideas. If love is one of their preoccupations—and it is, from dog love to house love—my writing, my work, is enabled by the fact that these elements in the world are themselves good to think with. This kind of work emanates from the university, belongs in the university, returns to the university and to the classroom. It's a place to which I always come home—and home to me means not only the university but also Shakespeare.

In summer 2007 I taught Shakespeare in summer school. The preponderance of my summer students were in secondary school, though some were in their forties and fifties, and a few were in college. The mix made for invigorating teaching. That fall I taught Shakespeare in the Extension School, or what is now called the Division of Continuing Education. The typical age of an evening school Shakespeare student was over fifty, though there were younger people present. Many of the evening students were lawyers, doctors, psychoanalysts, businesspeople.

The humanities are now a lifelong learning business, starting young, going on through and past retirement. We need to expand our notion of the world not just in space but over time, widening our sense of audience to include students of all ages. Those I taught in summer school may be back for more when they enter college in a year or two. Doctors and lawyers and high school teachers and other professionals, postcollege, return to the classroom with renewed commitment.

Before you say, "Oh, but Shakespeare is a universal language," I want to stress that both the summer school and the evening school are full of humanities courses—courses on the classics, on philosophy, and on fiction both old and new. Many of my colleagues teach these courses because they like the conversations with another age group, students who are there because they want to be and often at some personal cost. I also taught an evening graduate course on contemporary literary theory and criticism this fall, with a dozen students, some of whom came from quite far away and after a full day's work at another job.

I would also like to note that this kind of "inreach" program is enabled by changing technology. I once thought that *distance learning* was an oxymoron, but I have learned in the last couple of years that it can be a vital resource. If we do not learn to handle these new technologies, they will handle us instead. We've become accustomed to using and exploring the tools of the Internet for research. The Internet, for example, allows electronic examination of many rare books. *Digital humanities* is now a common phrase and a favorite one of deans and administrators. But it is not only our research tools but also our students who are distributed across the globe. The world is coming home to the university.

The work of the humanities in the world can include links between universities and arts institutions, on campus and beyond: theaters, museums, galleries, orchestras, dance companies. Bringing the arts into productive relation with scholars and students on campus is a way of making the humanities at work in the university into the humanities at work in the world. Bringing the practice of the arts as well as their history and interpretation into the curriculum—through courses, departments, and programs in writing, art making, film, dance, and theater—is part of this vital project for the future.

Good to eat, or good to think with? The humanities at work in the world or in the classroom? One of my favorite passages from Wallace Stevens articulates the choice that is involved in refusing the terms of this dichotomy:

> . . . it was not a choice
> Between excluding things. It was not a choice
>
> Between, but of. He chose to include the things
> That in each other are included . . .   (348)

"It was not a choice / Between, but of." The concept of the humanities at work in the world is like the quest for the bluebird: it gives pleasure, it provides exciting glimpses, and it may also lead us to recognize what we have overlooked at home. The idea of the humanities at work in the university may seem overfamiliar, a little drab, not quite blue enough, not the exotic thing we were seeking. But the university and the world are part of a single structure. In both places, in all places, there is a lot of work to be done—work that we are trained to do, that we are training our students to do. We might consider what lies between the university and the world not a boundary but a continuum or narrative: part of an ongoing and supervening plot, a *fort-da* structure, one of inevitable escape and return. Gone and there, loss and mastery: which is which?

And if what seems most desirable is always a little beyond reach—if the world seems the other of the university rather than its dream self—we might remind ourselves that this idea too is part of the quest narrative and that it underlies all research and writing, all the work that scholars and teachers do. The nearest bluebird may be right behind you, and it may not seem, at first, to be blue.

NOTE

1. The original French text reads: "Les animaux du totémisme cessent d'être, seulement ou surtout, des créatures redoutées, admirées, ou convoitées: leur réalité sensible laisse transparaître des notions et des relations, conçues par la pensée spéculative à partir des données de l'observation. On comprend enfin que les espèces naturelles ne sont pas choisies parce que 'bonnes à manger' mais parce que 'bonnes à penser'" (*Totémisme* 128).

WORKS CITED

Bacon, Francis. "Of Studies." *The Essays*. 1601. *Renascence Editions*. U of Oregon. 1998. Web. 13 June 2008.

Browne, Thomas. "Notes on the Natural History of Norfolk." *Miscellaneous Writings*. Ed. Geoffrey Keynes. London: Faber, 1931. 377–94. Print.

Jonson, Ben. "Inviting a Friend to Supper." *The Oxford Book of Seventeenth-Century Verse*. Ed. H. J. C. Grierson and G. Bullough. Oxford: Clarendon, 1934. 155–56. *Luminarium: Anthology of English Lit*. 7 Nov. 2006. Web. 13 June 2008.

Lévi-Strauss, Claude. *Totemism*. Trans. Rodney Needham. Boston: Beacon, 1963. Print.

———. *Le totémisme aujourd'hui*. Paris: PUF, 1962. Print.

Maeterlinck, Maurice. *The Blue Bird: A Fairy Play in Six Acts*. Trans. Alexander Teixeira de Mattos. New York: Dodd, 1911. *Project Gutenberg*. 1 Aug. 2005. Web. 14 June 2008.

Movers and Shakespeares. Web. 14 June 2008.

National Initiatives: The Big Read. Nat'l. Endowment for the Arts. Web. 14 June 2008.

Stevens, Wallace. "Notes toward a Supreme Fiction." *Collected Poetry and Prose*. New York: Lib. of Amer., 1997. 329–52. Print.

A Dean's Perspective

DAVID MARSHALL

As a dean of humanities and fine arts at a public university, I see it as part of my job to make the argument that the humanities are at work in the world. In his president's column about the Presidential Forum panels in the Winter 2007 *MLA Newsletter,* Michael Holquist referred to "the complex utility of the humanities" (3). There are risks in making utilitarian arguments about the value and values of the humanities, but there are also risks in not making such arguments, since other disciplines constantly make them, and the fate of the humanities within the university—the valuation of their labor, their market share of student enrollments, the respect for their research—depends on how the humanities are valued by the world outside the academy and how they are valued within the academy by students and colleagues in other fields.

I often talk about a 2002 *New York Times* profile of the only financial reporter to warn of Enron's fatal fiscal problems. The *Fortune Magazine* reporter Bethany McLean, at first the Cassandra of the business world, attributed her ability to read Enron's books while everyone else sang its fortunes to her liberal arts education, in particular to her double major in English and math. "'When you come out of a liberal arts background,' she said, 'you want to know why something is the way it is.' In accounting, 'there is no reason why. There is no fundamental truth underlying it.'" McLean credits her liberal arts background with enabling her to see

The author is professor of English and comparative literature, dean of humanities and fine arts, and executive dean of the College of Letters and Science at the University of California, Santa Barbara. A version of this paper was presented at the 2007 MLA convention in Chicago.

Enron's mathematical fictions and "the fundamental economic reality" that accounting ignored (Barringer). Her training in literature and math allowed her to deconstruct accounting's nonreferential system—as if her insight that there was no fundamental truth underlying Enron's economic reality had led her to discover that Arthur Anderson had hired Jacques Derrida to do Enron's books. Although literary critics have been accused of undermining our belief in truth and reality, meaning and value, McLean suggests that the spreadsheets of accounting contained empty fictions in which meaning had no value and value had no meaning, while literature allowed her to read the truth behind the figures.

Many economic arguments can be made about the work of the humanities in the world. Nonprofit arts organizations and activities add $5.4 billion a year to California's economy. American corporations spend $3.1 billion annually on remedial writing for their employees—and this expense doesn't include the cost of lawsuits caused by badly written e-mails. The California Economic Development Corporation has called for stronger requirements for foreign languages and cultures (*Arts*), and even the Department of Defense has called for the cultivation of stronger foreign language and cultural competencies in order to strengthen national security and economic competitiveness and to maintain our power in the global economy (see *Call to Action*). In a 2006 *Washington Post* article, Duke University President Richard Brodhead, addressing the question of whether higher education in the United States is "training the workforce needed to win in a global economy," especially in science and math, noted that Chinese educators envied the American system and feared that Asian higher education was "short on creativity and that the very strengths of their system may prevent the fostering of a versatile, innovative style of intelligence that will be the key to future economic advancement." Brodhead suggests that our "liberal arts model of education" promotes "initiative, independence, resourcefulness and collaboration."

What is at stake, of course, is more than economic competitiveness. McLean brought to *Fortune* the skills of someone trained in close reading and critical analysis. These modes of attention, along with communication and creativity, are crucial not only to the workforce that we need to compete in the twenty-first century but also to our democratic institutions. In our multicultural and multilingual global society (exemplified today by California) we need citizens who understand the languages and cultures of other traditions. Global challenges, as well as our increasing cultural diversity at home, necessitate the knowledge of the past and the comparative methods of interpretation that the humanities can teach us. One of the paradoxes for Americans in the information age is that globalization threatens to impose a culture of sameness throughout the world while simultaneously challenging us with a culture of difference at home. English dominates the Internet and asserts itself as the universal language, yet over three hundred languages are spoken by children in public schools in California alone. As we negotiate the complicated and unstable terms of identity and difference, we need to engage in acts of both linguistic and cultural translation.

Our literature departments have only begun to abandon their identities as national literature departments or foreign language and literature departments. In the age of *Google Translator,* the humanities must work to promote the necessity of translation while underlining the difficulty and even impossibility of translation, to assert the very foreignness of language at a time when the term *foreign* is increasingly unstable. In this context, it is important to think about Holquist's reminder that language is "the MLA's middle name" (3). The work of the humanities is threatened by the prospect that literature will be seen as a foreign language, an endangered language with few remaining native speakers. Yet it is also threatened by the prospect that literature will not be seen as foreign, that all language and media will be seen as (and expected to be) transparent. Part of our work is to return foreignness to language, to insist that meaning in the text and in the world must be found through acts of interpretation and translation, by reading and attending to the stories of both self and other and to the stories told by language itself. I suggest that teaching this familiar foreignness could allow us to rediscover our work in the world.

WORKS CITED

The Arts: A Competitive Advantage for California II: The Economic Impact of Nonprofit Arts and Cultural Organizations in California: Update to the 1994 Economic Impact of the Arts Report. California Arts Council. Apr. 2004. Web. 5 Aug. 2008.

Barringer, Felicity. "Enron's Many Strands: Early Scrutiny." *New York Times* 28 Jan. 2002. Web. 15 June 2008.

Brodhead, Richard H. "The U.S. Edge in Education." *Washington Post* 4 Sept. 2006: A19. Print.

A Call to Action for National Foreign Language Capabilities. Natl. Language Conf. 1 Feb. 2005. Web. 5 Aug. 2008.

Holquist, Michael. "The Humanities at Work in the World." *MLA Newsletter* 39.4 (2007): 3–4. Print.

Marshall, David. Introduction. *The Humanities and Its Publics.* ACLS Occasional Papers 61. New York: ACLS, 2006. 1–4. Print.

Steppin' Out: On Making an Animated Opera Called The Loathly Lady

WENDY STEINER

A few years ago, Carol Gilligan told me about a documentary she wanted to make about women professors who had stepped out of the university into the worlds of politics and the arts. She asked if I had any ideas for a title, and, without thinking, I answered, "Academic Freedom." As we went on talking, I imagined Washington and Wall Street types rolling their eyes: "What is it with these eggheads—they don't know a good thing when they get it. They wouldn't know freedom if it walked up and hit them over the head."

It is true that in certain ways we are a very privileged lot, with our long summer break and limited contact hours. And yet the freedom enshrined in the academy often seems to find expression in bureaucratic nit-picking rather than flights of creativity. What might an academic aspire to in the way of creative achievements? I decided to make a list, starting cautiously.

a. All your students get As.
b. Your students thank you for giving them Bs.
c. You organize a faculty revolt, and grades are abolished.

Or:

a. Every student for whom you write a recommendation gets a job, fellowship, or prize.

The author is Richard L. Fisher Professor of English and founding director of the Penn Humanities Forum at the University of Pennsylvania. A version of this paper was presented at the 2007 MLA convention in Chicago.

b. The MLA passes a resolution limiting recommendations to a hundred words.
c. Your university decides you've written enough recommendations for one lifetime and exempts you from having to write any more—ever.

Now I was getting somewhere. New possibilities sprang to mind:

a. The media declare that all the shortcomings of American culture are *not* to be blamed on the academy.
b. The trustees of the university hand over the endowment to your care and enroll en masse in literature courses.
c. Writers return from the grave (or Montauk) to thank you for your reviews and scholarly explications.
d. A Nobel Prize in Literary Criticism is established, and you . . .

Well, you see where this was going.

Is steppin' out just a matter of vaulting ambition? No question that it has an element of hubris, but I think it also has something to do with the title of this presidential panel: "The Humanities at Work in the World." Even academics who do not labor under the long shadow of Benjamin Franklin (as we at Penn patiently do) tend to believe that literary knowledge is useful for something other than its own perpetuation. The American public may not hold this view. Appalled at the disdain for the profession expressed during the culture wars, I founded the Penn Humanities Forum to demonstrate that humanistic thought was an untapped resource. It could put widely diverse disciplines into conversation with one another and enrich the lives of all citizens. With the forum's tenth anniversary approaching, this conviction has been amply borne out in the thousands of Penn and Philadelphia people who attend our programs each year.

But I must admit that no act of steppin' out has been as satisfying to me—or as challenging—as conceiving *The Loathly Lady*, an opera that someday, I hope, will be realized as a full-length animated film (fig. 1).

FIGURE 1 Illustration by John Kindness;
title for *The Loathly Lady*

FIGURE 2 Illustration by John Kindness; "Elf Queen,"
The Loathly Lady, act 1, scene 1

It began innocently enough. I stepped out of my field of twentieth-century literature to teach a survey course on major British poets: Chaucer to Donne. In the process, I read The Wife of Bath's Tale for the first time since graduate school and was bowled over: it could have been written yesterday. The disputes it staged between male and female characters were the feminist, traditionalist, and backlash arguments I had been hearing all my adult life. Before I knew it, those arguments were song lyrics, and Chaucer's tale had become an opera libretto.

I gave it a frame story: an elf queen steps out of a magic tapestry to become a real maiden (fig. 2). In retrospect, I realize this frame owes something to the triptych by Remedios Varo that Thomas Pynchon describes in *The Crying of Lot 49*. In its central canvas, maidens locked in a tower are

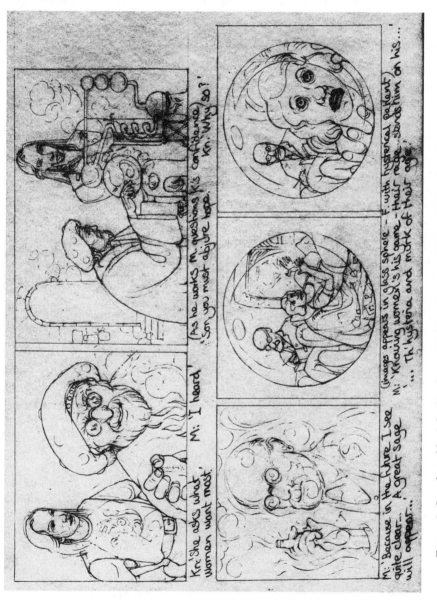

FIGURE 3 Storyboard by John Kindness; "Merlin Conjures Up Freud," *The Loathly Lady*, act 1, scene 4

weaving a tapestry that flows out the windows of the tower to become the world. By the final canvas, one of Varo's maidens has escaped the tower and is sailing toward some dangerous-looking cliffs. The escape of the Elf Queen proves dangerous, too: no sooner does she step out of her tapestry than Chaucer's Knight rapes her.

For this crime, the Knight is condemned to death in a year and a day, unless he can answer the question, What do women want most? I recalled that Freud had been bothered by the same question, and so I had Merlin conjure up the Viennese doctor to warn the Knight about the difficulties of the assignment (fig. 3). The Knight, a believer in sociological methods, pooh-poohs Freud's analytic approach and sets forth on a quest to interview representative women. Merlin has thoughtfully provided their addresses to the Knight in a medieval Filofax called "The Book of Dames" (fig. 4).

The Knight's informants, woven into the magic tapestry, come to life when he poses his question and tell him their heart's desire. Titania most wants a (changeling) child; Sheherezade wants passion and sings a tango to prove it; and Jane Austen's Emma yearns for a paragon of virtue, a Mr. Knightley. Unconvinced, the Knight continues on to the Lady of Shalott's tower, where two caryatids are holding up the doorway: Eliza Doolittle and Virginia Woolf (fig. 5). Eliza says all she wants is a room somewhere; the Lady of Shalott wants a room with a view; and Virginia of course wants a room of one's own. The Knight decides that what women really want is real estate.

Enter the Loathly Lady, who promises to give the Knight the correct answer if he will grant her a wish. He agrees and returns with her to

FIGURE 4 Illustration by John Kindness;
Virginia Woolf's page in "The Book of Dames,"
The Loathly Lady, act 2, scene 4

FIGURE 5 Storyboard by John Kindness; "Eliza Doolittle and Virginia Woolf as Caryatids at the Lady of Shalott's Tower," *The Loathly Lady*, act 2, scene 4

Camelot to report what she has told him: "Women most want mastery in marriage." Evidently this is the right answer, for the Knight's life is saved. But now the Loathly Lady reveals her wish: the Knight must marry her. In bed on their wedding night, he is distraught, and so the lady offers him a choice: she can stay as she is, ugly but faithful, or she can become young and beautiful but faithless (fig. 6). And now the Knight, suddenly inspired, gives the choice to the lady. She is so pleased to have mastery in marriage that she becomes young and beautiful *and* faithful, and the two live happily ever after. Merlin rejoices, but Freud is already fading back into the future via the Camelot airport, where "What do women want most?" is stenciled over the walls in the world's major languages.

It was a lot of fun to write this libretto, but I had no idea what to do with it. It sat around for a few years until my recorder teacher, John DeLucia, read it and saw an opportunity for early instruments to enter the realm of musical theater. But how to find a composer? Take out an ad in the American Music Center list, advised Michael Delaira, whom I ran into at a party. From the five dozen submissions I received, Paul Richards of the University of Florida, Gainesville, emerged: a master of pastiche and a wonderful collaborator. Responding to DeLucia's musical conception, Paul wrote the medieval scenes to sound like the *ars nova* music of Chaucer's day and orchestrated them for early instruments, whereas the scenes on the Knight's quest are musically appropriate to the various ladies—or at least to my idea of them. (I have yet to find hard evidence for the existence of tangos in Sheherezade's culture.)

Before Paul came on the scene, I had decided *The Loathly Lady* should

Figure 6 Illustration by John Kindness; "The Choice,"
The Loathly Lady, act 3, scene 3

be an animated film, and so Paul's commission was to write a film opera. The story was full of magic and whimsy, and since new operas come and go, I thought animation would give *The Loathly Lady* some needed shelf life. I showed the libretto to an artist friend, John Kindness, who was intrigued enough to paint and draw a whole series of still images and storyboards. All we had to do now, I figured, was scan them into a computer, launch an animation program, and watch out, Pixar!

It took very little time to discover that the costs involved in animation are astronomical. Computers make certain animation tasks easier, but the process is still unbelievably labor-intensive, as the credits scrolling down screen after screen at the end of animations should have warned me. And when by chance I found myself sitting next to a vice president of Walt Disney Studios at a luncheon, she did not seem to think *The Loathly Lady* had the makings of a cash cow.

This has been the hardest lesson of steppin' out: it is difficult to get things done out there if you have no track record, money, commercial sense, contacts—or, ahem, expertise. It is like setting up as a freelance scholar without taking the time to get a PhD. At a certain point, all you have is talented friends, a vision, and stubbornness. Still, these are not to be disdained. To date, *The Loathly Lady* project has brought into being a new opera with libretto, Paul's music, and full orchestration; a sheaf of Kindness's still images; a directing script that John and I dreamed up over the course of museum visits and studio sessions; and a seven-minute animated pilot film that was screened in the NewFilmmakers NY Summer 2008 Series.[1] And in April 2009, *The Loathly Lady* will have its concert première in Philadelphia.[2]

There are many kinds of "work in the world" that the humanities can perform, and among them, the rewriting of a Chaucerian tale as a contemporary opera is certainly not the most urgent. Yet that moment of being bowled over by The Wife of Bath's Tale was not just an opening for self-indulgence. To me, it explains why the humanities can do work in the world at all. When, after years of reading and teaching and thinking, the past steps out of its tapestry and speaks directly to us, the values of communication and human solidarity are powerfully served. That flash of understanding alters the world, or our being in it. As humanists, we strive on a daily basis to create such moments in our students and colleagues, but they are rare events, and mostly, we spend our time on grading and recommendations and rueful humility. But when the lightning strikes, how wonderful that the academy allows us—indeed, prepares us for—the immense pleasure of steppin' out.

NOTES

1. My adviser for the film was Joshua Mosley, an animation professor at Penn much celebrated during the 2007 Venice Biennale. Erinn Hagerty was the lead animator. Amey Hutchins, the manuscript librarian at Penn's Van Pelt Library, helpfully scanned sheets of vellum to provide backgrounds for Kindness's Filofax images. The sound track was recorded at a top New York studio, where the Yugoslav sound engineer, more accustomed to orchestras and rock bands, was overheard talking on his cell phone during a break: "You wouldn't believe what I'm working with here, man—all these weird things: krummhorns and rebecs and sackbuts and dulcians. It's awesome." The film will be available for viewing online in April 2009, at http://media.sas.upenn.edu/Humanities/ LL_Pilot_09_12_06_2.mov.

2. Julianne Baird will sing the title role, with Thomas Meglioranza as the Knight, Drew Minter as Merlin, and Susan Hellauer, Ruth Cunningham, and Jacqueline Horner as the many ladies inside and outside the tapestry. Gary Thor Wedow will conduct, and the early instruments will be played by the Renaissance wind band Piffaro and Parthenia, a consort of viols.

WORKS CITED

Chaucer, Geoffrey. *Wife of Bath's Tale*. *Luminarium: Anthology of English Lit*. 16 Oct. 2007. Web. 13 June 2008.

Pynchon, Thomas. *The Crying of Lot 49*. 1965. New York: Harper, 1990. Print.

The Humanities as an Export Commodity

PETER BROOKS

In proposing my title, I intended to reflect on three or so decades in which the interpretive disciplines in the humanities, in the wake of structuralism and poststructuralism, with the revival of psychoanalysis and the invention of feminist theory, and with the expanding universe of culture as the playground of study, did appear to generate paradigms of analysis and understanding that began to move across the border, sometimes with fanfare, sometimes in unmarked vans. There was a sense in the social science and professional republics at our frontiers that the humanities had developed methods (often themselves derived from such disciplines as linguistics and anthropology) that enabled important questions about the nature of the human animal as sign-bearing and sense-making.

To my mind, these questions—posed in the structural study of myth, for instance, or in the analysis of the narrative construction of reality—remain important today. A few weeks ago, some students in my introduction-to-narrative class, itself a creation of the 1970s, told me it had changed their lives. But I think the more common reaction was expressed recently by one of my colleagues at Yale Law School, who said she no longer looks to the interpretive humanities for inspiration. History, yes, but after that it's political philosophy and economics again. The notion that the law-and-literature movement, as it became known, was going to revolutionize the study of law through the incursion of the suspicion-laden methods of

The author is currently Mellon Visiting Professor at Princeton University. A version of this paper was presented at the 2007 MLA convention in Chicago.

reading associated with hermeneutics, psychoanalysis, feminism, and deconstruction may have come to very little in the long run, as Julie Stone Peters argued in the pages of *PMLA* three years ago. It's as if the body eventually rejected the transplant. If you have to go to court today, it is unlikely that your attorney will be citing Stanley Fish before the presiding judge. And while interpretive method from literary and cultural study has infected neighboring disciplines such as history and sociology, and farther provinces such as economics and even medicine (there is, for instance, a narrative-medicine movement), one nevertheless has the feeling that the humanities' big day as a cultural exporter is over.

I don't want to try to assess blame for this, though I would mention in passing that many who ought to have applauded and abetted the exportation of humanistic concerns and paradigms were the loudest in their denunciation of what the humanities had become: such guardians of the official humanities as William Bennett and Lynne Cheney; the anointed public intellectuals of *Commentary*, the *New Criterion*, the *Weekly Standard*, the *Wall Street Journal*; and those in our own ranks, from Camille Paglia to Frederick Crews, from Andrew Delbanco to Anthony Grafton, who chose to see academic humanists as having betrayed their commitment to transmit the great tradition and its values. I have agreed with certain critics of the humanities that a facile politics often replaces critical thinking and that critique aimed at the traditional father figures of Western thought is often mindless, but I refuse to shoot the piano player. The piano player may not be playing his or her best, but he or she needs protection from self-declared friends as well as enemies.

One of our problems, when we've seen the humanities as an export nation, has been the tendency outside and even inside to offer a kind of smarmy feel-good version of the humanities. Art, literature, and philosophy become value-added items, anodyne, enrichments of life, and they are low-cost. One must begin by urging the distinction between the humanities and humanity. The humanities as we know them descend from the *litterae humaniores*, a product of Renaissance humanism's concern to restore ancient texts and to learn to read them. The enterprise is human in that it deals with human reflections on the human condition. Being human ought to make the enterprise humanizing but doesn't necessarily. We know the reports of officers at Auschwitz who would listen rapturously to Mozart at the end of a day of killing. We also know that much great literature and art may be dedicated to false gods and carry in their current pernicious ideological flotsam: think of Richard Wagner, W. B. Yeats, Ezra Pound, Balzac, Dostoevsky, and a host of others. The student uprising at Columbia University in 1969 famously prompted Lionel Trilling to the response

"Modernism in the streets!" (see Diggins 267)—which I read as a recognition of the potentially violent and disruptive lesson of modernist writers. So many of our most prized beacons of modernism echo in some manner the old German Stein's advice to Jim in Conrad's novel: "In the destructive element immerse!" (246).

As secular scripture, literature is inadequate, subversive, at times dangerous. As Sartre put it in his autobiography, literature never saved anyone (211). The humanities can begin to make their address to the public sphere only when their proponents speak with a clear sense of what their work can and cannot do. It is not salvific, it won't necessarily make you a better person, it is not instrumental—it has precisely renounced the instrumental use of language and symbol in favor of something more reflective and mediated. What the interpretive humanities have to offer the public sphere is ultimately and basically a lesson in how to read—with the nuance, complexity, and responsibility that we practice most of the time in our classrooms. The study of poetry, and the study of what we are doing and learning when we study a poem, is a form of knowledge crucially important in the world now. I would inscribe myself in Shelley's camp, believing that poets are the unacknowledged legislators of humankind. But to be in that camp means to make an unremitting effort to say what poetry is and why its reading is a cognitive enterprise with real-world consequences.

Unfortunately the failure of responsible reading has put the United States into the camp of rogue nations, nations that are in violation of the most cherished principles of international as well as domestic law. I refer to the torture debate that has unfolded since it became apparent that the response to 9/11 included renditions, secret prisons, enhanced interrogation techniques. A host of commentators, not all on the right, not all stupid, have come forward to justify, in casuistic scenarios of apocalypse, practices and ideologies I thought were universally if tacitly recognized as wholly incompatible with the morality of American democracy. One of the most notorious documents to emerge from the hidden recesses of our Justice Department—only one among many, alas—is a memo dated 1 August 2002, addressed to Presidential Counsel Alberto R. Gonzales, signed by Assistant Attorney General Jay S. Bybee, and largely drafted by Professor John Yoo of Boalt Hall. It was eventually replaced but remains a monitory example of legal interpretive reading.

The memo expresses the interpretation of the Justice Department's Office of Legal Counsel, once a sanctum of authoritative legal opinion, of "standards of conduct under the Convention against Torture and Other Cruel, Inhuman, and Degrading Treatment or Punishment as implemented by Sections 2340-2340A of title 18 of the United States Code." It begins from the traditional premise that "when interpreting a statute, we must give words their 'ordinary or natural' meaning" (Leocal 382). The Supreme Court in 2004 reaffirmed this traditional commitment of statutory interpretation to the Plain Meaning Rule, affectionately known as the PMR (see Sinclair).

The Bybee-Yoo memo starts from the same premises. "The key statutory phrase in the definition of torture is the statement that acts amount to torture if they cause 'severe physical or mental pain or suffering.' In examining the meaning of a statute, its text must be the starting point" (Bybee 5). But, says Yoo, the statute doesn't define *severe*. Absent such a definition, he continues, "we construe a statutory term in accordance with its ordinary or natural meaning." To find that ordinary and natural meaning, he turns to *Webster's New International Dictionary* (in the 1935 edition, for some reason), then to the *American Heritage Dictionary* and the *OED*, to discover that *severe* "conveys that the pain or suffering must be of such a high level or intensity that the pain is difficult for the subject to endure." But this definition, however ordinary and natural, doesn't suit his purposes. So he searches for other possible uses of the phrase "severe pain" in the United States Code and discovers, as he puts it, "Significantly, the phrase 'severe pain' appears in statutes defining an emergency medical condition" (5). "Significantly" is his own transition word here—and we need to ask whether the use of "severe pain" in the medical context (for insurance purposes, for instance) is in fact more significant than any number of other uses of *severe*, in statutes and in ordinary usage. This slide into medical usage then allows Yoo to come up with his interpretation that the severe pain that defines torture must involve damage that rises "to the level of death, organ failure, or the permanent impairment of a significant body function" (Bybee 6). He now has us well into the emergency room.

Next, Yoo interprets the language used to define "severe mental pain or suffering" in the torture statute, which includes "the prolonged mental harm caused by or resulting from (A) the intentional infliction or threatened infliction of severe physical pain or suffering" (6). *To prolong*, his Webster's (1988 edition this time) tells him, is to "lengthen in time," and this definition permits him to segue to, "Put another way, the acts giving rise to the harm must cause some lasting, though not necessarily permanent, damage." This transition suggests to him that "prolonged mental harm" (words not used elsewhere in the United States Code) might resemble the posttraumatic stress disorder, lasting months or even years, noticed in torture victims. This argument is thoroughly circular. It leads, over the next three paragraphs, to the claim that torture, for it to be torture, requires a specific intent to cause prolonged mental harm by one of the predicate acts listed in the statute, thus the good-faith belief of defendants that the acts they committed would not amount to the acts forbidden by the statute constitutes a "complete defense to such a charge," of torture (8). We may uneasily sense that we are witnessing a free play of the signifier, the sort that literary critics and philosophers are sometimes accused of sponsoring.

The truly "deconstructive" cast of Yoo's interpretation of USC §2340 comes in the next section, which takes up "Harm caused by or resulting from predicate acts." These acts include, inter alia, "the administration or application, or threatened administration or application, of mind-altering substances or other procedures calculated to disrupt profoundly the senses or the personality." Since these substances are not further defined, Yoo sets out to make some distinctions. Here a longer quotation is necessary:

> This subparagraph, however, does not preclude any and all use of drugs. Instead, it prohibits the use of drugs that "disrupt profoundly the senses or the personality." To be sure, one could argue that this phrase applies only to "other procedures," not the application of mind-altering substances. We reject this interpretation because the terms of Section 2340 (2) expressly indicate that the qualifying phrase applies to both "other procedures" *and* the "application of mind-altering substances." The word "other" modifies "procedures calculated to disrupt profoundly the senses." As an adjective, "other" indicates that the term or phrase it modifies is the remainder of several things. *See* Webster's Third New International Dictionary 1598 (1986) (defining "other" as "the one that remains of two or more") Webster's Ninth New Collegiate Dictionary 835 (1985) (defining "other" as "being the one (as of two or more) remaining or not included"). Or put another way, "other" signals that the words to which it attaches are of the same kind, type, or class as the more specific item previously listed. Moreover, where statutes couple words or phrases together, it "denotes an intention that they should be understood in the same general sense." Norman Singer, 2A Sutherland on Statutory Construction § 47:16 (6th ed. 2000); *see also Beecham v. United States*, 511 U.S. 368, 371 (1994) ("That several items in a list share an attribute counsels in favor of interpreting the other items as possessing that attribute as well.") Thus, the pairing of mind-altering substances with procedures calculated to disrupt profoundly the senses or personality and the use of "other" to modify "procedures" shows that the use of such substances must also cause profound disruption of the senses or personality.   (10)

To use the "or" of "or other procedures"—which are of course supposed to be of the same sort—to argue that "disrupt profoundly" somehow controls and limits the meaning of "mind-altering" seems to me far from commonsensical, a parsing of vocabulary and syntax that is arbitrary and even a bit demonic. Whether or not this meaning was intended by Congress, the way

Yoo claims to find the meaning derives from an ungoverned and unscrupulous reading that uses—very selectively—dictionary definitions to produce arcane and obfuscating interpretations. It's like a parody of a deconstructive reading written by Frederick Crews.

I refrain from citing the next paragraph, which takes us into the meaning of *disrupt*, as "to break asunder; to part forcibly; to rend"—here we are back with the 1935 *Webster's* and a definition my 1975 *American Heritage* finds "obsolete": what about a more usual definition, such as "to upset the order of"? But Yoo needs to come out, at the end of his paragraph, with, "Those acts must penetrate to the core of an individual's ability to perceive the world around him, substantially interfering with his cognitive abilities, or fundamentally alter his personality" (11). Abu Ghraib doesn't make it on this definition, though the destroyed tapes almost surely would have put the interrogation of Abu Zabaydah over the line.

Yoo is providing the interpretation he knows his masters want. It's interpretation untethered by any ethics of reading, interpretation as domination, Humpty Dumpty style:

> "When *I* use a word," Humpty Dumpty said, in rather a scornful tone, "it means just what I choose it to mean—neither more nor less."
>
> "The question is," said Alice, "whether you *can* make words mean so many different things."
>
> "The question is," said Humpty Dumpty, "which is to be master— that's all." (Carroll 186)

When dealing with the torture memos, I find it hard to get beyond moral outrage, which I think is necessary but hardly sufficient. I really want to stress two points. First, it is important that we humanists remind the legal profession that legal interpretation stands in wider contexts of understanding and meaning. The law needs to cleanse itself in the humanistic tradition. Second, those trained rigorously in the reading of poetry— those who have taken seriously, for example, William Wimsatt's old essay "What to Say about a Poem"—could not permit themselves so arbitrary and phony an act of interpretation as Yoo performs. We do not necessarily export the humanitarian, but we can promote and enforce responsible reading.

Coleridge claims that he was taught a lesson by his "severe master," the Reverend James Bowyer:

> I learned from him, that poetry, even that of the loftiest and seemingly, that of the wildest odes, had a logic of its own, as severe as that of science, and more difficult, because more subtle, more complex, and dependent on more and more fugitive causes. In the truly great poets, he would say,

there is a reason assignable not only for every word, but for the position of every word. . . . (Brower 7)

We humanists do have reasons assignable. We still can and must be exporters of a responsive and responsible critical reading that says no to cover-up and cant and that calls torture by its name.

WORKS CITED

Brower, Reuben A. "Reading in Slow Motion." *In Defense of Reading*. Ed. Brower and Richard Poirier. New York: Dutton, 1962. 3–21. Print.

Bybee, Jay S. "Memorandum for Alberto R. Gonzales, Counsel to the President, Re: Standards of Conduct for Interrogation under 18 U.S.C. §§ 2340-2340A." 1 Aug. 2002. *The Bybee Torture Memo*. TomJoad.org. Web. 13 June 2008.

Carroll, Lewis. *Through the Looking-Glass*. New York: NAL-Signet, 1960. Print.

Conrad, Joseph. *Lord Jim*. London: Penguin, 1989. Print.

Diggins, John Patrick. *The Proud Decades: America in War and in Peace, 1941–1960*. New York: Norton, 1989. Print.

Leocal v. Ashcroft. 125 Supreme Court of the US 377, 382. 9 Nov. 2004. *FindLaw*. Web. 17 Oct. 2008.

Peters, Julie Stone. "Law, Literature, and the Vanishing Real: On the Future of an Interdisciplinary Illusion." *PMLA* 120.2 (2005): 442–53. Print.

Sartre, Jean-Paul. *Les mots*. Paris: Gallimard, 1964. Print.

Sinclair, Michael. *A Guide to Statutory Interpretation*. New York: Lexis, 2000. Print.

Wimsatt, W. K., Jr. "What to Say about a Poem." *College English* 24.5 (1963): 377–83. *JSTOR*. Web. 13 June 2008.

Safe Spaces in an Era of Gated Communities and Disproportionate Punishments

ROBERT F. BARSKY

I was going to propose a moratorium on the consequences of taking intellectual risks within and beyond the academy but deem it insufficient for the present task. In its place, I advocate a wanton disregard for arbitrary authority and an active promotion of lust and poetry; the purposeful secretion of fantasy; and the creation more than the critique of art, even in our classrooms.

I have spent most of my career bringing the tools from the humanities to bear on crucial social problems relating to Geneva Convention refugees (*Constructing* and *Arguing*), homeless people ("Stories"), and incarcerated migrants ("Activist Translation" and "From Discretion"). Nevertheless, I now firmly believe that we don't need to involve our students more directly in political debates as delineated in, say, the *New York Times*, because most of these so-called differences of opinion force us to take a stand on issues too obvious or superficial to really matter. We all have a view about an idea as bizarre as building a wall between the United States and Mexico in an era of much-vaunted free trade, but all the approaches to free trade take for granted our need to control the borders. This need leads otherwise perfectly reasonable human beings to promote freer movement of commodities as set forth by NAFTA, though they are incapable of imagining the fundamental first move of free trade, the elimination of the border between Mexico and the United States and between the United States and

The author is professor of English, French, and comparative literature at Vanderbilt University. A version of this paper was presented at the 2007 MLA convention in Chicago.

Canada, and though the European Union has done so between worlds that were once as divergent as the United Kingdom and Germany. We have also been forced to consider the value of torturing human beings in Abu Ghraib, Guantanamo, or down the street from us and have ended up reading Alan Dershowitz debating the fine points of the law as it applies to our citizens versus everybody else, instead of noting the insanity not only of torture but also of warehousing a prison population that exceeds two million people. We all want to live healthy lives whether or not we're employed but then with a straight face wonder whether universal health care, which works everywhere else in the world, is right for us. These are not debates, because frankly there is no serious intellectual content on either side of these so-called issues. We are being lured into this constructed pseudo-reality of trial balloons, nonchoices, and sensationalism designed to keep us—and our students—from debates worth having and from projects worth spending money on, using a resource like the trillion or so military dollars approved with nary a hesitation not only in Congress but also in our discussions at home, approved in the name of a smoke screen created through government-enforced fear mongering (on this point, see Melman). We need to change the terms of the discussion by bringing the glorious tools of creativity to bear on the fertile gardens of the mind, for it is time for the uncontrolled and unexpected.

Theodore Ziolkowski has written in a book on literature and law, "Justice gazes most often into her literary mirror when she has been disheveled by the winds of social and political upheaval, . . . when law finds itself out of phase with the prevailing community passions" (63), and, "It is at those moments when the tension between law and morality is increased to the breaking point that law is changed and its evolution lurches forward again" (16). This probably is a good time for justice to gaze into the literary mirror. Even more important, we must name the upheaval, note the disheveled, mark the tension, and observe the breaking point; we must provide the grounds for upheaval's creation.

So this is not a time for the complacency or self-satisfaction implied when the highbrow is invoked as a first gesture or when we take as our task the imposition of preordained, overriding, and all-knowing models of thought on our students and their work. Even Tzvetan Todorov is now bemoaning the efforts he and others put into structuralism, realizing that it has had the effect of destroying through a weak pseudo-science any pleasure people have in reading literature. So we need to go back to the pleasures of reading and the risks of creating, inside and beyond the classroom. These efforts will have to be conceived differently, because in the past, even relative to the Vietnam era or the cold war, we allowed policies that have raised the stakes of engagement and creative action to a level that is for most people unaffordable if not unfathomable.

As teachers, then, we can look back to those who made a difference to find some inspiration and evidence for the power of daring: Marquis de Sade, Emile Zola, Antonin Artaud, Henry Miller, Allen Ginsberg, Antonio Gramsci—examples of those whose public vilification was, to use the words of the prosecutor in the Gramsci trial, a conscious effort to stop the brain from functioning for twenty years (88). And we have the great contemporary model of Noam Chomsky, who was once asked, "You've been called a neo-Nazi, your books have been burned, you've been called anti-Israeli—don't you get a bit upset by the ways your views are always distorted by the media and by intellectuals?" His characteristically humorous but somewhat sardonic reply?

> No, why should I? I get called anything, I'm accused of everything you can dream of: being a Communist propagandist, a Nazi propagandist, a pawn of freedom of speech, an anti-Semite, a liar, whatever you want. Actually, I think that's all a good sign. I mean, if you're a dissident, you're typically ignored. If you can't be ignored, and you can't be answered, you're vilified—that's obvious: no institution is going to help people undermine it. So I would only regard the kinds of things you're talking about as signs of progress. (qtd. in Barsky, *Chomsky Effect* 52)

But maybe Chomsky's answer is from another era, another sign that we are in a different kind of crisis today, just as his pride in having been arrested for civil disobedience is a badge of honor that can no longer be worn in the way he did.

I was going to propose a moratorium on consequences, but the fact is, they are already here, and they're more nefarious than those Chomsky endured, because they're more insidious. Being labeled a *négationniste*, a Nazi, or an anti-Semite could be the kiss of death for our work, as "spook" was to Coleman Silk in Philip Roth's *The Human Stain* (6). And the jail time that many of us fondly invoke to prove our engagement can't be reasonably advocated to our students at a time when a criminal record can, in one fell swoop, obliterate their chances for travel outside the country, for certain kinds of employment, or for credit when they are starting their professional lives in massive student loan debt. The examples of how this works are astonishing: if one of our students chooses to participate in an illegal demonstration and gets arrested, charged, and sentenced, she may never have a chance to question any kind of authority again, ever. If while in prison doing time for the great crime of speaking out for what she believes in, she mistakenly makes a call to a cell phone, against the rules in prisons, the penalty can be two years of lockdown, two years at twenty-three hours a day in an 8'x10' cell where she both shits and sleeps.

So yes, it has been possible in recent years for Stanley Aronowitz, Norman Mailer, Seymour Melman, Noam Chomsky, Edward Said, and many others to use an affiliation to an institution like a university or to use a career like writing to protect them from the consequences of overt social criticism, and it has been okay for people like them to celebrate and re-call prison time for their dissidence. But it's much easier to advocate this course when the penalty is not lasting.

So how do we change the world, alter attitudes, fight for decency, get the humanities to work in the world? After a talk I recently gave about public intellectuals, one audience member suggested that convincing right-wing hawks that a course of violent action is wrong is impossible, for biological and chemical reasons. The only way we can challenge notions, he suggested, is through dramatic action, like an experiment with hallucinogenic drugs or a creative amorous exchange, both types having been practiced by our much loved and canonized poets and writers. But a productively turned-on Voltarine de Cleyre or Mary Shelley or Lord Byron or Allen Ginsberg could not function in the current security-minded setting: if they were alive today, these canonical authors could not travel, could not publish, and would likely have zero access to a public beyond the prison cell. They probably wouldn't even be brought to a much-publicized trial that could promote their actions or spread their ideas, as happened in previous generations, to people like Timothy Leary and Jerry Rubin. And using our critical powers to deconstruct the documents that those in authority have commissioned is ineffectual in an era when anything short of unrestrained action is deemed sissy, the hopeless "I told you so" of a lost cause.

Let us at least do what we in the humanities can do: delimit some safe havens for the planting of new ideas and the provoking of real ideals, within and therefore beyond the humanities. We can start by instilling in our students and ourselves the belief that the "future could fundamentally surpass the present," to cite Russell Jacoby in *The End of Utopia*, that "the future texture of life, work and even love might little resemble that now familiar to us," "that history contains possibilities of freedom and pleasure hardly tapped" (xi–xii). We as teachers and students need to know how to be free and in that freedom stimulate the unexpected, which means that we need to rethink rigid requirements and the idea of business as usual in the discipline—the word *discipline* is particularly apt in this context—and instead look to more promising experiments, like studying questions and catalyzing approaches to them in whatever genre or style one might think up. Such experiments can be practiced in our classrooms if we offer our students the possibility of addressing, say, literary questions creatively rather than programmatically.

Practice will be needed, though, because students are afraid of doing creative work in classrooms, in part because high schools are usually factories that teach them how to take tests and universities are often considered places that award certificates that facilitate social climbing, which suggests that students need only provide what the professors want to hear, just as the professors need only produce what the tenure committee wants to read. To teach freedom to students, to get them to drop their well-honed guard, to develop in the academy a saner relation to arbitrary, brutally enforced power, we must get over the problem of the outcome from the very beginning: without the concomitant risk of low grades, students might be willing to take the risk of real thought. A moratorium on consequences means teachers and students prancing in joyful embrace in fields of As, the mind-set of punishment for creative resistance no longer reinforcing the fear of real resistance to spending a trillion dollars a year in this fake and endlessly trumped-up obsession with the paper tiger's den called security. Creating safe spaces for intellectual risk taking in the humanities is a start.

If you are living in the United States illegally and are deported, your return will cost you three years. With a record of any kind, you could easily be looking at ten. It doesn't take much. We aren't protected from administrative regulations because we happen to be employed in the hallowed halls, particularly if we are immigrants. As a permanent resident, I have ten days to report a change of address; failure to report can lead to deportation proceedings—a tiny example of our newfound lust for government-sanctioned arbitrariness, brutality, violence, and disproportionate consequences for minor actions.

The moratorium I describe here only sets the ground; the earth to nourish the seeds of productive resistance and unexpected creation probably needs the sodomizing, psychedelic, far-fetched, orgasmic, fictional, exploded gesture whose nature I cannot even imagine. I think that to survive this era, we need to look to explosive examples from the past, hence the importance of recalling, rereading, and teaching *Sexus*, *Philosophie dans le boudoir*, *Lady Chatterly's Lover*, *Una vita violente*. Even more important, we all need to hear something unexpected, and it's our task as teachers, as catalysts in an era that promotes gated communities inside and outside our minds, to set out the spaces that will make this work possible, in the hope that the disease of freedom leaks from our classrooms and oozes its corrupting influence into our terrified worlds. I hope it's as contagious as can be.

WORKS CITED

Barsky, Robert F. "Activist Translation in an Era of Fictional Law." *Translation and Social Activism*. Ed. Sherry Simon. *TTR* 18.2 (2007): 17–48. Print.

———. *Arguing and Justifying: Assessing the Convention Refugee Choice of Moment, Motive and Host Country*. Aldershot: Ashgate, 2001. Print.

———. *The Chomsky Effect: A Radical Works beyond the Ivory Tower*. Cambridge: MIT P, 2007. Print.

———. *Constructing a Productive Other: Discourse Theory and the Convention Refugee Hearing*. Amsterdam: Benjamins, 1994. Print.

———. "From Discretion to Fictional Law." *SubStance* 109 (2006): 116–46. Print.

———. "Stories from the Court of Appeal." *Dis/Locations*. Ed. Mike Baynham and Anna de Fina. Manchester: St. Jerome's, 2005. 217–38. Print.

Dershowitz, Alan M. *Preemption: A Knife That Cuts Both Ways*. New York: Norton, 2006. Print.

Gramsci, Antonio. *Prison Notebooks*. Vol. 1. Ed. Joseph A. Buttigieg. New York: Columbia UP, 1992. Print.

Jacoby, Russell. *The End of Utopia*. New York: Basic, 1999. Print.

Melman, Seymour. *War, Inc.* Spec. issue of *AmeriQuests* 5.2 (2008). Web. 14 June 2008.

Roth, Philip. *The Human Stain*. New York: Vintage, 2000. Print.

Todorov, Tzvetan. *La littérature en péril*. Paris: Flammarion, 2007. Print.

Ziolkowski, Theodore. *The Mirror of Justice: Literary Reflections of Legal Crises*. Princeton: Princeton UP, 2003. Print.

A Clash of Deep Memories

JAMES V. WERTSCH

In April 2007 Tallinn, Estonia, witnessed some events that were almost un-imaginable in that orderly and peaceful city. Over the course of two nights, riots broke out, leading to one fatality; a hundred injuries, including those sustained by thirteen police officers; and a thousand arrests. These riots were not about a policy for the future but about a dispute over the past, a dispute between two mnemonic communities over a memorial to what is known in Russia as the Great Fatherland War of 1941–45. One commu-nity was the million ethnic Estonians who compose most of the country's population, the second was the half million ethnic Russians who make up most of the remaining portion.

The spark for these riots was the decision by Estonian authorities to move the Bronze Soldier statue from a small park in the center of the city to the Tallinn Military Cemetery on its outskirts. This memorial was erected in 1947 to commemorate the Red Army's arrival in Tallinn in 1944, and it is something of a sacred site for Russians. In addition to the statue, the old location for the memorial included the graves of thirteen Soviet troops who died in 1944 and 1945.

In the months leading up to April 2007, this memorial setting saw an increasing number of commemorative events such as field trips for chil-dren from Russian regions of Estonia. On some occasions these children carried red flags and portraits of Stalin, acts viewed by Estonians as pro-

The author is Marshall S. Snow Professor in Arts and Sciences at Washington University. A version of this paper was presented at the 2007 MLA convention in Chicago.

vocative displays of Russian nationalism and likely to spark conflict. In response, Estonian politicians and authorities discussed plans to move the memorial out of the center of the city, and the riots broke out when work began to make the move. Workers not only dismantled and moved the statue but also disinterred the remains of the soldiers buried in the surrounding park and either reburied them in the Tallinn Military Cemetery or turned them over to the families in Russia who requested that they be buried elsewhere.

The Bronze Soldier was officially known as Монумент освободителям Таллина ("Monument to the Liberators of Tallinn"), and many Russians viewed it as part of a larger liberation story. Many ethnic Estonians, in contrast, viewed it as a symbol of Soviet and Russian oppression of their nation, which had been independent for two decades before being forcibly annexed by Stalin in 1940 under the secret protocols of the Molotov-Ribbentrop Pact. Estonian feelings were so strong about Soviet occupation that in private some referred to the Bronze Soldier as the unknown rapist.

Disputes between the parties responsible for these two readings of the monument were kept largely under wraps until the late 1980s, but with the breakup of the Soviet Union, they became very public. For Russians, it is simply wrong—indeed offensive—to suggest that 1944 was the beginning of oppression directed at Estonians. While many Russians might agree that oppression was part of postwar life in the USSR, they take this as not being directed toward or perpetrated by any national group in particular. In this view all citizens of the USSR were victims of Soviet authorities: Estonians suffered, but so did Russians and members of all other groups in the USSR. Further, Estonians should be grateful for having been liberated in 1944 from the much more brutal Nazi oppressors.

Ethnic Estonians view the statue quite differently. For them it was a reminder of the oppression that came with the return of Soviet forces in 1944, and they find evidence for this in the statue itself (shown in its new location in illus.), pointing out that instead of an image of triumph and victory the sculptor produced a figure who was pensive if not depressed about the fate of his nation. The boundaries of the Russian mnemonic community that objected to moving the Bronze Soldier extended well beyond Estonia. The reaction in Russia may have been more intense than in Estonia. Speaking in Red Square on 9 May 2007, the holiday for commemorating the Soviet victory in 1945, Russian President Vladimir Putin pointedly referred to the April events by saying, "Those . . . who desecrate monuments to war heroes offend their own people and sow discord and new distrust between states and people" (Kramer). On that same day a massive cyber attack from computers in Russia reached its peak and almost

The Bronze Soldier in the Tallinn Military Cemetery

shut down government and banking services in E-stonia, one of the most highly wired countries in the world (see Landler).

Russian anger continued in the months that followed. In July 2007 the Russian nationalist youth group Наши ("Ours") held a large rally in Moscow to commemorate the death of the twenty-year-old Russian who had been killed in the April riots in Tallinn. A more extremist Russian religious group, Union of Orthodox Citizens, called this young man "a hero of Russia" who died defending the memorial in Tallinn "in a war between the Orthodox 'Third Rome' [Moscow] and the occult Nazi 'Third Reich'"("Orthodox Prelate"). In general, the widespread and vehement Russian reaction to moving the Bronze Soldier came as a surprise to many. The authorities' failure to anticipate it is one reason why the April events in Tallinn got out of hand.

The key to understanding the strong Russian reaction is a national narrative that frames the view of the past by this mnemonic community. But just what sort of narrative is at issue? Was this community concerned with the story of those who had perished in 1944 and been buried at the site? Was its focus the story of what happened more generally in Tallinn in 1944? There is little to suggest that Russian anger had to do with either of these events or even with the story of the Great Fatherland War of 1941–45. In fact, few Russians in Estonia or elsewhere know very much about the first two of these events, and there are indications that some young Russians don't have a firm grasp even of the larger war.

What, then, gave rise to such outrage? To answer this question, it is useful to distinguish between two levels of narrative organization: "specific narratives" and "narrative templates" (Wertsch 60). Specific narratives give particular dates, settings, and actions such as the arrival of the Red Army in Tallinn on 22 September 1944 or the Battle of the Kursk in the summer of 1943. Narrative templates are more generalized and schematic structures that do not give such specific information. They are cookie-cutter plots that can be used to generate narratives that contain concrete settings, actors, and events.

The notion of a narrative template grows out of ideas that have long been part of the humanities and social sciences. Among its predecessors are the ideas of Vladimir Propp on textual functions found in folk tales and Frederic Bartlett's notion of schema in the psychology of remembering. Narrative templates are the cultural tools that mediate what can be termed deep collective memory. This form of memory is deep both in the sense that it is largely inaccessible to conscious reflection and in the sense that members of a collective tend to have a strong emotional attachment to it. Questioning a collective's narrative template is often tantamount to a personal attack on the members of the collective. The Russians' vehement reaction to the decision to move the Bronze Soldier is an example.

The notion of a template suggests that a story line is used repeatedly to interpret or emplot many events. Evidence of this tendency in Russia can be found in the name Великая Отечественная Война ("Great Fatherland War"), which echoes the "Fatherland War," known in the West as the Napoleonic War of 1812. The parallel between the two wars becomes all the more apparent when one considers that the description of Hitler as a second Napoleon has long been widespread in the Russian mnemonic community.

The narrative template here covers a much broader range of events than these two wars. Consider the classic 1938 film *Alexander Nevsky*, in which the Soviet director Sergei Eisenstein suggests that the looming danger from fascist Germany can be viewed through a lens from the thirteenth century. In his film, invading Teutonic knights are referred to as немец ("the German") and depicted wearing helmets that come straight from the uniform of the invaders in the impending conflagration in 1941. The list of parallels goes on, as Russians speak of the conquests by numerous foreigners, including Tatars, Germans, Swedes, Poles, Turks, and Germans again.

What these events have in common for the Russian mnemonic community is a narrative template that can be labeled "the expulsion of foreign enemies," whose elements I summarize as follows:

1. The initial situation: Russia is peaceful and not interfering with others.
2. Trouble: a foreign enemy viciously attacks Russia without provocation.
3. Russia loses nearly everything, suffering defeat at the hands of an enemy that attempts to destroy it as a civilization.
4. Through heroism and exceptionalism, against all odds and acting alone, Russia triumphs and expels the foreign enemy.

This narrative template fits the pattern of what Bartlett called the "effort after meaning" (20); it is widely understood and employed by Russians when making sense of events both past and present. It provides a plot line for specific narratives, which take the shape of the same story told again and again with different characters.

All this is not to say that the specific narratives associated with this template are simply fabricated or figments of the imagination of the mnemonic community. Russia obviously *has* suffered at the hands of foreign enemies on numerous occasions. But "the expulsion of foreign enemies" provides a powerful interpretive framework that guides the thinking and speaking of the members of this community, to such an extent that their interpretations of some events are quite striking to those coming from other mnemonic communities. For example, it is surprising for members of other communities to hear Soviet Communism described as a foreign enemy, this time in the form of Western ideas that the heroic Russian people finally managed to defeat and expel. This story line is by no means new. A nineteenth-century version of it can be found in the "demons" of

Dostoevsky's imagination, where alien ideas had to be cast out of Russian society in order for it to avoid a descent into nihilism and godless inhumanity.

Some might question whether "the expulsion of foreign enemies" template is peculiarly Russian. At least some of its elements would appear to be in the repertoire of cultural tools used by members of other mnemonic communities. The American view of the 1941 attack on Pearl Harbor, for example, is built around the notion of an unprovoked attack. That such a question arises reflects the first basic property of narrative templates: their abstract, schematic nature. Precisely because they are abstract, they are consistent with a range of specific narratives, including those from more than one mnemonic community. Nonetheless, the Russian mnemonic community is distinguished from most others in its predilection for this template, which provides the outlines of the official account of many events from Russia's past and is often quickly invoked to make sense of incidents in the present. Other narrative templates are likely to be used by members of, say, the American mnemonic community, where story lines about manifest destiny or a reluctant hegemon are more commonly harnessed to interpret events (resp., Lowenthal; Kagan).

A second basic property of narrative templates restricts their tendency toward generality and binds them strongly to unique mnemonic communities. Standing in opposition to the tendency toward schematic abstraction, which suggests that narrative templates are generalized and relatively neutral "cognitive instruments" (Mink) available to any group wishing to use them, is the tendency for national narratives to be what Jan Assmann calls "monoperspectival, ethnocentric, and narcissistic" (21). This is not a matter of simple selfishness; indeed in some cases the story is one of selfless service to a broader community or to all of humanity. *Narcissism* here means that events, including those initiated by others, are really all about one's own collective. This view is often coupled with a collective's claims about the uniqueness of its story and hence of itself. It can easily lead to difficulties in understanding that other legitimate interpretations of an event can exist.

From the perspective of the Russian mnemonic community, for example, the annexation of Estonia in 1940 had nothing to do with Estonia; it was part of a larger story about Russia—the effort to prevent, or at least delay, yet another invasion by a foreign enemy. In this view the delay was part of a strategy that allowed Russia to prepare for the German invasion and that ultimately led to a victory over fascism for Russia and for human civilization. Obvious as this interpretation is to Russians, it is of course not the only one that can be used to make sense of the 1940 annexation. Members of the Estonian mnemonic community typically view the annexation as another episode in a long history of Russian territorial expansionism and domination of smaller neighbors.

The combination of schematic abstraction and narcissistic particularity of narrative templates is not as confused or syncretistic as it at first appears. Being abstract, narrative templates are difficult to falsify and hence ideal instruments for supporting beliefs that cannot be challenged by counter-evidence. They are therefore powerful cultural tools in national discourse. They mediate deep collective memory in a way that makes it possible for members of a mnemonic community to interpret a wide range of events from a strongly held narcissistic perspective and to remain convinced that they are simply telling "what really happened."

As Hayden White reminds us, any narrative introduces a subjective perspective, a moralizing impulse into our understanding of the world. The notion of a narrative template calls on us to examine the workings of this impulse at the level of deep collective memory, a level that seems to motivate many of the emotional and seemingly intractable conflicts in Russia but of course is also at work everywhere else in the world.

In conclusion, I point to three implications of this line of reasoning. First, the outrage of a national community can easily be sparked by a challenge to narratives about the past, but such challenges are often not really to specific narratives. Most threatening is to call into question the template that lies at the core of collective identity. What binds a mnemonic community together is not so much a set of specific narratives as a pattern of making meaning that is general and schematic, on the one hand, and quite local and narcissistic, on the other.

Second, this combination of properties of narrative templates gives the templates staying power. They maintain their integrity over long periods and resist change even in the face of massive social and political transformation. The specific narratives about World War II that one finds in official Russian accounts today are strikingly different from those found in the Soviet period (Wertsch), but "the expulsion of foreign enemies" narrative template seems to have remained intact.

Third, in certain circumstances the combination of properties of narrative templates can create a toxic mix that gives rise to stark, nonnegotiable opposition between two mnemonic communities. Such an opposition was manifested in the events in Tallinn in 2007 and in their aftermath. A more dangerous version can be found in Nagorno-Karabakh, the region disputed by Azerbaijan and Armenia. As outlined by Thomas de Waal, the "sealed narratives" in this dispute are part and parcel of a permanent standoff that could reerupt at any time into further bloody conflict (225).

National narrative templates are not always destined to play a nefarious role. They are often used for the common good of a community or even the broader world. Regardless of how they are harnessed, however, we need to understand them better—and perhaps even help control some of their more dangerous tendencies.

WORKS CITED

Assmann, Jan. "Cultural Memories and National Narratives: With Some Relation to the Case of Georgia." Negotiating a New National Narrative in Georgia: Rockefeller Foundation Bellagio Conf. Aug. 2005. *Caucasus Context* 3.1 (2007): 21–23. Print.

Bartlett, F. C. *Remembering: A Study in Experimental and Social Psychology.* Cambridge: Cambridge UP, 1932. Print.

de Waal, Thomas. *Black Garden: Armenia and Azerbaijan through Peace and War.* New York: New York UP, 2003. Print.

Dostoevsky, Fyodor. *Demons: A Novel in Three Parts.* Trans. Richard Pevear and Larissa Volokhonsky. New York: Knopf, 1995. Print. Trans. of *Besy.* 1872.

Eisenstein, Sergei, dir. *Alexander Nevsky.* Image Entertainment, 1998. DVD.

Kagan, Robert. *Dangerous Nation: America's Place in the World from Its Earliest Days to the Dawn of the Twentieth Century.* New York: Knopf, 2006. Print.

Kramer, Andrew E. "Putin Likens U.S. Foreign Policy to That of Third Reich." *International Herald Tribune* 9 May 2007. Web. 13 June 2008.

Landler, Mark. "Hot Technology for Chilly Streets in Estonia." *New York Times* 13 Dec. 2005. Web. 7 Aug. 2008.

Lowenthal, David. "Identity, Heritage, and History." *Commemorations: The Politics of National Identity.* Ed. John R. Gillis. Princeton: Princeton UP, 1994. 41–57. Print.

Mink, Louis O. "Narrative Form as a Cognitive Instrument." *The Writing of History: Literary Form and Historical Understanding.* Ed. Robert H. Canary and Henry Kozicki. Madison: U of Wisconsin P, 1978. 129–49. Print.

"Orthodox Prelate Decries Exhumation of Communist Soldiers: Two Stories." *Directions to Orthodoxy News Center.* 3 May 2007. Web. 13 June 2008.

Propp, V. *Morphology of the Folktale.* Trans. Laurence Scott. Austin: U of Texas P, 1968. Print. Trans. of *Morfologija skazki.* 1928.

Wertsch, J. V. *Voices of Collective Remembering.* New York: Cambridge UP, 2002. Print.

White, Hayden. "The Value of Narrativity in the Representation of Reality." *On Narrative.* Ed. W. J. T. Mitchell. Chicago: U of Chicago P, 1981. 1–23. Print.

On Being Wrong

NANCY K. MILLER

It was early in the fall semester of 1985, and I was lying in bed reading the *New Yorker*. During most of the 1980s I ran the Women's Studies Program at Barnard College and taught there. But I also taught on occasion in the graduate school at Columbia, where I had studied French during the high theory days of the 1970s. I had been leafing through the magazine on a Friday night trying to relax, when my eye was caught by a story that began in the following way: "It was easy to find an apartment in New Haven, even though my classes in feminist criticism were starting in just a few days and most of the other grad students had arrived at Yale the week before" (Janowitz 30). Hey, I elbowed my husband, who was reading on the other side of the bed. A story in the *New Yorker* by a woman writer about feminist criticism. I sat bolt upright in amazement.

Then feminist criticism disappeared for a while, until well into the third page of the story, when the narrator, a young woman named Cora, after supplying some family background for the reader (a dead sister, a father living in New Zealand), mentions that she had been accepted into the Women's Studies Program at Yale. I was newly excited. But not, as it turned out, for long. "I was sitting in class, taking notes as usual," the narrator complains about her seminar in feminist criticism, "when it became apparent that not one word that was being said made the slightest bit of sense" (32).

More than twenty years after the fact, it's hard for me to slow down my initial reaction enough to replicate it here. I confess that I had been

---

The author is distinguished professor of English and comparative literature at the Graduate Center, City University of New York.

---

so enchanted by the prospect of reading about a feminist criticism class at Yale (Yale!) that I temporarily lost my critical cool. Hadn't I been taught to distinguish the sign from the referent? literature from the thing itself? All training flew out the bedroom window as I read on, enraptured. "The teacher, Anna Castleton" (who could that be?), "a well-padded, grayish woman with clipped-poodle hair" (that doesn't sound like Margaret Homans, the one feminist professor at Yale I could think of), "was discussing a conference she had attended the week before—a Poetics of Gender colloquium—where she was severely attacked for her presentation" (32). No, wait, that's not Margaret Homans, I thought, my readerly pleasure sliding into heart-pounding paranoia. Well-padded? Poodle hair? It sounded like me. But wait, I struggled for sanity—this doesn't make sense. The Poetics of Gender conference had taken place at Columbia in the fall of 1984—I ran the conference, I hadn't been attacked, and no one fitting that—my?—description had been either. On the other hand, the laundry list of notes composed by the student narrator did ring true:

> Status of empirical discourse.
> Post-structuralist account of dissolving subject precludes formation of female identity.
> The notion of the subject in progress.
> It was assumed she was calling for a return to fixed identity.
> Post-gendered subjectivities.
> If gender is constructed, a gendered identity ninety-nine per cent of the time is built onto person who has a sex. (32)

If on the page of the magazine the words sounded excruciatingly familiar, it was because I remembered having spoken them, or words like them, at the Feminism/Theory/Politics conference held at the Pembroke Center the previous spring.[1] My talk had been about authorship, female authorship after the famous "death of the author" argument, taking as my example Charlotte Brontë's feisty feminist heroine Lucy Snowe; I had ended on what I meant to be an ironic turn inspired by the novel.[2] Unfortunately, my irony badly misfired, and a member of the audience, a young British theorist famous for her poststructuralist views, stood up and denounced me in a statement she had managed to take the time to write out. Her words and her tone left me gasping. In the *New Yorker* story version of the conference, what happened to the feminist professor, according to the heroine's seminar notes (reproduced as such in the story), was that "without using the word 'class,' she argued for a more complicated view of women as historical subject. Yet she was attacked for this—brutally attacked" (32). And in a brief, disingenuous flash of sympathy, the narrator speculates about what the professor might have felt: "I wondered whether the teacher had burst into tears following the attack on her. The two hours of class were devoted to a retelling of the attack in this language which so gracefully circled a subject without ever landing to make a point" (33). I had not cried at the event at the Pembroke Center. I was too shocked for tears. But I was forced to admit then that women, feminists, could be as violent toward one another as any men in academia. In the seminar I was teaching that semester, I had talked about my disillusionment.

Recalling the scene as I read in bed, I did feel like crying, though, because it was clear that the writer of the story was taking no hostages either and that what I thought was so wonderful—a story about feminist criticism in the *New Yorker*—was the opposite of wonderful. All the more so because it was written by a woman, Tama Janowitz, a young writer who had already received a great deal of thrilled literary attention, although it was only the following year, when her story collection *Slaves of New York* appeared, that she attained celebrity as a female member of the literary brat pack. I hated the author's portrait of me. Was it true? Had I not even made my point? My mortification deepened. I was not only a pathetic, jargon-ridden joke in the eyes of the student narrator, I had big hips and bad hair. I got out of bed and poured myself a serious drink.

But the story—of reading the *New Yorker* story—isn't over yet. Once I (likened in Cora's notebook doodle to a "beaver, paddling frantically, with a tree stump clutched in its large buckteeth" [32]) had been dispatched to utter ridicule, the narrator turned the spotlight on herself, on the presentation she had made in the same seminar later in the semester, an oral report on "mysticism and Eastern philosophy and some of the similar themes that emerge in the writings of Virginia Woolf" (33). I actually remembered the presentation quite vividly and recalled that it wasn't in fact the author, whom I had begun in my mind's eye to see in her place around the seminar table, but another young woman in the class who had discussed Woolf and Eastern mysticism. As I began to revisit the scene in memory, I slowly realized that this story was not going to be just about me. "I had hoped to please the teacher," Cora confesses. "Throughout my report she wrote furiously in a notebook." And, she goes on, "when I finished, she looked up and said, 'You're wrong'" (33). By then I was not only wide awake, I was shocked again, although in an entirely different way. For one thing, I now had to recognize that the "seminar in feminist criticism" at Yale was actually a seminar on women's writing and feminist theory at Columbia that I had taught several times with my friend and mentor Carolyn Heilbrun. Carolyn and I had been literarily fused into one "well-padded, grayish," generic feminist professor: Anna Castleton. I remembered this scene with absolute clarity, because I had been a spectator to it. Carolyn was the Woolf expert, and in our alternation I naturally deferred to her authority. I too watched and waited as Carolyn gave her response. "The other women in the class," the narrator continues, "all turned to catch my reaction. I felt as if I had been electrocuted on a television game show" (33).

Now Carolyn/Castleton had not said, "You're wrong," in anger, or even theatrically, like a game show announcer. But she had said it, and the words echoed in the seminar room on the sixth floor of Philosophy Hall, a wood-paneled room hung with the portraits of famous dead male professors of English. She had said it not so differently from the way my thesis director in the French department on the fifth floor of Philosophy Hall used to interrupt students making presentations after a few words if they were not to his liking: "*Non,*" he would say, "no." Sometimes the student would leave the classroom in tears. Once, when I criticized him for the way he treated students in his seminar, he said, "This is not a charitable institution." Like Virginia Woolf's angry professor in *A Room of One's Own*, the man saw no need to apologize.

Hold on. How can I even put the feminist and the patriarch together in the same sentence? The patriarchal professor's explanation typically would compare the student's inadequate analysis to his own masterful theory of the literary text, to the one correct reading, as he saw it. With my friend and colleague, a recognized authority on Virginia Woolf's writing, the explanation was couched in feminist terms, referring to theories of gender and power. The student, she explained, as the narrator tells it, "had fallen prey to a traditional male put-down: placing women in the category of weak, dreamy mystics and then denying them power" (33). Soon after this episode, which leaves her perplexed and demoralized, Cora gives up on graduate school and returns to live in New York.

Why revisit that story now? A story that at the time I prayed no one I knew would see, or if they did, would think, as I had, that Anna Castleton taught at Yale. Rereading the tale as I thought about the question of feminist pedagogy, what surprised me was how little feminist criticism—or, as it is referred to in the *New Yorker*'s online abstract, "feminine criticism"—how little the classroom scene had to do with the story's arc, which mainly turned on the heroine's decision to return to New York and not marry a kind of strange slacker guy, hence the title "Engagements." After her disappointing semester at Yale, Cora temporarily lives with her mother, as she tries to figure out what to do next.

In 1985, when I finished reading the story, I called Carolyn at her country house in the Berkshires. She had not seen it; she was cynical about the *New Yorker*, the few women they published. She was sure I was overreacting and even chuckled a bit as she recalled the seminar moment. Naturally, that was not how she saw the matter at all, though the report had definitely irritated her. Her comments were meant to be instructive, to expose the ideological foundations of the framework the student had chosen to support her interpretation. Her intent was to help the young woman understand the presuppositions that had led her to an erroneous view of Virginia Woolf. If the student was devastated by what she experienced as a feminist put-down, by what she perceived to be an unfair exertion of authority, that was because she wasn't sufficiently tough-minded. Besides, it was just a story, a *New Yorker* story at that, why take it so seriously? Being reminded that I had succumbed to the perils of the referential fallacy was no help at all.

Mean as Janowitz's story was (and it has not stopped, despite the passage of time, feeling very mean), I found that I could not so easily dismiss its portrayals. In real life were we feminist professors nobler than the author had made us out to be? The student who had given the report in the seminar didn't think so, and Janowitz had defended her with the tools of her trade: in print. Maybe we were even. But surely that's the wrong metaphor: keeping score. Still, if it's easy to see what is not feminist in a professor's "You're wrong!," what would be the better way to perform a critique when a critique is what seems called for? And aren't there times when to say "You're wrong!" is what needs saying?

At a recent tribute to Tillie Olsen, organized by the Feminist Press, Olsen's youngest daughter, Laurie, evoked an episode from her mother's life. While a fellow at the Radcliffe Institute in Cambridge, Olsen attended a lecture given at her daughter's high school during parents' weekend. Inspired by his reading of *The Lord of the Flies*, John Kenneth Galbraith, then professor of economics at Harvard, was holding forth on the lessons of the novel, concluding that "human beings by nature are wired to be individualistic, and to crush those in the way as they strive to get to the top of the heap and to look out for themselves." At this point, Laurie Olsen described her mother rising from the audience, interrupting the speaker's peroration to declare in a voice that echoed throughout the room, "You are wrong, sir!"

Olsen, in her daughter's words, then proceeded to put forward her own countervision of humanity. "Have you never observed young children when they hear another child cry? Have you never seen them reach out to comfort each other? That impulse," she went on to explain, "to feel and respond to another's pain is one of the deepest human impulses, wired into the human spirit. The room was stunned," the daughter recalled, "as Tillie continued for some time." After the lecture many women came up to her mother "with tears in their eyes." Olsen never feared identifying injustice, her daughter concluded, protesting what was wrong.

What's the difference between Tillie Olsen's interrupting Galbraith to set the record straight and Carolyn Heilbrun's saying (Heilbrun also often spoke out against injustice, especially toward women), "You are wrong," to the student in her seminar? Is it as easy as concluding that it's OK for a woman to tell a man, a figure of authority, that he is wrong, to speak truth to power, but not for a woman professor to tell a woman student that the student is wrong? Or not for a feminist professor to say that to a feminist student? It has happened to me, as to all of us, that it sometimes becomes necessary to convey that something indeed is wrong. What options do we have in those circumstances, which are, after all, matters of interpretation?

I recently taught a seminar called The Ethnic I, in which we read first-person fiction and nonfiction works from the early twentieth century to the present, by authors of Asian, Jewish, and Latino/Latina origins. We began with an autobiography from 1912, *The Promised Land*, by Mary Antin. Her best-selling autobiography is often considered to be the first true account of the Eastern European immigrant experience in America. She emigrated from Russia in 1894, and her family settled in Boston. In *The Promised Land*, Antin tells a story that in its broadest outlines conforms to the classic arc of immigrant literature, of the narrator's transformation from immigrant to citizen through the education plot, of success in school leading to success in the wider world. Hers is a story of vocation in which she becomes a writer through her belief in the ideals of American democracy. Her hero was George Washington.

In the session devoted to *The Promised Land*, which was our first text for the semester, one student analyzed a passage that had bothered her. Antin recalls being bullied as a child by a boy "who was the torment of the neighborhood." Her father, she explains, proudly, "determined to teach the rascal a lesson for once, had him arrested and brought to court. The boy was locked up overnight, and he emerged from his brief imprisonment with a respect for the rights and persons of his neighbors" (203). For Antin, the "moral of the incident" was not her revenge on the bully but what she "saw of the way in which justice was actually administered in the United States." This was the opposite of what might have happened in Russia, she explains, if a Jew sought justice against his attacker.

In America—she continues, educating her American reader—the "evil-doer was actually punished, and not the victim, as might easily happen in a similar case in Russia." And she sums up the occasion with a patriotic salute to her new country, "three cheers for the Red, White, and Blue!" (203–04).

Why did the student select this episode for commentary? She chose the passage, she said, because something about the language of Antin's characterization made the student pause as a reader. The bully is described as a "great, hulky colored boy," the two groups who attend the trial as two mirrored communities defined through metonymy by physical differences: "bearded Arlington Street against wool-headed Arlington Street" (204). The student, whose comments were thoughtful, nuanced, and historically astute, brought the scene with all its problems of representation to the class, because what felt like unconscious racism on the part of the author left her as a twenty-first-century reader feeling, as she nicely put it, "unsettled." In my rereading of the autobiography, I had been bothered by the passage myself—so bothered, in fact, that I inadvertently changed the adjective "hulky" (a strange-sounding adjective in English; "hulking" would have been more expected) to "husky" when I responded to the student's presentation. In my eagerness to find something "wrong" with the student's analysis, to quell my own discomfort, I had stumbled over the signifier. In Antin's narrative of childhood lessons in American democracy, I insisted, after admitting my mistake and trying to turn it to my advantage, what matters is size: Antin is a little girl; the bully is a big, *hulking* boy. It's anachronistic to accuse Antin of racism, I argued, hoping to settle the matter with history. (Of course, it was in fact the oddity of the signifier that caused both of us to pause, as my earliest training as a structuralist had taught me, but to make that case seemed just as anachronistic.)

Now this is not a case where the student was wrong, either in her choice or in her interpretation. On the contrary. If anyone was wrong, I was. But I cite this example to invoke another kind of seminar interaction. As the professor who had chosen the reading, I wanted to justify Antin, so that she would not be considered wrong in the eyes of the students. I showed the class how later in the chapter she refers to a "Chinky Chinaman" (though there Antin herself places scare quotes around the phrase to indicate the language of her group of girlfriends [204]). I desperately wanted to make the case for a historicized reading of racialized stereotypes, of language we no longer considered acceptable. Didn't Fitzgerald and Hemingway refer to "kikes" without anyone's impugning their integrity as writers?[3] I didn't want this linguistic bump to ruin my author's reputation. I wanted to erase what was making me uncomfortable in my own eyes and perhaps also implicating me, who had assigned the text, as sharing Antin's unconscious racial bias. I too descend from Russian Jewish immigrants, and racism is not what I want my legacy to include.[4]

Let me use the question of anxiety and discomfort to move back to the earlier question my anecdotes raised: How as teachers and students can we learn to respond to what's wrong—what feels wrong—without recourse to a rhetoric of blame, without sending the offender to jail for the night? How can we tolerate disagreement among ourselves, particularly when, which is usually the case in the humanities, right and wrong are often a matter of interpretation and just as often of politics? What would make it possible for us to occupy the same space, acknowledging our differences and disagreements but without policing one another?

Here, therefore, though it may seem paradoxical, I return to the work of Carolyn Heilbrun, who wrote poignantly about what connects and separates women, about the need for justice, and about the difficulty of taking feminist positions in postfeminist times.[5]

This essay will appear soon after the fifth anniversary of Heilbrun's suicide. What I most want now to say to my friend is, "You are wrong!" There are always many reasons—or feelings translated into reasons—that lead people to suicide. One cause of Carolyn's published despair was the difficulty of continuing to be a feminist teacher, an older feminist teacher to younger feminists. She was often discouraged by the women students who thought feminism was over, that the battles were won, that they had heard it all before. This was the theme of one of her last books, *Women's Lives: The View from the Threshold*. Oddly, this was also a book in which she put forward one of her boldest and potentially most optimistic ideas: that of liminality, a concept borrowed from the great anthropologist Victor Turner. Heilbrun writes:

> The word "limen" means "threshold," and to be in a state of liminality is to be poised on uncertain ground, to be leaving one condition or country or self and entering upon another. But the most salient form of liminality is its unsteadiness, its lack of clarity about exactly where one belongs and what one should be doing, or wants to be doing. (3)

Liminality is a good description of what it means to be a graduate student, like Janowitz's protagonist, Cora. "Liminal entities," Turner observes, "are neither here nor there; they are betwixt and between . . . " (qtd. in Heilbrun 36). Liminality, another Turner proponent puts it, helps women "find viable alternatives to patriarchy" (Driver qtd. in Heilbrun 37). But Cora doesn't stick around long enough to figure out what might emerge from the lack of clarity.

In the penultimate episode of "Engagements," Cora goes shopping with her mother on Thirty-Fourth Street. She has just had an unsettling encounter with Ray, who told her he's getting married to another woman. As consolation, though Cora professes not to really care about the wedding announcement, her mother buys her two pairs of shoes, "gray pumps, with a medium heel, and a pair of purple sandals, which resembled, at least as far as I was concerned, those worn by French prostitutes. They weren't practical," she observes of the sandals, "but I liked them" (Janowitz 38). Cora implicitly dismisses the "gray pumps" as she rejects her gray feminist professor, preferring, as stereotypes go, the sandals of a French prostitute. There's a lot to be said about the therapeutics of shoe shopping, but that's not where I want to end.

I turn for a final image to Virginia Woolf's last novel, *Between the Acts*, written during World War II and published after her suicide. The thread I want to pull out is the portrait of Miss La Trobe, the author of a play whose performance is at the center of the novel. La Trobe is a middle-aged woman described in terms that Carolyn enjoyed because they rejected stereotypes of gender and especially of female beauty: "Very little was actually known about her," Woolf writes. "Outwardly she was swarthy, sturdy and thick set; strode about the fields in a smock frock; sometimes with a cigarette in her mouth; often with a whip in her hand; and used rather strong language—perhaps, then, she wasn't altogether a lady? At any rate, she had a passion for getting things up" (58). One of the main things Miss La Trobe gets up is the play, whose meaning baffles the audience. Mr. Streatfield, the minister, tries to sort out the confusion: "To me at least it was indicated that we are members one of another. Each is part of the whole. . . . We act different parts; but are the same. That I leave to you" (192). The audience struggles to understand: "He said she meant we all act. Yes, but whose play? Ah, that's the question! And if we're left asking questions, isn't it a failure, as a play?" (200). As a title, *Between the Acts* points to the condition of liminality and to the entanglement of contradiction that comes from being betwixt and between: "It was Yes, No. Yes, yes, yes, the tide rushed out embracing. No, no, no, it contracted" (215). Yes and no coexist in the liminal world. A no doesn't mean a yes can't come later; a yes is always only provisional.

The professor Heilbrun evokes at the end of her book is an aging feminist faced with young women students who do not see the world as she does. I have felt this myself at times, the loneliness of being the one in the "gray pumps with the medium heels" watching the girls in purple sandals go dancing. But the one thing that Heilbrun does not imagine here is the possibility of change coming from the very terms of her analysis of the threshold: in the provisional suspension of codes and conventions that liminality entails, feminist genealogy might evolve differently. Change and continuity could emerge simultaneously through the movement of a feedback loop, in which, for instance, students and teachers alike resist the need for certainty, for being right.

The liminal, as Turner has shown, is often the site and the occasion for a rite of passage, a ritual attended by witnesses. That would be another way to understand the dynamics of the graduate seminar. For each student, the oral report is a rite of passage witnessed by fellow participants. The performance of the student is not solely a pas de deux with the teacher. Rather, the presentation, like any rite, makes sense within a collective frame. "In this view," writes another commentator on liminality, "life is a series of individual passages from group to group, while the groups [of witnesses] . . . remain stable, like standing waves" (Beels 121). What happens in these rites can be unsettling. "Transformations occur in this in-between space," Gloria Anzaldúa writes, a threshold space where we are in a "constant state of displacement—an uncomfortable, even alarming feeling" (Anzaldúa and Keating 1).

In the liminal classroom—a space that Heilbrun anticipates when she concludes her argument with a metaphor reminiscent of Woolf's—we are no longer actors in a "carefully structured drama, a play in which our parts are written for us" (102). Rather, we become performers in a space of invention and tolerance for the alarming, in which, for instance, a student presentation like Cora's would lead to flashes of electricity, and not electrocution, to the illumination of another way—other ways—of thinking.

After the audience disperses, Miss La Trobe ponders the play's reception: "'A failure,' she groaned" (209). But Woolf does not leave her author in despair. As night begins to fall, Miss La Trobe is on the move: "She took her voyage away from the shore, and, raising her hand, fumbled for the latch of the iron entrance gate" (211). She finds herself at the "threshold, . . . the place where as women and creators of literature," as Heilbrun puts it, unconsciously, perhaps, reprising Woolf's final vision in the novel, "we write our own lines and, eventually, our own plays" (102). At the end of *Between the Acts*, lonely, but not bereft, Miss La Trobe proceeds into a pub, orders a drink, and listens to the words circulating around her. As she listens, new words of her own form in her head, the dialogue of her next play.

NOTES

This essay was originally presented at the Second Feminist Pedagogy Conference 2007, called "What's Feminist about Feminist Pedagogy?" (Oct. 2007). The conference was organized by Jen Gieseking, Antonia Levy, and Jennifer Gaboury, students in environmental psychology, sociology, and political science at the Graduate Center, CUNY. I am grateful in particular to Gieseking, who invited me to speak at this student-organized occasion. I'd also like to thank two of my former students, Kevin Ferguson and Victoria Rosner, for their comments on earlier drafts of this essay, as well as the students in The Ethnic I seminar at the Graduate Center for the example of their practice.

1. Clearly, this conference was, as Jane Gallop suggests, a "memorable" moment in the history of feminist criticism (186). For me it was memorably contentious.

2. I published the final version of this paper as "Changing the Subject: Authorship, Writing, and the Reader" in *Subject to Change* (102–21).

3. The very next week we read *The Great Gatsby*, where "kyke" appears in the mouth of Mrs. McKee (38) but, more interesting, where Tom Buchanan objects to Daisy's use of "hulking": "a great big hulking physical specimen of a. . . ." Tom replies, "I hate that word hulking, . . . even in kidding" (16).

4. When I showed this essay to the student who had made the Antin presentation, she told me that she in fact had shared my anxiety about the passage because she shared my background. In class, on the basis of assumptions I had made about her name, Jessica Wells Cantiello, it did not occur to me that her discomfort with the text might have common roots with my own.

5. The emergence of a so-called postfeminist generation was already being diagnosed in 1982, just as I was starting to run the Women's Studies Program at Barnard (see Bolotin).

WORKS CITED

Antin, Mary. *The Promised Land*. New York: Penguin, 1977. Print.

Anzaldúa, Gloria, and Annalouise Keating, eds. *This Bridge We Call Home: Radical Visions for Transformation*. New York: Routledge, 2002. Print.

Beels, C. Christian. *A Different Story: The Rise of Narrative in Psychotherapy*. Phoenix: Zeig, 2001. Print.

Bolotin, Susan. "Voices from the Post-feminist Generation." *New York Times* 17 Oct. 1982: 28+. Print.

"The Feminist Politics of Interpretation." Feminism / Theory / Politics. Conf. Pembroke Center, Brown U. Mar. 1985. Addresses.

Fitzgerald, F. Scott. *The Great Gatsby*. New York: Simon, 1995. Print.

Gallop, Jane. "The Historicization of Literary Studies and the Fate of Close Reading." *Profession* (2007): 181–86. Print.

Heilbrun, Carolyn G. *Women's Lives: The View from the Threshold*. Toronto: U of Toronto P, 1999. Print.

Janowitz, Tama. "Engagements." *New Yorker* 2 Sept. 1985: 30–38. Print.

Miller, Nancy K. *Subject to Change: Reading Feminist Writing.* New York: Columbia UP, 1988. Print.

Olsen, Laurie. "A Memorial Tribute to Tillie Olsen." 11 Sept. 2007. *Audio Archive.* Center for the Humanities, Graduate Center, CUNY. Web. 20 June 2008.

Woolf, Virginia. *Between the Acts.* New York: Harcourt, 1969. Print.

A Clash of Civilizations: Religious and Academic Discourse in the English Classroom

PETER KERRY POWERS

A colleague teaching at a public university recently told me of a conversation with her chair as he lamented the large number of fundamentalist students on his campus and in his classes. He informed my stunned colleague, a Christian, that part of their job as professors of English was to move these students away from their faith.

On the surface such candor seems to confirm what a great many cultural and religious conservatives believe already: that higher education as it exists in the United States purposefully erodes the fundamental values of those it seeks to educate. Indeed, conservative religious people can view themselves as a threatened minority. According to the First Amendment scholar J. M. Balkin, conservative students increasingly articulate this sense of embattlement in terms of broad First Amendment protections and view their inability to speak in class as a form of censorship (169; qtd. in Sherwood 56).

It may well be that this phenomenon is overstated. Nevertheless, I want to avoid the tendency to blame our students for their failures to learn and to feel at home in the academic worlds that we have created. Maybe we should be forthright and admit that we are often uncomfortable with our students' religion and that we often don't know what to do with it in the classroom. Having taught at both state universities and faith-based institutions, I can say with some confidence that this discomfort runs across the

The author is professor of English at Messiah College.

academic board, though with different specifics in different circumstances. In some instances, intellectuals at faith-based institutions may be even more troubled by such students, who remind them vividly of the fundamentalists they once were or avoided becoming. Secretly, perhaps guiltily, many of us, whether secular or religious, think it might be easier if our students didn't have the faith they in fact have. Wouldn't we be better off if they were stripped of it or at least kept it under wraps, where we wouldn't have to deal with it in all its messy reality?

My general sense is that this question projects an educational program and pedagogy that are not only implausible but also at odds with the ideals most educators share. In this essay, I examine the sources and teleology of academic discomfort with religion in the classroom. Why is it there, what are its consequences, and what if anything should be done about it?

Although I'm interested mostly in the educator, I'm not arguing that the religious commitments of students can't present genuine problems for teachers. Scholarship on teaching religious students regularly poses the problem of the aggressive, usually white, usually male student who creates a disagreeable atmosphere with simplistic references to the Bible and judgmental condemnation of others, a student whom I imagine all of us have had to engage. My most dramatic encounter with this type involved a student who pretended to vomit into his book after I told a class that James Baldwin was gay. Let's just say we didn't get far that day in our understanding of Baldwin or sexuality, or even religion. Such students shape our belief that religion in the classroom is a problem.

Nevertheless, the attention given to this kind of student as typical of religious students in general may betray a much larger problem, which is shared by faculty members and students alike, a problem Stephen Prothero calls religious illiteracy. He defines religious literacy in terms akin to cultural literacy, as "the ability to understand and use in one's day-to-day life the basic building blocks of religious traditions—their key terms, symbols, doctrines, practices, sayings, characters, metaphors, and narratives" (11–12). We are, Prothero argues, "a nation of religious illiterates" (21).

Indeed, too often our most aggressive religious students also appear to be desperately unfamiliar with the traditions and complexities of their own religion. It's not impossible that their aggression masks the anxieties that accompany this lack of competence, especially if they already feel incompetent in the classroom. Unfortunately, their professors too often share their illiteracy. When culturally illiterate, we reduce the unfamiliar to the simplest and perhaps most egregious stereotypes, missing the complexity of different cultural and subcultural formations. We tend to assume that one student's clumsy or offensive behavior represents a group, even if we vaguely know better. When religiously illiterate, we view religion in the classroom through the single lens of our loudest and most obnoxious student, assuming that he speaks not for himself but for religion as such. Why, we ask ourselves, doesn't he have the common decency to keep his faith quiet and to himself like all the other religiously anxious students in the classroom?

And they are, in fact, in the classroom. Research suggests that religious convictions and religious curiosity are important to student self-conception as students enter our college classrooms, that students in general—not only those who are fundamentalist—want to understand how our subject matters relate to their religious lives (Braskamp 8). However, we have yet to develop a pedagogical ethos that seeks to understand religious backgrounds with the same professional seriousness that we have learned to bring to the question of a student's race, gender, or sexual orientation. While there has been a much-vaunted turn to religion in literary and cultural studies, it's unclear that this intellectual interest has affected our perceptions of and relationships with the students sitting in front of us.

Teaching at a faith-based institution, my colleagues and I regularly assume that the vast majority of our students are Christians, but this assumption doesn't make us more aware of the particular languages and histories of faith that students bring to the classroom. Roman Catholics, mainline Protestants, and others can feel at some distance from the broadly white Protestant evangelical consensus on our campus. Even more religious diversity is in play at public universities. Teaching at George Mason University, I was as likely to engage Hindu faithful as atheists. Perhaps more likely. One of my most vivid memories of teaching there is of my engagement with a student who insisted on interpreting T. S. Eliot through Islamic creation stories, which to her were cold, hard facts. Completely unfamiliar with Islam, I dismissed her observations as unrelated to Eliot's religious concerns and thus as an illegitimate opening into the poetry.

Of course, as Prothero rightly notes, we cannot possibly be literate in every single religious culture and language (12). But being culturally competent in every student culture is not a prerequisite for sensitive attentiveness to student differences. I teach with an awareness that students work out of ethnic and racial frameworks, even when I am not always conversant with those frameworks. My awareness that students have certain kinds of cultural competence that I do not makes me more open to the knowledge they bring to the table. By analogy, attending to the fact that students speak, think, and write out of different religious cultures might change the way we imagine our pedagogical responsibilities and might change as well our responses to the personal knowledge they bring to the classroom. Had I brought a simple humility to my Islamic student's observations, I might have seen her comments as a doorway rather than as an irrelevancy.

Religious discourses, beliefs, and practices should be understood more clearly as cultural formations out of which students think and act and through which they form a sense of themselves as human agents. However, in the normal course of academic business we perceive religious literacy as a private literacy (if that is not an oxymoron), an idiolect that belongs to the student's private world rather than to the public conversation of the classroom. I have written elsewhere of how, until very recently, religion and literary studies—ethnic literary studies in particular—seemed to find no way of meshing, despite the overt religious content and form of a good deal of ethnic literature. Moreover, some of the basic professional tools used by professors of American literature—anthologies, literary histories, and the like—could well lead one to suspect that religion was not an aspect of American culture at all, or at least that it ceased to be somewhere around the Civil War (1–19). Such assumptions drive our sense that while religion may once have been socially important, it is now a private matter best left to student ruminations in the dorm.

The result is an implicit censorship of the religious equipment for living that students bring to bear on their experience of literature, a censorship that professors may not even recognize, because it embodies the normal course of doing literary business. While we've come to recognize and even celebrate the ways in which students' ethnicity or gender inflects their understanding of a text and contributes to our public knowledge of its action in the world, we don't readily transfer this understanding to students' religious identity—even in classrooms focused on religious subject matter. For instance, in a recent literary theory course, one of my students remarked on her experience in a course on Milton that induced a personal crisis of faith. Academic discourse allowed her to engage with the structural features of Milton's work and its context, but she had no language, or even opportunity, to engage what to her seemed more important. Similarly, while I was teaching James Baldwin's *Just above My Head* at George Mason, an African American woman informed me that the explicit sex in the novel violated her standards as a Christian woman. The demographics suggested that most of my class had some form of personal religious commitment, so I assumed that this student was not the only one struggling with the material. Yet I could not see how her sense of spiritual violation could become a part of the discourse of the class, given that the normal range of literary discourse was well established.

I don't want to argue that classes on Mark Twain ought to become open forums for our students' anxieties about heaven and hell. But it would be worth recognizing that for a fair number of students in the classroom, Huck's declaration that he would go to hell (Clemens 168–69) is not simply an exercise in literary or cultural history; it is a cultural and religious problem, one that can't be divorced from the problem of reading. As a young person who believed earnestly in a burning hell and a shining heaven, I was astonished at the gravity of Huck's declaration and wondered whether I myself wasn't a little closer to burning simply for reading—and liking—what everyone else seemed to think was merely a classic work of literature. Seeing Huck's declaration as only an occasion for knowing laughter may make us miss some of Twain and a good deal of some of our students.

Ultimately, an implicit censorship of religion in the classroom is intellectually indefensible and pedagogically ineffective. It is intellectually indefensible because it prepares students for a world that nowhere exists: a world in which religion is absent. It is pedagogically ineffective because it both inhibits our efforts to educate religious students and feeds the attitude of fundamentalists that they are an embattled minority. Studies by Paul Bramadat, among others, indicate that conservative Christian students at public universities, feeling threatened, are likely to withdraw and become yet more conservative in their theological and cultural views. Without recognition of their religious identity as part of the life of a public institution, they protect that identity vigorously. Ironically, the hope that we might rid ourselves of our fundamentalist students likely ensures that they will persist in their least accommodating forms.

We must do what we can to become more literate in the various religious backgrounds of our students. In the tradition of good rhetoricians, we can do more to understand our audience instead of expecting them to understand us. Addressing such issues can be uncomfortable and lead to messy missteps. Moreover, religious discourses and academic discourses may sometimes be simply incommensurate. However, in the discourses of literary pedagogy and basic professional competence, we already have resources that suggest the encounter between religious students and literary studies can be more than a clash of civilizations with no quarter asked and none given.

To begin, we can do more to take seriously our role as both a sympathetic and a demanding audience for student scholars. In the process we may not only teach ourselves more about our students' religious contexts but also enable students to become more effective negotiators of the borderland between religious and academic discourse. Gerald Graff has argued that academe too often leaves its students "clueless" as to how academic discourse works, why it works the way it does, and what purposes it serves. As an audience for student intellectual work, we should see ourselves as an audience whose features students do not yet recognize and whose grammar they do not understand.

Thus, we might talk with students about how truth claims made on the basis of the Bible may affect different audiences differently or about how the Bible or other religious texts might be used effectively in the context of intellectual or political argument. Why do certain kinds of religious appeal—say, those of a Martin Luther King, Jr.—have a powerful effect on academic audiences when others do not? This question presumes, of course, a better grasp of the uses of religious rhetoric than most of us now have. Further, we might remind students of what they know about religious language in different contexts. For example, Christian students know the language of traditional hymns differs from the language of Christian hip-hop, and this could clarify why a sermon might work in church on Sunday morning but not in Comp 101 on Tuesday afternoon. As both Chris Anderson and Priscilla Perkins have suggested, doing this kind of work can make religious students more reflective and sophisticated rhetorical agents in the context of their own systems of belief. At the same time it can make them more thoughtful interlocutors of those who have other religious positions or no religious position at all. If this is so, then the classroom can be the laboratory for effective civil discourse that most of us would like it to be but that it rarely is.

Such a strategy might also recognize anew the validity of religious discourse as a form of personal knowledge and the importance of narrative as a resource for intellectual and public discourse. At one point in the past the very idea of including the personal as a valid form of knowledge would have seemed peculiar, but it is now common. Similarly, many academic quarters now accept the notion that knowledge is narratively and culturally based rather than transcendentally given or discovered. These two developments in the shape of academic discourse point to productive ways of opening ourselves to student religious discourse, while also opening those students to the difficulties posed by academic discourse and by the fact of religious differences in the world they must engage.

Remaining within the contours of contemporary academic discourse, we recognize that the personal—the space to which religion is often relegated—is never merely private. What we conceive of as personal is culturally and socially produced. The stories of our lives, including our religious lives, spring from the effort to narrate our relation to the many larger stories that have made our individual stories possible. We already seek to help students understand how their personal stories can be resources for rhetorical action and doorways to intellectual inquiry. It is not so hard to imagine helping students find ways to make similar uses of their religious histories, convictions, and cultures. A course on Frederick Douglass might be bold enough to ask students to write a journal on their own crisis of faith and how it compares with that discussed by Douglass in his *Narrative*. How do the similarities and differences tell them something about the cultural world in which Douglass operated? Similarly, his peroration on the role of dual, and dueling, Christianities in a divided America might be enlivened by student reflections on how they have imagined the relation between religious and national identities. Students could be asked how Douglass might respond to our current crises of religion and culture, where his audience would include Buddhists, agnostics, and atheists rather than Christians alone. Such reflections can have the ironic effect of making students at once more articulate practitioners of their own religious rhetoric and more effectively engaged citizens of a pluralistic polis. They will become more religiously literate while at the same time becoming better readers of themselves, of others, and of literature.

As popularly portrayed, religion is the root of much violence, irrationality, and repression globally. The understandable reflex is to assume that there is too much religion everywhere, to feel we would be better without more, especially in our classrooms. Like Plato, we imagine that the religious are better remanded, with the poets, outside the walls of the good republic, that our public is safer with less talk about such matters. This reflex is a cultural and political mistake, and a pedagogical one. The religious, like the poets, show no sign of disappearing. Our good republic may be better served by a pedagogy that gropes, even if half blindly, toward a discourse that recognizes rather than regrets their presence.

WORKS CITED

Anderson, Chris. "The Description of an Embarrassment: When Students Write about Religion." *ADE Bulletin* 94 (1989): 12–15. Print.

Balkin, J. M. "The American System of Censorship and Free Expression." *Patterns of Censorship around the World*. Ed. Ilan Peleg. Boulder: Westview, 1993. 155–71. Print.

Bramadat, Paul A. *The Church on the World's Turf: An Evangelical Christian Group at a Secular University*. New York: Oxford UP, 2000. Print.

Braskamp, Larry A. "The Religious and Spiritual Journeys of College Students." *The American University in a Postsecular Age: Religion and Higher Education*. Ed. Douglas Jacobsen and Rhonda Hustedt Jacobsen. Oxford: Oxford UP, 2008. Soc. for Values in Higher Educ. Web. 17 Mar. 2008.

Clemens, Samuel Langhorne. *Adventures of Huckleberry Finn*. Norton Critical Ed. 2nd ed. Ed. Sculley Bradley, Richmond Croom Beatty, E. Hudson Long, and Thomas Cooley. New York: Norton, 1977. Print.

Graff, Gerald. *Clueless in Academe: How Schooling Obscures the Life of the Mind*. New Haven: Yale UP, 2003. Print.

Perkins, Priscilla. "'A Radical Conversion of the Mind': Fundamentalism, Hermeneutics, and the Metanoic Classroom." *College English* 63.5 (2001): 585–611. Print.

Powers, Peter Kerry. *Recalling Religions: Resistance, Memory, and Cultural Revision in Ethnic Women's Literature*. Knoxville: U of Tennessee P, 2001. Print.

Prothero, Stephen. *Religious Literacy: What Every American Needs to Know—and Doesn't*. New York: Harper, 2007. Print.

Sherwood, Steve. "Censoring Students, Censoring Ourselves: Constraining Conversations in the Writing Center." *Writing Center Journal* 20.1 (1999): 51–60. Print.

The Depths of the Heights: Reading Conrad with America's Soldiers

GEOFFREY GALT HARPHAM

For one who has spent his entire adult life in academic settings, a trip to Colorado Springs, Colorado, seems like an inverted *Heart of Darkness*: instead of going deeper in toward the horror, the horror, you ascend to space and light. The skies are open above you, and the air, while there's not much of it at six thousand feet, is clean and clear. You find yourself constantly looking up, thinking large thoughts or no thoughts at all. To the west are the Garden of the Gods and the immensity of Pike's Peak. Just to the north is the campus of James Dobson's vast Focus on the Family, a corporate headquarters, gift shop, and museum of its own history. A couple of miles north from there is the New Life Church founded by the now-disgraced and departed Ted Haggard, both mall and amusement park, filled with milling youth groups on their way to another large room, another inspiring message delivered by a guy in blue jeans who was lost and now is found. And just over there, at the end of that road that winds toward the Rockies, and below the spot where those tiny figures are gently descending to earth (no matter when you happen to glance up), is the gleaming, geometrical Air Force Academy, where I was invited to lead a seminar—on *Heart of Darkness*, as it happens—with faculty members from humanities departments.

Going up Academy Boulevard was like traveling to some primal nexus of mystic patriotism, military service, and evangelical Christianity. I found

The author is director of the National Humanities Center.

myself worrying that the seminar I was about to lead—one week, nearly twenty hours on one text—might create cognitive dissonance in this place, although they, not I, had chosen the text. The Academy is not known for its dedication to literary study; what it has become known for over the past few years is series of metastasizing scandals concerning religious harassment by evangelicals, cheating, and unpunished sexual assault. All this might put it in the same category as Brussels as represented in Conrad's book, a city that makes Marlow think of a "whited sepulchre" (9), a phrase from the Gospel of Matthew that describes scribes and Pharisees, who "appear beautiful outward, but are within full of dead men's bones, and of all uncleanness" (23.27 [King James Vers.]).

The more I reflected on the upcoming seminar, the more starkly its Conradian implications stood out. Of course, to a Conradian, all situations are Conradian, but still, it cannot be denied that *Heart of Darkness* has an exceptional representational plasticity. So primal is the situation, so elemental the narrative form (up the river, down the river), so compellingly does the text capture the general theme of modernity and its other, that there are, it sometimes seems, more metaphoric hearts of darkness in the world than any other body parts or than hearts of any other hue. Modernity generates hearts of darkness with an efficiency, and on a scale, that could only be called modern. Google "Heart of Darkness" and "Joseph Conrad," and you get fewer than 400,000 entries; leave off Conrad so that you are looking not for a text but a concept, and you get nearly 2,000,000. And the characters in the text are so iconic and are presented with such hyperreal clarity—one at a time, with each occupying a segment of the text—that they seem almost allegories of some aspect of selfhood, like figures in *Pilgrim's Progress*. No matter who you are, you should be able to find yourself somewhere in *Heart of Darkness*.

In fact, you can probably find yourself in several places. Depending on the circumstances, you can float from one icon to another. One moment, you can feel yourself to be an African mistress, wild and free and full-bodied; but then, you discover, the kaleidoscope has turned a tiny bit, and you are actually the Intended—desiccated, deceived, betrayed, and pathetic. Or you could approach a given task in an uncommitted Marlovian spirit as a job involving a bit of adventure with no historical or ideological burden at all—but then find that you are Kurtz, the exemplar of the horrors of modernity laid bare. This actually happens to Marlow, who finds, to his deep discomfiture, that he is insistently linked with Kurtz: the two of them, he hears, are both considered part of "the new gang—the gang of virtue" (25). Everything in the text has, it seems, a heart that both negates and expresses it.

So what was I at this moment, and what was my heart? I was an academic going to lead a seminar. An innocent undertaking—but what precisely was my job, in its deepest essence? Specifically, what was my relation to the war in which the nation, with the assistance of the Air Force Academy, was currently engaged? Was my real assignment to humanize the military, at a time when the conduct of the war was widely seen as degrading the nation that had undertaken it? Which of us was the agent of enlightenment, the military that was hard at work creating the conditions of democracy in a distant land or I? Was I supposed to darken the imperial mission by introducing doubt, fiction, language, and the exposure of ideology into a scene of unreflective patriotism? Did my small mission have a colonial character of its own? If so, how could I accomplish, excuse, or refuse it? Had this mission really been thought through? It seemed the best thing to do was just to keep driving up that road to the hotel and go to bed.

And so, the following morning at 8:30 a.m. on a crystal-clear day in July, with questions thronging in my head, I took my seat in a clean but windowless room, along with eighteen members of the Academy faculty. They ranged from a sixty-eight-year-old senior professor, a civilian who had spent most of his distinguished career at Dartmouth and the University of Maryland, to an undergraduate cadet, with colonels, lieutenant colonels, majors, captains, and some civilian professors in between. They were in the unfamiliar but for them refreshing situation of being the students, while I was in the unfamiliar and discomfiting situation of being addressed as "sir" by uniformed personnel. Dissonance all around.

But a seminar is a seminar, and so we began. This book, I said, is about someone who leaves the familiar world and ventures into the unknown. Conrad himself did this, not just by going up the Congo River on a steamer but also by leaving Poland as a teenager and joining the French merchant marine. What, I asked, might motivate a person to do that?

In an American undergraduate classroom, this question might merely have served to get people talking, but since most people in the room would have gone down the expected path, from one protected environment to another, their answers might not have been particularly productive. The question would not have been taken as an invitation to talk about oneself. Here, it provoked a dozen or more narratives that attempted to map Conrad's and Marlow's experiences onto their own decisions to join the military. Each story that unfurled had a strikingly individual trajectory. The military might be a subculture in which the individual is regarded as an impediment to trust or discipline, something to be broken down rather than fortified, but each person in the room had come to the military in his or her own way. The Academy for them had represented an honorable solution to some difficult problems, a bracing summons to patriotic duty, a way of carrying on a family tradition, a gateway to the world, a life of order and clarity, a way of experiencing managed risk, an opportunity to take pride in oneself, or simply a decent job. "I know exactly why I'm here," one said. "If I hadn't joined the military, I'd be driving a milk truck in Auburn, California." The seminar included those who themselves had graduated from the Academy, as well as those who had joined out of college, during the first Gulf War, at the invasion of Afghanistan, and more recently. Not all were from small towns; not all were escaping grinding poverty or lack of opportunity. In fact, the lone cadet in the seminar was a rogue debutante from North Carolina who had astonished her family by forgoing an easier life in favor of military service. All seemed to assume that *Heart of Darkness* was written by a man, Conrad, whom they could understand and who understood them; a man who escaped from unpromising circumstances by joining an institution with an honorable tradition of discipline and service; a man who, as a boy, had wanted to see the world. More pointedly, the book was about a man, Marlow, who found himself caught up in a much larger and different narrative than any he had foreseen. It was also about a man, Kurtz, whose commitment to discipline—"the discipline that makes the soldiers of a free country reliable in battle," as the inscription on the dormitory at the Academy reads—had failed. And it was about an imperial power pursuing an unworthy mission that was justified with rhetoric appealing to the highest universal values.

Like Conrad and Marlow, the members of the seminar were acutely aware of their own marginal status in the institution they had joined. As humanist professors, they represented the academy part of "military academy," Athens rather than Sparta, their task being to teach not engineering, aeronautics, or military strategy but literature, history, and philosophy. But their position on the edge of the main mission gave a certain edge to their comments. Professionally sensitive both to rhetoric and to danger, they were, I noticed, also sensitive to the powerful link between idealistic pronouncements made by high officials and violence visited on others, including themselves. The Norton edition we were using included a passage of soaring rhetoric attributed to Leopold II, the Belgian sovereign who administered the Congo as a personal possession, with an eye to maximum profit from ivory regardless of the human cost borne by Congolese natives. In a piece entitled "The Sacred Mission of Civilization," Leopold contended that "if, in view of this desirable spread of civilization, we count upon the means of action which confer upon us dominion and the sanction of right, it is not less true that our ultimate end is a work of peace" (119). A connection was immediately drawn to President Bush's 2003 Christmas message to American troops: "You are confronting terrorists abroad so that . . . people around the world can live in peace." When military people hear talk of world peace, they prepare for deployment. "As Walter Benjamin said," a uniformed colonel commented (out of the blue, it seemed to me), "there is no document of civilization that is not also a document of barbarism." In general, I began to realize, the participants in this seminar had a highly developed capacity for detecting connections between civilization and barbarism, idealism and violence. Again on the first day, someone asked what a gifted man like Kurtz was doing in the jungle. Someone else mentioned the Intended, his fiancée back in Brussels; another noted the piano in her apartment, with its ivory keys. After a pause, one young officer, who had been entirely silent until then, ventured her first comment, and it was startling and decisive: "She killed him."

Having taught Conrad many times before, I found myself constantly bumped off balance by comments indicating, for example, considerable sympathy for Marlow as a man who found himself on a mission more problematic than the one he had signed up for and who had to decide whether this new mission still commanded his loyalty; and even for Kurtz, as a man tested by isolation and the deep corruptness of the task he had been assigned. There was less sympathy for Edward Said and Chinua Achebe, authors of two critical texts also included in the Norton edition, texts that have been so firmly attached to Conrad's in American teaching practice that they almost seem part of it. Said charged Conrad with an inability to imagine a state of affairs in which Europeans were not dominating Africans; Conrad, he said, could not "grant the natives their freedom" (428). In American colleges and universities, this argument generally sweeps all opposition aside; here, it met resistance. "The natives don't want 'freedom,'" a captain said; "they just want the Belgians to go away. And freedom wouldn't be Conrad's to grant anyway." This critique seemed to be clinched when it was aligned with President Bush's description of liberty as "God's gift to humanity," a gift America was divinely charged with delivering. Achebe's famous accusation that Conrad was racist received a respectful hearing but was ultimately dismissed on the grounds that racism in the modern sense did not exist in Conrad's day. It appeared that, from the seminar's point of view, both Said, a Palestinian, and Achebe, a Nigerian, were "too American" in their perspectives.

Shortly after we reached this comfortable affirmation of the superiority of creative artists over critics, however, we hit a snag. I had wanted to talk about how Marlow insistently turns things inside out. The first instance occurs in his very first words, when he gestures upriver toward the English heartland and says, "This also has been one of the dark places of the earth"

(5). Again and again, I noted, Marlow casually offers his listeners a thought experiment involving a total reversal of present circumstances. Another example would be his explanation of the curious fact that his party encountered no natives on their two-hundred-mile tramp to the Central Station. I read the passage: "Well if a lot of mysterious niggers armed with all kinds of fearful weapons suddenly took to traveling on the road between Deal and Gravesend catching the yokels right and left to carry heavy loads for them, I fancy every farm and cottage thereabouts would get empty very soon" (19–20). On this day, Wednesday, we had another participant, a young black woman who was only able to attend this one session. She had been looking attentively at me, but at this point she stared down at the book and did not look up for another hour, until the session ended. Two days later, I spotted her at the end of a hallway during one of our breaks but wasn't able to make contact and never saw her again. Conrad presents such difficulties. Once, some years ago, I was phoning the university bookstore, ordering that semester's texts, including *The Nigger of the "Narcissus."* "The . . . Nigger . . . of . . . the . . . 'Narcissus,'" the bookstore employee repeated very slowly as she wrote it down, with, I thought, a certain accusatory emphasis.

The distance between the past horrors of the Congo Free State and the enlightened politics of the present day in America had in a sense made things easy for us. The morality of the case may have troubled Marlow, but after a century of universal condemnation of Leopold's administration, it did not trouble us: the issue was settled. The pastness of the past, and the consolidation of history's judgment, can have an anesthetic effect on discussion. On the last day, however, the anesthesia wore off as we took up Coppola's *Apocalypse Now*, which translates *Heart of Darkness* into terms that American military people could understand immediately. On this day, the conversation, which had been so free, candid, and direct, became stressed and troubled. In an undergraduate classroom, the discussion might center on Brando's Kurtz; here, it fastened immediately and almost exclusively on Robert Duvall's Lieutenant Colonel Kilgore, an Army officer (First Squadron, Ninth Cavalry) who, in a famous scene, leads a helicopter attack on a Vietnamese beach village, with speakers blaring "The Ride of the Valkyries." Weathering VC mortars and machine-gun fire, he wipes out the village and lands Willard (Martin Sheen) on the river so he can hunt Kurtz down. Mission accomplished, Kilgore adds a gratuitous napalm strike ("I love the smell of napalm in the morning") that improves the surfing. The helicopters, like the playing cards Kilgore places on the corpses of his victims, bear the motto "Death from Above."

In ways the participants appreciated, Kilgore was an excellent officer.

He had, as Willard notes, a "weird light around him. You just knew he wasn't gonna get so much as a scratch here." He was devoted to his men and had earned their trust. Under him, they felt motivated and safe. And yet, as one of the women in the seminar pointed out, he deliberately chose to land at a place he knew to be defended in preference to another location where there was no surfing, and lost both men and equipment as a consequence. And while he was a passionate surfer, he killed with a disturbing indifference. Was there a problem? The nation was at war, and some of the Vietnamese, at least—hard to tell which—had the means and the motivation to kill Americans. What did we think of Kilgore?

As a way of approaching, or avoiding, this question, we took up the issue of "Death from Above," which was after all what the Air Force was all about. In one sense, a colonel said, death from above is easier and cleaner to inflict than "grime on the ground" (the Army's job), because there is greater distance between one's action, in a plane or a silo, and its consequences. Another participant noted that more imagination is required for the Air Force soldier to grasp what he or she is doing—but, she seemed to imply, because of the increased risk, almost a certainty in some cases, of civilian casualties, there is a greater shock to the conscience for those who do grasp it. That kind of shock is not good: you can, as one put it, lose your mojo and become tentative, doubtful, or uncommitted, placing yourself and others at greater risk.

About one-third of all Air Force personnel have been to Iraq in recent years, but I was reluctant to ask whether any in the room had actually dropped or launched weapons. When they spoke, they focused on training missions. A female lieutenant colonel recalled being trained to turn the key that would launch a missile from a silo. When she subsequently visited Moscow on an arms control mission, it struck her that if that training session had been real and if the target had been Moscow, everything around her would be toxic rubble. Another participant, a male captain, noted that the key used in training was not spring-loaded like the real key and had a different feel. Pause. Another recalled sending a man whose wife had just given birth to twins on a dangerous assignment during the invasion of Grenada because he was "the most qualified person available," a decision that still troubled him over twenty years later. He did not say whether the man returned, but he did note that the officer who took his place in that decision-making position committed suicide two months after returning home.

Diverted into channels of personal reflections, the conversation seemed to be losing its way, in search of the main current. There were longer pauses between comments—greater depth but sluggish progress, albeit with moments of sudden clarity emerging from the fog. After nearly an hour circling around Kilgore, a lieutenant colonel with a PhD in English from the University of Michigan (dissertation on Seamus Heaney's treatment of violence) and a refugee from the milk trucks of Auburn, California, broke the silence by saying—as I recall—the following:

> I wear this uniform because I believe that, in the end, our way of life is better than any other at defending the *sanctity of the individual*. My understanding of history teaches me that violence is always going to be part of human existence, and my moral sense says that managed violence, in the service of the right principles, is better than the alternatives. What we try to do here . . . is train . . . *reluctant killers*. We teach them how to do things that will haunt them for the rest of their lives. That's what we do. We stand there in front of our cadets, and we train them to do things they would never do if the nation didn't ask it of them. And even though the nation asks it, and no matter how disciplined they are, they will still be haunted by what they've done. And they have to be. If they aren't, then we've only trained Kilgores, murderers without a conscience.

After a long silence during which we all stared at the table, we took a break.

The humanities have been the subject of an immense quantity of elevated rhetoric. Distinguished people have described and defended the need for a national investment in the study of literature, history, philosophy, and the arts. I have read many of these testimonials and have written some myself. I do not recall seeing this particular approach taken before. But the lieutenant colonel's statement grasped the nettle with a boldness that grew in the mind during that long silence, and thereafter.

What are the humanities about if not the cultivation of an informed conscience, a habit of reflection in which the flow of thoughtless action and means-end calculation is interrupted by an examination of historical contexts and ethical considerations, by an imaginative awareness of the character and consequences of action, by a deep investment in the human condition and its possibilities? If those with such knowledge and such capacities do not assume some kind of responsibility for worldly action, including the management of violence, then that responsibility passes to the Kilgores and Kurtzes of the world.

Those who serve in the military do not always, much less naturally, think in these terms. Hard training is required in order to achieve an understanding so deeply counterintuitive. What this training inculcates is not simply competence in destruction but also the proper attitude to have toward it. The stated mission of the English department at the Academy includes instilling in cadets "an appreciation for the culture they've

promised to defend" even as they carry out the violence that culture occasionally requires (Dept. of English). Insofar as humanistic study imbues
people with a moral imagination, the real burden of the humanities, as
opposed to their manifold pleasures and benefits, does not fall on professors, students, or the culture-loving population in general. That burden is
allocated to those whom society charges with the conscience-testing task
of sanctioned killing. In a democracy with a volunteer military, the weight
falls on that small number of people who have chosen to bear it by en-
listing. For them, it is, as Marlow put it, always "a choice of nightmares"
(62). For the rest of us, the key is never spring-loaded, the flights are all
simulated.

We spent a good deal of time over the course of the week talking about
the ways that honorable people get ensnared in and somehow committed
to large patterns of action that they would not, if given the option, choose
or approve of. Marlow continually remarks on how insistently he is identified with the ivory trade, Belgian rapacity, and Kurtz. It struck me on
our final day that despite never having worn a uniform, I was now part of
the American military mission, part of homeland defense, even of Opera-
tion Iraqi Freedom. My honorarium had been approved by the Pentagon
(I was a very small unit in the Wide Area Workflow), which expected me
to provide professional development for those whose job was to produce
soldiers who would kill with an attitude worthy of a morally enlightened
democracy committed to the sanctity of the individual. This mission was
implicitly informed by the conviction that a conscience with the capacity
to be deeply disturbed, even traumatized, is a precious thing, an indicator
of democratic principles and ethical values.

In a culture whose commitment to the freedom of the individual often
seems to begin with the freedom from guilt, the military perspective on
the humanities is well worth pondering.

WORKS CITED

Achebe, Chinua. "An Image of Africa: Racism in Conrad's *Heart of Darkness*." Conrad
336–49.
Apocalypse Now. Dir. Francis Ford Coppola. Zoetrope Studios, 1979. Film.
Bush, George W. *Presidential Message*. White House. 24 Dec. 2003. Web. 25 June
2008.
Conrad, Joseph. *Heart of Darkness*. Norton Critical Ed. 4th ed. Ed. Paul B. Armstrong.
New York: Norton, 2006. Print.
Department of English and Fine Arts. United States Air Force Acad. Web. 25 June 2008.
Leopold II. "The Sacred Mission of Civilization." Conrad 119–20.
Said, Edward W. "Two Visions in *Heart of Darkness*." Conrad 422–29.

Will the Circle Be Broken: The Rhetoric of Complaint against Student Writing

DAVID GOLD

In his summer 2008 President's Column, Gerald Graff, who has been teaching composition since he began his career in 1963, called attention to the tenuous place that writing instruction still has in the profession:

> One of the most depressing moments for me at MLA job interviews is when candidates are reassured that, if they get the job, they "won't have to teach comp." The only thing more depressing is when colleagues who are revolted at the very thought of teaching composition complain that their students write poorly. They blame bad student writing on the high schools or on their own campus writing programs and take no responsibility for the problem themselves.

Given that for much of the twentieth century, the MLA largely ignored pedagogy as a scholarly pursuit, such attitudes are perhaps not surprising. Before 1900, approximately ten percent of the articles in *PMLA* treated pedagogy. After 1903, however, when the MLA eliminated its pedagogical section to focus on literary scholarship, such articles largely disappeared from its pages (Goggin 22; Brereton 24; Bartholomae, "Composition" 1950–53). Even as rhetoric and composition reemerged as a vibrant discipline in the 1970s and 1980s—by 1986, twenty-four percent of listings in the MLA *Job Information List* were in composition and rhetoric (Bartholomae, "Composition" 1952)—it was still infrequently represented in *PMLA* (and remains so). While the last decade has done much to bring rhetoric

The author is assistant professor of English at the University of Tennessee, Knoxville.

and writing back from the margins, as Graff notes, old attitudes toward writing instruction and student writing linger.

Indeed, we have all heard the complaints against student writing. As one colleague bitterly complained to me of her freshmen, "They can't write, they can't reason, they can't punctuate, they can't spell." These complaints are often born out of legitimate frustration at the difficulties of teaching writing. Our workloads are high, our classes large. Our students are often underprepared or exhibit such a wide range of preparation that we find ourselves teaching three classes in one. We ourselves may have had little training in writing pedagogy or lack the time to keep up with advances in the field. As Herbert Lindenberger noted in response to Graff's column, "[E]ven if you understand how important these courses are[,] they take a lot more work to teach than lit courses." In courses in which writing is not the primary focus, we may resent the time that writing issues take from other subject matter. Is it any wonder we complain?

I do believe that the overwhelming majority of us who are privately frustrated with student writing, in whatever course we encounter it, are sincerely committed to improving it. However, there is an important difference between venting by the photocopy machine among our colleagues and taking our complaints public. And yet each school year brings another round of bitter published invective against student writing from college English teachers. One critic finds students victims of a "cool consumer worldview," complacent in their ignorance (Edmundson 40). Another argues they "don't know how to—or care to—express their views" (Gerhardt), while another claims they engage in "illiterate and semiliterate scribbling" when they try (Clio). So "atrocious" are their grammar and logic, writes another, that most "are not writing even at the level of competence that was once required of third-graders" (Blue). Such invectives rarely make reference to the vast body of literature in rhetoric, composition, pedagogy, linguistics, and literacy studies that explains why students may have difficulty writing—and offers proven strategies for helping them.

We should know better. Since English was introduced as a university subject, hardly a generation has gone by without national hand wringing over an impending literacy crisis. In 1987, E. D. Hirsch warned that our nation was on the brink of cultural illiteracy. In 1975, *Newsweek* fretted that Johnny couldn't write (Sheils). In 1955, Rudolf Flesch proclaimed that Johnny couldn't read. Over a hundred years ago, professors at Harvard sounded the alarm at declining standards. In 1892, forty-seven percent of students taking Harvard's entrance exam "passed unsatisfactorily," and twenty percent failed (Berlin 100). Complained one faculty member, "The average theme seems the work of a rather vulgar youth with his light gone out" (Briggs 30). A generation earlier, English studies itself was an upstart discipline, regarded with suspicion by classics faculty members doubtful that the study of mere belles lettres in the vernacular could ever match the character-building discipline of studying Latin and Greek grammar. Even Harvard President Charles Eliot felt compelled to publicly make the case for English, which he acknowledged was difficult to teach well (206), as a cornerstone in the new liberal arts curriculum.

Contemporary critics of student writing tend to locate the golden age of literacy at about the time when they were in school, before the corrupting influence of whatever feature of modern life most appalls them. Stanley Ridgley condemns "strange literary theories, Marxism, feminism, deconstruction, and other oddities in the guise of writing courses." Writing in the *Atlantic Monthly*, Professor X laments that his students "don't really share a culture" (73); that is, they haven't read the literary texts he deems to constitute one. Allan Bloom faults the 1960s for promoting moral relativism. Tina Blue wishes for the rigor of her third-grade teacher in 1958, who "took off points for *everything* we did wrong." For Pamela Gerhardt, the violence at Woodstock '99—and her students' apparent indifference to it—symbolizes the anomie of an entire generation. Writing in the *Washington Post*, she attributes her students' refusal to share her outrage to a decline in their thinking skills over her teaching career, which, at the time of writing, had spanned a mere six years.

LAYING THE BLAME

Who is to blame for the supposedly sorry state of student writing? A common strategy is to blame high school English teachers. Writing pseudonymously in the *Chronicle of Higher Education*, Max Clio, who teaches at an open admissions university where, as he dismissively puts it, "anyone . . . can take a whirl," insists that "[h]igh schools no longer prepare most students to express ideas coherently or follow accepted English, let alone carry on serious intellectual work." He is in venerable company. Responding to the recent overhaul of the SAT to include more questions on grammar and copyediting, the Harvard dean of admissions, William Fitzsimmons, argued that the new test will catch those who otherwise might have managed to slip by the gatekeepers with their polished entrance essays and that high school teachers, who "haven't been doing a good job in teaching writing," will now be forced to become responsible (qtd. in Lewin). In 1892, the Harvard Committee on Composition and Rhetoric also blamed poor high school instruction for the inadequacies of the school's freshmen (Adams, Godkin, and Quincy). Instead of longing for a nonexistent past, perhaps we should simply admit that eighteen-year-olds frequently write poorly, and consider it our job to take it from there.

Of course, it is easier to blame students. Gerhardt sneers at the student who wants to do an essay on what she considers the "'problem' of the instant replay." But for the discourse community of sports fans, the instant replay *is* a widely debated, historically significant, and rhetorically rich problem, as is the use of performance-enhancing drugs, the Bowl College System, and, yes, even the question of whether cheerleading is a sport. Why shouldn't students write about such topics?

It serves little good to condemn students for their lack of passion for our passions. Mark Edmundson, for example, excoriates contemporary students for being unwilling and unable to engage in serious debate:

> For the pervading view is the cool consumer perspective, where passion and strong admiration are forbidden. . . . [I]s it a shock that the kids don't come to school hot to learn, unable to bear their own ignorance? For some measure of self-dislike, or self-discontent . . . seems to me to be a prerequisite for getting an education that matters. My students, alas, usually lack the confidence to acknowledge what would be their most precious asset for learning: their ignorance.   (42, 47)

Though his frustration may be sincere, it is also silencing. I think it telling that when Edmundson published his essay, the most thoughtful critique came not from a fellow English professor but from one of his former students, Lisa Kijewski:

> I believe that I can explain the "generic" responses and lukewarm evaluations he garnered from students. I have encountered few classes in my university career whose objectives were so poorly defined and whose assignments were so amorphous and ill-explained. Edmundson, with his obvious contempt for undergraduates, wasted my time and my money, and then used his experiences in front of the classroom as fodder for a sardonic critique of my generation's intellectual incompetence and consumerist attitude. . . . If Edmundson wants his students to be "changed by the course," perhaps he should try teaching with a modicum of passion, enthusiasm, and respect for his students.

If we expect our students to share our passions, we must also acknowledge theirs.

Student Writing Today

I do historical work on rhetorical education, largely at marginalized institutions. Part of the thrill is discovering a fine piece of writing done by a student in 1900 or 1920—and there are many such examples. Here is a delightful defense of slang from 1914, by Marie Erhardt, a Texas Woman's University student:

> Why it is perfectly shocking to any nice young lady to think the latest, good-looking man can speak perfect English and find nothing in stock except second-rate discarded jabber that he has used ever since Taft's administration. Just think of a grown up man saying, "I should worry," when anybody would know that "Ish Ka Bibble" is the proper form. It should be the height of everyone's ambition to make the language they use sound like a musical comedy. Everyone should strive to speak so that it would be easy to enter into a conversation in which neither of the persons would understand the other. (189)

I get examples as lively today. A freshman from Texas, who persuasively argued for the uniqueness of her state's culture: "Have you ever seen a bumper sticker saying, 'I wasn't born in Iowa but I got here as fast as I could'? How about tortilla chips in the shape of Montana?" A junior from Los Angeles, who dreamed from childhood of playing in a professional ballpark but then had the worst performance of his life when he finally got the chance in a high school all-star game: "I sucked," he concluded, "but at least I sucked in Dodger Stadium."

Not all my students, of course, will emerge from freshman composition— or even from my graduate seminars—writing error-free prose. But writing well is a complex skill that develops slowly over time and not necessarily in linear fashion. At times of frustration we should take comfort that empirical research has shown that students today do not make significantly more errors than students did in the past, about 2.26 per 100 words in 1986 (well after the effects of open admissions) compared with 2.11 in 1917 (Connors and Lunsford 406). Given that then only an elite fraction attended college, we're doing pretty well.

It is also worth remembering that the tasks we give our students in freshman composition are far more complex than those given elite Harvard students a century ago. Then, freshmen were commonly asked to write simple narratives or descriptive sketches, such as "A Morning in Tarrytown Harbor":

> While we were eating, a glorious breeze sprang up, and, moreover, it was down the river. The tide, also, was going out. Now for a sail! The waves danced round the boat; white-caps were omnipresent. Our nerves tingled with delight as we hurried about to make ready for the start. Hurrah! we're off! The sails caught the breeze, and the small craft bounded over the waves as if she too were glad to be released from her moorings.
> (qtd. in Copeland and Rideout 112)[1]

The then-dominant emphasis on form and correctness often led to formulaic essays as well. Consider this expository example from a 1922 Berkeley freshman, which placed him in the top quarter of the entering class:

> The choice of an automobile depends primarily upon the purse of the prospective purchaser. There are three classes of automobiles to be considered: the high priced, medium priced, and the cheap cars. Each has its advantages and disadvantages. Cheap cars are not easy riding. Expensive ones are easy enough to ride in but their cost is prohibitive to the majority. The medium priced car strikes the happy medium: and decreases the disadvantages of each of the extremes while yet partaking of the advantages of each of them. (qtd. in Brereton 533–34)

In rhetorically grounded freshman composition classes today, students are commonly asked to write original, research-based arguments that synthesize and respond to multiple points of view, incorporate a variety of textual evidence, and seek to persuade a specific audience in a specific rhetorical context, in addition to following the conventions of edited English. Here's a paragraph from a recent essay arguing that hip hop, contrary to popular opinion, actually promotes positive images for women:

> Today a super slim woman is the norm. As one 16-year-old girl said, "How thin you are is associated with success and how big you are reflects low self-esteem and being unsuccessful" (Martino and Pallota-Chiarolli 103). However, the black community condones just the opposite. The "thick" woman is idolized, being defined as having a large gluteus maximus and a big bust without excess fat elsewhere. This image is depicted throughout the hip-hop industry, representing that the average woman can be her normal weight and still be attractive. The most infamous example is Mo'nique, a big comedian who made a career out of embracing her size and has helped many big women everywhere to love themselves regardless of negativity. The hip-hop culture promotes physically diverse women that can do anything they put their minds to. The uniqueness of all women's bodies is accepted.[2]

While this student's syntax and word choice might lack the belletristic influence of her turn-of-the-twentieth-century counterparts, I would argue that the student is better prepared for the rigors of academic and public argument.

A century ago, English professors had no trouble telling students their work was "very elementary," "wretchedly loose," "discreditable," or "entirely inadequate." Today, though we might privately long for that freedom, we are less likely to insist on our gatekeeping function. Indeed, as a discipline we are committed to a democratic vision of literacy as the linchpin of citizenship. Why then such resistance to student writing, such bitter, public complaint? It is the public nature of the complaint I find so troubling. I believe that this discourse speaks less to our students' capabilities than to our own fear of and discomfort with writing. Thirty years ago, Richard Young argued that many English instructors suffer from the lingering Romantic ideal of writing as a mysterious process, and the dichotomy he spoke of still remains. My graduate students often maintain that writing is an inborn talent, that there exists in us an authentic voice not subject to modification by rhetorical exigencies, even as they nod in agreement at scholarship that suggests that writing is a teachable skill and that success in writing is highly dependent on learning and adapting to the often implicit rules of a discourse community.[3] What we have learned about writing as informed scholars and teachers does not always correspond to what we believe about writing as lifelong readers.

Whatever our reasons, by dismissing student writing we abdicate responsibility for our own failures as teachers, in particular our responsibility to teach *all* students, to take on anyone who wants to "take a whirl." Michael Ryan, writing in the *Houston Chronicle*, laments that students "don't know how to apply grammar and punctuation rules; to write strong summary sentences; to use direct quotations and dialogue; to organize essays effectively; to be creative; or to recognize the difference between good and bad research." If this is indeed the case, then why not show them how? Grumpily insisting that educated people should write everything well, "even a grocery list," or returning "without a response" student e-mails "that contain errors" will not cause students to spontaneously understand comma splices. Nor will insulting them. "The poor souls," Ryan quips, "couldn't write literate essays even if they knew failure meant they'd be shipped off to write reviews of Thomas Hardy novels." Given his attitude, his students might be forgiven for not wanting to learn how to write or for believing that writing is nothing more than a checklist of arbitrary and obscure rules designed to expose their ignorance. The pseudonymous Professor X concludes early in the semester that a forty-something returning student will fail. Yet he does little to help her: instead of showing her how to use the Internet to do research, he tells her she has "skills deficits" (71) and pushes her off on a librarian; instead of modifying the assignment so that she can research a contemporary issue she does understand, he insists she do a historical one she does not, though either assignment would seem to achieve his goal of having students address scholarship on both sides of an issue; instead of giving her a topic, he lets her flounder through several topic changes so as to preserve the integrity of the assignment; instead of working with her through multiple drafts, giving her feedback on her progress, he lets her turn in a single failing one.

Obviously we cannot reach all students. And certainly it is frustrating when students do not share our conviction that writing is important, that we are important, that we have something to offer. But that frustration is part of the background noise of teaching. Many students also do not believe that math or science or foreign languages are important. But do Spanish teachers publish editorials lamenting their students' inability to use the subjunctive? Indeed, does any other profession so openly mock the population it serves? Blaming the victim is not just misguided, it's unethical.

Our students do not come to us, as one of my colleagues puts it, "shellacked" after taking first-year composition, perfectly preserved in the minutiae of mechanical conventions. By dismissing student writing, we thereby dismiss the teaching of writing as either an impossibility or a mere mechanical skill that can be fobbed off on graduate students, lecturers, and junior faculty members, who then provide us with a convenient scapegoat for the poor student writing we subsequently encounter in upper-level classes. Moreover, by dismissing student writing, we dismiss student writers and the possibility that they have something to tell us.[4] Such blame can only come back to haunt us. While we fault students, parents, high school teachers, television, and text messaging for the inability of students to write, the culture at large is busy indicting us for the supposed national crisis of poor writing.

John Trimbur argues that the discourse of crisis masks the anxiety of the middle class over its socioeconomic status and its complicity in the perpetuation of inequality through the adoption of a privatized literacy that serves corporate ends. Our promulgation of crisis as teachers serves a similar function. Where there is crisis, there is crisis management, thus the increased reliance on standardized writing exams to counter the supposed failures of English teachers to teach English. The new "writing skills" section on the SAT tests not writing skills but decontextualized knowledge of prescriptive grammar, while the new timed writing exam—a twenty-five-minute response to a generic prompt—is an affront to nearly everything we teach in writing courses.

Unfortunately, contemporary debate about student writing and language and literacy education is not driven by academic journals. As scholars and teachers, we need to do a better job of publicly discussing what is right with student writing, of getting the message out to those same popular journals and newspapers for which the naysayers write—and that a wide audience reads. We need to take up the call of the Council of Writing Program Administrators, in its Network for Media Action, and contact misinformed education reporters, write letters to the editor in response to misleading reportage and op-ed invectives, and write op-eds ourselves. We need to stop smiling our tight, polite, tolerant smiles when strangers, on meeting us and discovering we are English teachers, begin to rail against the grammar of kids today. In response to our students, we need to adopt what Kevin Porter terms a pedagogy of charity, not severity—not because it feels good, but because it works. As George Hillocks has demonstrated, optimistic English teachers who trust their students' abilities are far more likely than pessimistic ones to engage in the kinds of "environmental" classroom practices that improve student reading and writing; they allow group and independent work instead of relying on lecture, they spend more time on instruction and less on management and assessment, and they spend more time on content and less on mechanics (41–52). Finally, we need to embrace a vision of English studies as not just literary studies but also literacy studies and recognize that the teaching of writing, no matter what our subdiscipline, is part of our job description. After all, as Thomas Miller reminds us, our discipline began not in elite institutions such as Oxford or Harvard but in eighteenth-century Scottish public schools, "provincial institutions serving students who were often marginally literate in the language of the learned" (1). We have an obligation to serve such students today.

The trouble with English is that, more than any other subject, it carries the weight of our society's anxieties and fears about education and is the most visible emblem of both our failure and success. As English teachers, we are asked to do more than we possibly can. Yet students can and do learn to read, write, reason, and even punctuate and spell. Most of them, in fact. That most do is a message worth sharing. If we fail, at the very least these shortsighted invectives serve one pedagogical purpose: promoting student engagement. When I assign such essays to my students to analyze, they respond with enthusiasm, opening up lively discussions about argument, evidence, ethos, audience, voice, diction, and even grammar. Would Edmundson feel the same way if he taught at a commuter school rather than an elite university? Does the length of time Gerhardt has been teaching help or hurt her ethos? Does her tone make her more or less persuasive? Do we lack a shared culture, as Professor X suggests, and if so, is that a problem? So to these invectives I am grateful. As long as they continue to be published, our students will never lack for inspiration to write.

NOTES

1. The instructor evaluated the first draft of this fortnightly theme as "pleasant and readable" (qtd. in Copeland and Rideout 109) though requiring sharper and more vivid detail, which the student appears to have supplied in the subsequent draft.

2. I graded this essay a B, finding the argument to be focused, well organized, and engaged but somewhat underdeveloped in its address of counterarguments.

3. For an excellent introduction to the challenges freshmen writers face in negotiating the demands of the academic discourse community, see Bartholomae, "Inventing."

4. Peter Elbow writes poignantly of the need to respond to students not merely as teachers but also as readers: "As teachers, we need to think about what it means to *be an audience* rather than just be a teacher, critic, assessor, or editor. If our only response is to tell students what's strong, what's weak, and how to improve it . . . we actually *undermine* their sense of writing as a social act. We reinforce their sense that writing means doing school exercises, producing for authorities what they already know—not actually trying to say things to readers" (65).

WORKS CITED

Adams, Charles Francis, Edwin Lawrence Godkin, and Josiah Quincy. *Report of the Harvard Committee on Composition and Rhetoric.* Cambridge: Harvard U, 1892. Print.

Bartholomae, David. "Composition, 1900–2000." *PMLA* 115.7 (2000): 1950–54. Print.

———. "Inventing the University." *When a Writer Can't Write: Studies in Writer's Block and Other Composing Process Problems.* Ed. Mike Rose. New York: Guilford, 1985. 134–66. Print.

Berlin, James A. *Writing Instruction in Nineteenth-Century American Colleges.* Carbondale: Southern Illinois UP, 1984. Print.

Bloom, Allan. *The Closing of the American Mind.* New York: Simon, 1987. Print.

Blue, Tina. "How Long Does It Take to Grade an Essay?" 26 Nov. 2003. Web. 1 May 2008.

Brereton, John C. *The Origins of Composition Studies in the American College, 1875-1925: A Documentary History.* Pittsburgh: U of Pittsburgh P, 1995. Print.

Briggs, Le Baron Russell. "The Harvard Admission Examination in English." *Twenty Years of School and College English.* Ed. Adams Sherman Hill, Briggs, and Byron Satterlee Hurlbut. Cambridge: Harvard U, 1896. 17–32. Print.

Clio, Max. "Grading on My Nerves." *Chronicle of Higher Education Online* 21 Nov. 2003. Web. 1 June 2008.

Connors, Robert J., and Andrea A. Lunsford. "Formal Errors in College Writing; or, Ma and Pa Kettle Do Research." *College Composition and Communication* 39.4 (1988): 395–409. Print.

Copeland, C. T., and H. M. Rideout. *Freshman English and Theme-Correcting in Harvard College.* New York: Silver, 1901. Print.

Erhardt, Marie. Editorial. *Daedalian Monthly Annual Issue. Daedalian Yearbook, 1914.* 189. Print. Texas Woman's U Archives.

Edmundson, Mark. "On the Uses of a Liberal Education: I. As Lite Entertainment for Bored College Students." *Harper's Magazine* Sept. 1997: 39–49. Print.

Elbow, Peter. "Closing My Eyes As I Speak: An Argument for Ignoring Audience." *College English* 49.1 (1987): 50–69. Print.

Eliot, Charles W. "What Is a Liberal Education?" *Century Magazine* 28.2 (1884): 203–12. Print.

Flesch, Rudolf. *Why Johnny Can't Read—and What You Can Do about It.* New York: Harper, 1955. Print.

Gerhardt, Pamela. "A Higher Degree of Indifference." *Washington Post* 22 Aug. 1999. *Lexis/Nexis.* Web. 1 Sept. 2007.

Goggin, Maureen Daly. *Authoring a Discipline: Scholarly Journals and the Post–World War II Emergence of Rhetoric and Composition.* Mahwah: Erlbaum, 2000. Print.

Graff, Gerald. "Bringing Writing In from the Cold." *MLA Newsletter* 40.2 (2008): 3–4. *From the President* Apr. 2008. MLA. Web. 1 June 2008.

Hillocks, George. *Ways of Thinking, Ways of Teaching.* New York: Teachers Coll., 1999. Print.

Hirsch, E. D., Jr. *Cultural Literacy: What Every American Needs to Know.* Boston: Houghton, 1987. Print.

Kijewski, Lisa J. Letter. *Harper's Magazine* Dec. 1997: 6–7. Print.

Lewin, Tamar. "College Board Announces an Overhaul for the SAT." *New York Times* 28 June 2002. Web. 1 June 2008.

Lindenberger, Herbert. "Gerald Graff on Freshman Writing." 28 Apr. 2008. Member comment in response to "Bringing Writing In from the Cold." *From the President* Apr. 2008. MLA. Web. 1 June 2008.

Miller, Thomas P. "The Formation of College English: Literacy Studies from the Republic of Letters to the Information Economy." 2008. TS.

Porter, Kevin J. "A Pedagogy of Charity: Donald Davidson and the Student-Negotiated Composition Classroom." *College Composition and Communication* 52.4 (2001): 574–611. Print.

Professor X. "In the Basement of the Ivory Tower." *Atlantic Monthly* June 2008: 68–73. Print.

Ridgley, Stanley K. "College Students Can't Write? What a 'Scoop.'" *National Review Online* 19 Feb. 2003. Web. 1 June 2008.

Ryan, Michael. "Why Johny Cant Write, Its a Generasionel Thing." *Houston Chronicle* 5 May 2004. Web. 9 May 2004.

Sheils, Merrill. "Why Johnny Can't Write." *Newsweek* 8 Dec. 1975: 58–65. Print.

Trimbur, John. "Literacy and the Discourse of Crisis." *The Politics of Writing Instruction: Postsecondary.* Ed. Richard Bullock, Trimbur, and Charles Schuster. Portsmouth: Heinemann, 1991. 277–95. Print.

Young, Richard E. "Paradigms and Problems: Needed Research in Rhetorical Invention." *Research on Composing: Points of Departure.* Ed. Charles R. Cooper and Lee Odell. Urbana: NCTE, 1978. 29–47. Print.

Stopping Cultural Studies

WILLIAM B. WARNER AND CLIFFORD SISKIN

For those of us who were looking to leave the canonical home of literary studies in the late twentieth century, cultural studies was a hitchhiker's dream. Fresh from one crossing—the Atlantic—it promised another one: a journey beyond the then current horizons of literary study. For those who climbed aboard, cultural studies offered a way to make good on the poststructuralist insight that language and other symbolic systems play a constitutive role in the production of meaning; rather suddenly, there were few objects in the world that could not be usefully read as texts. Cultural studies also allowed us to overcome the limitations of a literary study that restricted itself to literary history, author-centered study, and various species of formalism (genre theory, close reading, rhetorical analysis) to decipher the meaning of the literary work. It demonstrated that discourses of knowledge (like literary studies) could not be separated from effects of power (Foucault). Finally, cultural studies aimed not to abandon literature but rather to inscribe literature into the amorphous but expansive term "culture." Because feminist and British Marxist cultural studies understood culture as a contested terrain (of the high and low, elite and popular, hegemonic and emergent, spiritual and material), the term "culture" gave our critical interventions an immanent political valence. Not only would the horizons of literary study expand, but what was done within them would somehow *be* political.[1]

If being political is to participate actively in the processes of change, then

William B. Warner is professor of English at the University of California, Santa Barbara. Clifford Siskin is professor of English at New York University.

this essay is a political act with a nod to cultural studies. It is a nod of thanks and a nod goodbye. Cultural studies pulled into our disciplinary home at just the right time; we begin this essay by describing how a disparate set of imperatives aligned to put North American literary studies and cultural studies on the same path. But we then argue that it's time to pull over. The new horizons that cultural studies has helped us open reveal a landscape that it cannot help us to traverse. The strategic vagueness of the term and concept "culture," which was so important to the inclusiveness, emancipatory promise, and growth of cultural studies, can no longer take literary studies where it needs to go. We don't pretend to know exactly where that is, but profound change is not always a matter of prophetic change. Equally important—in fact, often more important—is knowing what and when to stop. It's time to write cultural studies into the history of stopping.

A Brief and Selective Account: The Emergence of Cultural Studies within Literary Studies

Theorize!

The early adapters of the bold new world of French theory confronted a vexing practical problem of application, a problem that made us feel as though we were skating on thin ice. On the one hand, many of the concepts found in the writings of Roland Barthes, Jacques Derrida, Michel Foucault, and Jacques Lacan—the text, difference, discourse, the subject—could be used to explicate literary texts, and many of us proceeded to do so. However, we were not unaware that the central arguments of these theorists unsettled, or put in question, many of the grounding concepts of literary studies: the *work/book* as a bounded thing; the *author* as the unique agent of creation; the *aesthetic* as a locus of beauty and value; and, finally, *history* as the frame for a narrative within which to place literature. The disciplinary variety of these theorists (Barthes was a literary critic, Derrida a philosopher, Foucault a historian of sorts, Lacan a psychoanalyst) and the range of new texts they invited us to read (Nietzsche, Hegel, Freud, Kant, Marx, etc.) made the precincts of the literary studies that we had inherited seem parochial. To write a new literary history, as in the title of the journal that introduced much of this work to the United States, one had to retheorize literature as well as history. In retrospect this theoretical turn in literary studies helped clear conceptual and canonical ground for cultural studies. When feminist film theory and British cultural studies introduced distinct versions of cultural studies to North American literary studies, theory had already rendered many forms of resistance futile.

Politicize Knowledge Work!

By the 1970s, feminism offered the most influential model for how cultural studies might politicize academic work. Feminist criticism and literary history exposed the misogynistic underpinnings of a broad arc of literary studies: the startling exclusion of women's writing from the canon; a particular way of representing marriage and death, old maids and women's rage; a use of pronouns that made man the general type of the human; the marginalization of women in the profession, to name just a few. The exemplary political power of this body of academic work came from the way critique moved from literary history to practices of reading to styles of address to hiring practices. In her long 1974 introduction to Derrida's *Grammatology*, for example, Gayatri Spivak slyly invested that high theoretical text with a feminist political horizon by inserting this sentence in her overview of Derrida's philosophical project: "Here are a few provocative examples, which I append so that the reader may sense their implicit or explicit workings as *she* reads the *Grammatology*" (Derrida xxviii, our emphasis).

The debates among feminist scholars during the 1970s and 1980s showed how theoretically energized discourse generated in one area of literary studies could raise the political stakes for the discipline as a whole— giving it an edge that proved conducive to the spread of cultural studies. Books exploring the difference between oppressive patriarchal representations of women and the experiences narrated by women themselves (Ellen Moers, Kate Millet, Sandra Gilbert and Susan Gubar, Elaine Showalter) were soon subject to critique in the work of emerging critics such as Mary Jacobus, Shoshana Felman, and Toril Moi who used Derridean deconstruction and what came to be called French feminist theory to challenge the essentialism of this earlier writing. They argued for looking at how women's difference is constituted in language itself, woman as language's other. The limits of this way of locating difference were in turn made visible in books by Cherrie Moraga and Gloria Anzaldúa (*This Bridge Called My Back*) and by bell hooks (*Ain't I a Woman*), which emphasized the significance of differences created by race and class.[2] The triumvirate of race, class, and gender thus came to preside over the political union of literary studies and cultural studies. Now politically as well as theoretically empowered, literary-cultural discourse recast the earlier debates about gender in terms that called the category of gender into question. In *Gender Trouble* and *Bodies That Matter,* Judith Butler joined other queer theorists in adding "sexual preference" to the political agenda and then, through an antiessentialist critique of "identity politics," reinscribed both gender and sexual identity *as* performance.

Performativity, with its emphasis on the temporality of the categories that seemed most fundamental, highlights how our third imperative
came into play: the confluence of theory and politics turned many critics
to history. Although Edward Said's writing had helped introduce French
theory to literary scholars, by the late 1970s Said openly complained that
the intellectual subtlety of theoretical work should not be harnessed only
to ever more refined readings of passages of Jean-Jacques Rousseau. (This
was a gentle reproach to his friends—members of the Yale school, Paul
de Man and Derrida and their influential students.) As a model for politically engaged reading, Said published a study in 1979 that would become
a founding text of postcolonial studies: *Orientalism*. By offering politically inflected readings of a range of European texts about the Orient—
eighteenth- and nineteenth-century anthropology, literature, and travel
narratives and the most recent scholarship—Said isolated a historical, discursive concept, "orientalism," the phantasmatic idea of the Orient within
the Occident, with which to lay bare the co-implication of knowledge,
power, and imperialism. Like Said, Fredric Jameson had helped introduce
French theory to American critics. Jameson's influential monograph *The
Political Unconscious: Narrative as a Socially Symbolic Act* offered a flexible
tool kit for politicizing the study of literature: an advanced concept of literary form, a nuanced alternative to Marxist ideology critique, and models
for reading romance and novels as symbolic acts. Through this kind of
reading, literature was posited as always already political, but in a way that
would support a theoretically advanced dialectical conception of both literature and history.

Historicize!

In *The Political Unconscious* Jameson famously declared that "History is
what hurts" and that "History itself becomes the ultimate ground and un-
transcendable limit of our understanding in general and our textual interpretations in particular" (102, 100). While the Hegelian-Marxist aura with
which Jameson invests History (it's his capital H) convinced many scholars
of the political urgency of historical analysis, his readings did not offer
a way to revise received literary histories. Most literary scholars continued to understand literary texts in relation to a received literary historical
narrative: the shift from medieval to Renaissance, the rise of the novel,
the emergence of the deep romantic subject, and so on. What was needed
was a way to relate literature to history so that history was not naively
construed as a pregiven context for the text, the radical critique of advanced theory was embedded in its reading procedures, and the imperative
to politicize literary history was met. Stephen Greenblatt's monograph

Renaissance Self-Fashioning, the founding of the journal *Representations* (1983), and the programmatic development of new historicism helped make good on these imperatives. Much has been written to explain new historicism's enormous popularity. It turned ingenious close readings of literary and historical texts into political allegories; it linked an expansive concept of history—indebted to poststructuralism, Marxism, and a version of Foucault—to an unapologetic, undertheorized affirmation of the aesthetic value of literature. For its political critics, who wanted more class conflict and ideology critique, new historicism enabled professors to feel radical without jeopardizing their cultural capital. For its traditional critics, new historicism's concept of history was fundamentally incoherent, and its set of obsessions (race, gender, power, ethnicity, etc.) told us more about the late twentieth century than about the epochs new historicists claimed to study (Myers 27–36).

Despite these critiques, new historicism had legs—legs specifically suited to the terrain of cultural studies. New historicism allows literary scholars to cast what they do—interpreting literature—as invested with the specific imperatives we've described: political relevance and a new, theoretically rigorous connection to history. To make this connection, Greenblatt argued for the usefulness of a broad, anthropological concept of culture. To link the symbolic meaning-making at work in "social life" to that same process in literature, Greenblatt quotes the anthropologist Clifford Geertz, but gives Geertz's definition of culture a characteristic torque toward the question of power: "customs, usages, traditions, habit clusters [but also] . . . a set of control mechanisms—plans, recipes, rules, instructions . . . for the governing of behavior" (3). To accommodate the literary text and the social world in their complex co-implication, Greenblatt called for the practice of a "cultural poetics" that would be conscious of the impossibility of exhaustively reconstructing the culture it studies (5). New historicism helped broaden literary studies by convincing a generation of literary scholars to go into the archive to find diverse noncanonical and nonliterary texts to link to the canonical literary texts they teach and study.

Go beyond the Literary!

In retrospect there is nothing more distinctive about the inchoate enterprise called cultural studies than the sanction it gave to going beyond canonical literary texts. In the 1980s and 1990s this expansion took many forms. Within historical areas of literary studies the quirky nonliterary text suddenly seemed to be the key to literary meaning, so a canonical text like Shakespeare's *Much Ado about Nothing* might be read against odd Renaissance medical treatises on sexuality (Greenblatt, "Fiction"), or Richardson's *Pamela* might be illuminated through seventeenth- and eighteenth-century conduct books for women (Armstrong). Feminist scholars showed how Harlequin romances, which traditional critics had loved to spurn, might be read and revalued as women's popular culture (Modleski; Radway). British cultural studies had originated in the study of working-class reading practices, like Richard Haggart's pioneering *The Uses of Literacy*. But cultural studies also ventured beyond textual objects. In his influential *Subculture*, Dick Hebdige studied the meaning-making at work in the stylistic invention of beats, mods, skinheads, punks, and Rastafarians. In "Fragments of a Fashionable Discourse," Kaja Silverman made use of the feminist psychoanalytic theory of the gaze (e.g., Laura Mulvey) to make a feminist case for female arts of adornment in the popularity, during the mid-1980s, of vintage clothing and the retro style (Silverman).

However, whoever sought to incorporate nonliterary texts or nontextual objects into their studies soon discovered the tenuous connections between the objects under study. So, for example, when William Warner (coauthor of this essay) embarked on a study of the relation between *Rambo* and Reaganism, he studied the first two Rambo films (*First Blood* and *Rambo: First Blood II*), the journalistic reception of the second film as an expression of Reagan's hypermacho foreign policy, Maya Lin's design of the Vietnam Memorial (1982), the odd staying power of the legend of the existence of MIA (missing in action) POWs being held by the enemy Vietnam, and, finally, the remarkably unheroic masochism of Rambo. Going beyond literary objects implied the necessity of a term to authorize the looseness (and potential inexhaustibility) of the many terms he sought to understand in their relation to one another. Stuart Hall's theory of "articulation" helped him claim that "culture" was already making the linkages between Rambo and Reaganism, between masochism and anger, that he found in his materials. Many of the most influential essays of this period—for example, Donna Haraway's "A Cyborg Manifesto" and Butler's "Gender Is Burning: Questions of Appropriation and Subversion" (on *Paris Is Burning*)—implied a concept of culture in order to read a phenomenon, like cyborg subjectivity or "queer performativity," that was not in any obvious way literary.

The Power of "Culture"

For those who followed the imperatives that we have just delineated—theorize, politicize, historicize, go beyond the literary—the reward was a new sense of community. By 1990, enough scholars had gathered under the conceptual tent of culture to justify an actual gathering. Cary Nelson, who had, with Larry Grossberg, assembled a huge conference on Marxism at the University of Illinois and published it as *Marxism and the Interpretation of Culture*, worked with Grossberg and Paula Treichler to convene an equally ambitious conference focused on cultural studies. The event may be usefully compared to a prairie revival meeting and the Catholic Church's convening of the Council of Trent in the mid–sixteenth century to refute the proliferating innovations of Protestantism. The conference, and the volume that was published from it in 1992 with the title *Cultural Studies*, resisted the anything-goes liberal pluralism of the American academy by affirming the historical and doctrinal priority of British cultural studies. While the conference gathered a broad spectrum of scholars from many different academic disciplines, the conference and volume insisted, with some of the explicitness of a catechism, on the political goals of cultural studies: "Cultural studies thus does believe that its practice does matter, that its own intellectual work is supposed to—can—make a difference" (Grossberg, Nelson, and Treichler 6). This statement of creed is linked to an origin story: cultural studies has its founders (Raymond Williams, E. P. Thompson, and Richard Hoggart), its precursor institution (the Centre for Contemporary Cultural Studies at Birmingham), its guiding theoretical texts (Marx, Althusser, and Gramsci), and, most important, its guiding contemporary intellectual (Stuart Hall, who spoke at the conference). This gathering of scholars also had impressive international reach, many scholars coming from Britain and the various countries of the Commonwealth. While Grossberg, Nelson, and Treichler resisted offering a reductive definition of cultural studies in their introduction to the conference volume, the emancipatory desires of this version of cultural studies, with its critique of power and its intellectual support for subject peoples, are everywhere evident. In the last decade of the twentieth century, various degree programs in cultural studies were founded at the University of Pittsburgh; George Mason University; the University of California, Davis; and Indiana University, and some are still functioning, especially in fields outside literary studies.

An Equally Brief and Critical Account: The Problem with Cultural Studies Is Culture

The Problem with Culture I: The Politics of the Political

The same suspicion once directed at deconstruction has now been raised in relation to cultural studies: doesn't this very proliferation of cultural studies mean that its dispensation was essentially liberal, in the classical sense of plural, tolerant, and market driven? In other words, hasn't cultural studies' big tent been just that—a convenient venue for every kind of cultural approach that scholars in English wished to attempt? The overt political agenda of some cultural studies led to the complaint that its find-ings were not so much part of a research project as part of a predetermined agenda. At a meeting in spring 1993 to initiate the Cultural Studies Cau-cus in the American Society of Eighteenth-Century Studies, the historian Dena Goodman complained, "For a long time historians have been study-ing the kinds of social and cultural difference that suddenly interest you folks in English; isn't 'cultural studies,' whatever its intellectual interest or political salience, just one more way for English to seize the politi-cal high ground and assert your priority in defining ethical values?" But there is another, more fundamental reason to worry about the costs of cul-tural studies' political desires. In *Reassembling the Social: An Introduction to Actor-Network Theory*, Bruno Latour argues that theory-driven sociological analysis, guided by its long-standing commitment to a nineteenth-century emancipatory politics, repeatedly reduces the complex networks of human beings and objects that it studies. Thus to explain "religious fervor," critical sociology will replace

> statues, incense, tears, prayers, and pilgrimages by "some stuff" like "so-cial cohesion" . . . [believing] that there must exist "behind" the variet-ies of religious experience another deeper, stronger force that is "due to society" and which explains why religious fervor holds "in spite of the fact" that entities mobilized in prayers (gods, divinities) have no "real existence." Similarly, since objects of art have no intrinsic properties, the passions they trigger must come from some other source.   (102)

The implications for cultural studies are clear: as with the concept of the social in sociology, our emancipatory deployment of culture may empty and simplify the objects it examines.

The Problem with Culture II: The Culture in Culture

In taking on the "social," Latour is challenging the institutional forma-tions that the term has long underwritten: sociology, in particular, and the social sciences, in general. The social is easy to find. Culture, however, is a moving target. Although, as noted earlier, cultural studies has fostered its own programs and groupings, many of them have not survived or flour-ished. And the rubric itself has not, as many either anticipated or feared, reconfigured the MLA *Job Information List*. Cultural studies appears to be easier to do than to institute—a problem with roots in its vexed relation to the established disciplines. For some of its practitioners that vexation is enabling. In his introduction to the influential 1993 *Cultural Studies Reader,* for example, Simon During begins his short history of British cultural studies with a seemingly remarkable concession: cultural studies "is not an academic discipline quite like others" because it possesses "neither a well-defined methodology nor clearly demarcated fields for investigation" (1). During presents this idea not as the dirty secret of cultural studies but as part of its inviting flexibility.

To gauge whether that flexibility comes with a debilitating price, however, we need to know more than the fact that cultural studies is *not* a discipline. What *is* its relation to the disciplines from which it emerged? That answer lies not just in the brief history of cultural studies itself but in the history of its core term: the longer history that "culture" shares with those disciplines. In *Keywords* and in his earlier *Culture and Society* Raymond Williams argued that our current notions of culture date back only to the late eighteenth century, having evolved from an earlier sense of culture grounded in the agricultural sense of the term. That evolution, however, was, crucially, twofold. First, on the basis of that earlier usage as "a noun of process," specifically "the tending of natural growth" (*Keywords* 87), culture played a crucial role in the natural and conjectural histories of the Enlightenment—narratives in which everything a society does contributes to its transition from nature into a product of the process of culture—that is, into the state of *being* a culture. For Herder, for example, "culture" had to be in the plural, for every society was—or was developing into—one. Today we simply assume that culture is always already there; it is the tool with which we totalize all the activities of every people, period, and group—even humanity itself—that we encounter.

In David Radcliffe's words, "while cultural practices are thought to vary, all literatures and societies are thought to behave as cultures" (x–xi). But if the enterprise of cultural studies values difference—theoretical, political, historical, and literary—then why depend on a concept that "applies to all literatures and societies indifferently"? The answer lies in a startling twist in the historical development of the term itself. At the same moment in the late eighteenth century that "culture" assumed its totalizing function, it took on a second meaning. Reorganizing internally the very unity that it helped contrive, "culture" also came to signify a subset of itself. Among the totality of activities that we call a "culture," is "culture": in Williams's words, "the works and practices of intellectual and especially artistic activity" (*Keywords* 90) that we now valorize as the specialized subject matter of the humanities and fine arts. This historical doubling—the lining up of culture within culture—is what configures the current relation of cultural studies to literary studies. Culture in its capacious sense lures us from our disciplinary home; culture in its specialized sense draws us right back. To do cultural studies, you have to walk the line.

If, as Johnny Cash recommends, we "keep [our] eyes wide open all the time," we'll see that what we're doing is reenacting the logic of the modern disciplines: the price of encyclopedic knowledge is specialization. Thus the Enlightenment gave us "culture" as comprehending "all" the "products of human work and thought" (*American Heritage Dictionary*) *and* as the select subset of those products. Culture and disciplinarity, in other words, are bound historically to each other. To grasp the consequences for cultural studies now, just think of the line that we've been walking as a cord—a bungee cord. The thrill of following through on the late-twentieth-century imperatives we've described—of going theoretically, politically, historically, and canonically beyond what the discipline had been doing—is like the thrill of bungee jumping. Better yet, to do justice to the grandeur of its ambitions, think of cultural studies as a variation of that sport—one in which you start off by first stretching the tether like a slingshot—stretching it in the hope of empowering a scholarly flight that really will transcend previous limits. The danger, of course, as in an episode of reverse bungee jumping one of us actually saw on television, is that the upward flight ends in a collision with the bottom of the platform, a jarring return to the solidity of disciplinarity. What both enables the flight from discipline and enforces disciplinary limits is the tether of "culture" itself: the object of knowledge—culture—and the way we know it—disciplinarity—are inextricably linked through the term itself (Siskin, *Work* 71–88).

AN EVEN BRIEFER ACCOUNT OF THE FUTURE: STOPPING AND STARTING

Stopping

For some scholars, the return to the platform has not been jarring. It's a relief. Hoping to find and keep the comforts of their disciplinary homes, they've been telling an already familiar set of lessons-learned tales about each of our imperatives. "After theory" is a been-there, done-that turn from the imperative to theorize. "New belles lettres" promises pleasure free of the friction of politicizing, while the "new biography" has made "History" "hurt" in a way Jameson did not anticipate, subjecting us to feigned lives of everyone from Shakespeare to James Frey. And then there's "Literature and . . . ," the homeland security solution to the dangers of going beyond the literary: secure the borders first, then encounter the other (e.g., science, medicine, religion, or any other other).

Other scholars have been less interested in defending current bound-aries than in putting "the literary" into history. Starting again with Wil-liams, what we have found is that "literature" changed meanings at the same time as, and in a similar manner to, "culture." The word that re-ferred through most of the eighteenth century to all kinds of writing—*Britannica* still defined "literature" in the 1770s as simply "learning or skill in letters"—came, in the space of a few decades, to signify a subset of itself. This second usage, let's call it *Literature*, narrowed and hierarchized those kinds of writing, admitting only certain texts within certain genres. It came to define, that is, the specialized subject matter of literary studies (Siskin, "More" 810–11).

Despite these parallels, those who have been enthusiastically remap-ping literature—and thus reopening literary studies to newly capacious enterprises such as Williams's "history of writing" (*Writing* 1–2)—have floundered when it comes to culture. It's the Teflon category. We fret over it—everyone complaining at one time or another that it doesn't quite do the job—but the complaints don't stick because it's so easy to use. We sim-ply don't know what we would do without it. But our point here is that ease of use carries hidden costs: culture *is* the problem with cultural studies. As long as we entrust our differences to its totalizing indifferences—and give it the energy of our imperatives—it will keep us in the same categorical bind, always doubling us back into its own disciplinary agenda. What the metaphor of reverse bungee jumping cannot convey is the everyday frus-tration this entails. Doing cultural studies is like doing Groundhog Day: you think you're getting somewhere different, in this case institutionally, but then you always find yourself back where you started. You never get to do what cultural studies is supposed to do: change literary studies. That task requires some conceptual breathing room—we need to give "culture" a rest so that we can wake up to a working day that actually turns out to be different.

So what should we start doing? We have two answers. The first is just to stop. Why put the burden of prophecy on everyone who advocates change? Many important changes might never have happened—and many more opportunities have certainly been lost in just this fashion—if argu-ments for stopping had to be matched by arguments for what to do next. Knowing what needs to be stopped and when can be a hard enough task. Think of William Wordsworth's timely injunction to stop the "style" of his predecessors, particularly the use of personifications and elitist diction. That act of stopping was a crucial intervention on its own. Feeling the bur-den of prophecy, he did try to follow up with "a more exact notion of the style in which it was my wish and intention to write," but it was anything but "exact" in detail or even in its connection to "style": "I have at all times endeavored," he wrote mysteriously, "to look steadily at my subject."

Starting

We can be less opaque about our agenda by taking our cue for the future from the past we have just described. The disciplinary transformations of culture and literature occurred in the context of an abrupt and startling proliferation of print in the final decades of the eighteenth century—the take-off that transformed British society into what is often called print culture. Only a few decades later, we get the first mention of English departments. The function of this new organizational grouping was to facilitate that transformation. The business of English departments from their inception was to mediate society's relation to the newly mature technology that now saturated it (Siskin, *Work* 12, 226–27). Anthologies, the canon, the aesthetics of taste, interpretative close reading, and other now familiar features of English were the means to that end—not ends in themselves. Mesmerized by the newly empowered umbrella terms under which those means gathered—"Literature" and "culture"—we've lost track of how we started and what our business still might be.

The popularity of the term "print culture" illustrates the ongoing nature of this problem. The power of the noun—its ease of use—draws our attention from the issue posed by the adjective: technological change. Whereas our new electronic databases have helped break the spell of "Literature" by recovering the true scope of "literature" in its earlier comprehensive sense, "culture" remains the ubiquitous term that still occludes our past and our future. If we stop making it the object of our studies, then important historical continuities and discontinuities materialize. In the early twenty-first century, English departments are still in the business of mediating society's relation to the dominant technologies for reading and writing. Print remains the core business but with a crucial twist: print is being remediated by the new technologies—electronic, digital, algorithmic—that are now saturating our society. All the familiar forms of literary study—novels, newspapers, poems, plays—are being transformed.

The challenge for English departments, then, is to transform ourselves to meet the historical challenge of remediation. Our relevance to universities and to society at large depends on a retooling that mixes some established means of mediation with new tools—and that then deploys both across the newly altered and expanded range of literary activity. The purpose of this essay is to free up some of the space, in our toolboxes and in our heads, that we will need for this new work—which is, in fact, our old work. To stop cultural studies is not to give up our past or our values but to reclaim what made our enterprise valuable in the first place.

NOTES

1. Many thanks for friends from the cultural and theory wars who were kind enough to advise us on earlier drafts of this essay: Devon Hodges, Felicity Nussbaum, Nancy Armstrong, Len Tennenhouse, Abdul JanMohamed, and Alan Liu.

2. We want to thank Devon Hodges for her help in formulating the rhythms of this debate within feminist cultural studies.

WORKS CITED

The American Heritage Dictionary of the English Language. 3rd ed. Boston: Houghton, 1992. Print.

Armstrong, Nancy. *Desire in Domestic Fiction: A Political History of the Novel.* Oxford: Oxford UP, 1987. Print.

Butler, Judith. *Bodies That Matter: On the Discursive Limits of "Sex."* New York: Routledge, 1993. Print.

———. *Gender Trouble: Feminism and the Subversion of Identity.* New York: Routledge, 1990. Print.

———. "Gender Is Burning: Question of Appropriation and Subversion." Butler, *Bodies* 121–40.

Cash, Johnny. "I Walk the Line." *Sixteen Biggest Hits.* Sony, 1999. CD.

Derrida, Jacques. *Of Grammatology.* Trans. and ed. Gayatri Chakravorty Spivak. Baltimore: Johns Hopkins UP, 1974. Print.

During, Simon, ed. *The Cultural Studies Reader.* London: Routledge, 1993. Print.

Greenblatt, Stephen. *Renaissance Self-Fashioning: From More to Shakespeare.* Chicago: U of Chicago P, 1980. Print.

———. "Fiction and Friction." *Shakespearean Negotiations: The Circulation of Social Energy in Renaissance England.* Berkeley: U of California P, 1988. 66–93. Print.

Grossberg, Lawrence, Cary Nelson, and Paula A. Treichler, eds. *Cultural Studies.* New York: Routledge, 1992. Print.

Hoggart, Richard. *The Uses of Literacy: Aspects of Working-Class Life.* Harmondsworth: Penguin, 1957. Print.

Haraway, Donna J. "A Cyborg Manifesto." *Simians, Cyborgs, and Women: The Reinvention of Nature.* New York: Routledge, 1991. 149–82. Print.

Hebdige, Dick. *Subculture: The Meaning of Style.* New York: Routledge, 1979. Print.

hooks, bell. *Ain't I a Woman: Black Women and Feminism.* Boston: South End, 1981. Print.

Latour, Bruno. *Reassembling the Social: An Introduction to Actor-Network Theory.* Oxford: Oxford UP, 2007. Print.

Jameson, Fredric R. *The Political Unconscious: Narrative as a Socially Symbolic Act.* Ithaca: Cornell UP, 1981. Print.

Myers, D. G. "The New Historicism in Literary Study." *Academic Questions* 2 (1988–89): 27–36. Print.

Modleski, Tania. *Loving with a Vengeance: Mass-Produced Fantasies for Women.* New York: Routledge, 1982. Print.

Moraga, Cherríe, and Gloria Anzaldúa, eds. *This Bridge Called My Back: Writings by Radical Women of Color.* New York: Kitchen Table / Women of Color, 1981. Print.

Nelson, Cary, and Lawrence Grossberg, eds. *Marxism and the Interpretation of Culture.* Urbana: U of Illinois P, 1988. Print.

Radcliffe, David. *Forms of Reflection: Genre and Culture in Meditational Writing.* Baltimore: Johns Hopkins UP, 1993. Print.

Radway, Janice. *Reading the Romance: Women, Patriarchy, and Popular Literature.* Chapel Hill: U of North Carolina P, 1984. Print.

Said, Edward. *Orientalism.* New York: Vintage, 1978. Print.

Silverman, Kaja. "Fragments of a Fashionable Discourse." *Studies in Entertainment: Critical Approaches to Mass Culture.* Ed. Tania Modleski. Bloomington: Indiana UP, 1986. 139–52. Print.

Siskin, Clifford. "More Is Different: Literary Change in the Mid and Late Eighteenth Century." *The Cambridge History of English Literature, 1660–1780.* Ed. John Richetti. Cambridge: Cambridge UP, 2005. 810–11. Print.

———. *The Work of Writing: Literature and Social Change in Britain, 1700–1830.* Baltimore: Johns Hopkins UP, 1998. Print.

Warner, William. "Spectacular Action: Rambo, Reaganism, and the Cultural Articulations of the Hero." Grossberg, Nelson, and Treichler 672–88.

Williams, Raymond. *Culture and Society: 1780–1950.* 1958. New York: Columbia UP, 1983. Print.

———. *Keywords: A Vocabulary of Culture and Society.* New York: Oxford UP, 1976. Print.

———. *Writing in Society.* London: Verso, 1983. Print.

Wordsworth, William. "Preface to the Second Edition of *Lyrical Ballads.*" *Wordsworth's Poetical Works.* Ed. Thomas Hutchinson. Rev. Ernest De Selincourt. 1936. London: Oxford UP, 1967. 735–36. Print.

From Literary Theory
to Critical Method

RITA FELSKI

Courses in literary theory, once decried for damaging or distorting students' appreciation of primary works of literature, are now a staple of university course catalogs around the country. Having taught more than my share of such courses, I view them as essential resources not just for English majors or graduate students but for anyone eager to learn about key intellectual trends of the last few decades. Theory can no longer be dismissed as an arcane subspecialty when references to Baudrillard and Derrida crop up in best-selling fiction, Salon.com, and the pages of the *Village Voice*. And yet the conventional theory course, I've come to realize, has certain built-in limits: it tends to obscure rather than illuminate issues of method that are significant in their own right and especially germane for graduate students seeking to define and refine analytic procedures that will guide the writing of their dissertations. A course in critical method thus offers a valuable complement to the standard theory class, yet its function is not just additive but also transformative. Thinking seriously about critical method cannot help but alter our view of literary studies, putting pressure on the overly ambitious claims sometimes advanced in the name of theory.

The "introduction to theory" course offered at many institutions conforms to a familiar generic model, grouping course materials according to criteria of philosophical orientation or political affiliation. At the University of Virginia I teach a survey that starts with intellectual background on New Criticism, F. R. Leavis, and Russian formalism before moving

The author is William R. Kenan, Jr., Professor of English at the University of Virginia.

briskly through a spectrum of recent theories: structuralism, psycho-analysis, Marxism, deconstruction, feminism, African American and post-colonial theory, queer theory, and cultural studies. While the details of such courses obviously hinge on the interests of individual professors and the requirements of particular departments—one year Heidegger gets in, another year new historicism drops out—versions of such a format are now ubiquitous in both graduate and undergraduate education.[1] A similar structure defines most primers and anthologies of literary theory currently on the market. Take, for example, *A Reader's Guide to Contemporary Literary Theory*, an example picked randomly from the numerous textbooks sent to me by publishers seeking course adoptions. This guide by Raman Selden and Peter Widdowson contains chapters on New Criticism, Russian formalism, reader-oriented theories, Marxist theories, structuralist theories, poststructuralist theories, postmodern and postcolonial theories, and feminist theories. Within these categories, approaches are further subdivided by political stance (Marxist feminism as distinct from liberal feminism) or historical or cultural location (second-wave feminism, American deconstruction). Most textbooks of literary theory follow an analogous pattern, organizing their material according to the political or philosophical tenets of their proponents.

Such presentations of literary theories are not surprising; they echo how theories conventionally present themselves. In this sense, *literary theory* is something of a misnomer, given that the dominant figures in the theory canon are typically concerned not just with literature but also with language, history, identity, society, politics, the nature of being. Indeed, more often than not, their most provocative theses were originally forged for purposes quite unrelated to the academic study of literature. Learning how to perform a psychoanalytic reading of a literary work means acquiring a working familiarity with a terminology originally devised for the milieu of the therapeutic session. Introducing Marxist aesthetic theory in the classroom means bringing students up to speed on political and economic fundamentals such as ideology and class. Literary theory thus expands students' intellectual horizons beyond the category of literature, offering a substantive challenge, both its defenders and its critics would agree, to any notion of the autonomy of art.

While this embedding of literary interpretation in a bigger picture strikes me as highly desirable if not indispensable, it also possesses certain drawbacks. Namely, it can inspire an exclusive focus on why we read—to what political or philosophical end?—at the expense of how we read. In consequence, it can obscure striking convergences of method between very different frameworks. Critics at opposite ends of the theoretical or ideological spectrum, in other words, can share a common commitment to specific styles of interpretation. The technique of close reading defines the work of apolitical or traditionally minded critics such as Helen Vendler or Denis Donoghue, but it also characterizes the writings of queer theorists such as Eve Sedgwick or Joseph Boone. The political beliefs of these two groups of critics may be worlds apart, but their methods of interpretation overlap, even as the critics draw different conclusions from these methods. Conversely, critics with shared political affiliations may opt for divergent modes of interpretation: one feminist scholar is drawn to a Foucauldian, neohistoricist framework; another adopts a form of analysis that is psychoanalytic and symptomatic. The styles of reading of these two feminist critics, their conception of the relation between text and context, and their view of what counts as evidence reveal little common ground.

In other words, if we focus less on what critics say (their avowed beliefs and political or philosophical commitments) and more on what they do (their method of interpreting, analyzing, and evaluating texts), the map of literary theory begins to shift and change, as predictable groupings give way to less familiar constellations and affinities. Yet the rationale for requiring a course on critical method at the graduate level is not just to offer a fresh perspective on current intellectual debates but also to make students more aware of interpretative choices that help define the structure, shape, and plausibility of their own research projects. In general, I've found graduate students much more savvy about the intellectual content of contemporary theories than about the implications of those theories for method, more confident weighing up the pros and cons of models of hybridity versus models of identity, for example, than explaining how exactly an interpretation grounded in reflection theory differs from one based on symptomatic reading.

A course on critical method, then, focuses on how expansive claims about language, truth, or power-discourse relations are translated into particular forms of interpretation and argument. It quickly becomes evident that the relations between political or philosophical worldviews and methods of reading are complex, contingent, sometimes asymmetrical, and not always predictable. While particular theories influence how we read, the reverse also holds true: practices of reading, governed by their own distinctive logic, rhythms, and history, covertly mold how theories are interpreted, taken up, and used. Participants in the so-called theory revolution of the last few decades often extolled the iconoclasm of their intellectual interventions, yet in practice these theories rarely if ever spawned entirely new ways of reading, but modified and fine-tuned techniques of interpretation that had been developed over decades, in some cases over centuries.

We may be reminded, at this point, of the frequently made observation that deconstruction's success in the United States derived from its ability to latch on to, while burnishing with new glamour and prestige, techniques of close reading popularized during the heyday of New Criticism. Yet the tone of such observations is typically reproachful, even accusatory, lamenting the co-option of high-wattage theories by mundane interpretative practices and everyday academic routines. My inclination is to view such practices less judgmentally, to regard them as significant, determining, and revelatory in their own right rather than as phenomena that should be automatically subjugated to, and measured against, the claims of theory. Modes of reading, like other habitual activities, are often deeply ingrained in the form of practical rather than theoretical knowledge—we learn to interpret by following the examples of teachers or peers, not by consulting a rule book or drafting a general statement of principles. This approach holds true both for commonsense or everyday reading and for academic methods of literary interpretation. These methods are often transmitted unconsciously and by example: the student learns by modeling the teacher, by voicing similar observations and making analogous arguments, often without either participant's being fully aware of the processes of transmission that are under way.

For this reason, the claim sometimes made by theory's defenders, that every reading of a text is by default a theoretical reading, needs qualification. The merit of such a claim lies in forcing us to recognize that every act of interpretation depends on a host of tacit assumptions about meaning and significance that speak philosophical and political volumes, that there is no neutral interpretation, no possible access to the "text itself." Yet it is also misleading, in that it obscures the differences between forms of knowledge conveyed through intellectual argument and theoretical precept and forms of knowledge communicated by example and by doing. The activity of reading, to an extent that has not been fully acknowledged, often falls into the latter camp, as a form of knowing how rather than knowing that. As a practice that is semiconscious and deeply ingrained, providing a pleasurable sense of mastery through the exercise of acquired expertise, it can prove remarkably resilient and resistant to change. Hence the not uncommon scenario of the scholar who, in a weighty theoretical preamble, advertises his conversion to Deleuze or Stuart Hall, only to subsequently fall back into a mode of interpretation methodologically indistinguishable from his undergraduate analyses of *Heart of Darkness*. The impact of new theoretical pictures on actual reading practices is more attenuated, mediated, and unpredictable than we have been willing to recognize.[2]

Instead of lamenting such lapses, I am intrigued by what they reveal about the relations between theory and practice, between visionary ideas and everyday activities, and about the inevitable messiness and hybridity of scholarly work. They intimate that our view of how knowledge operates is too rarefied and abstract, that we do not attend sufficiently to the grounding of thought in the semiconscious routines, practices, and pleasures of a particular habitus. In this sense, while theory often draws us away from the disciplines, espousing styles of thought that claim general authority and disregard conventional intellectual boundaries, a course in critical method draws us back to the disciplines. It asks us to think about how the ingrained assumptions and taken-for-granted conventions of particular fields of study exercise a powerful influence on our arguments, shaping the ways in which theoretical claims are played out. Such ingrained methodological preferences shape readings not only of literary works but also of theoretical texts, which—whether their provenance be philosophical, anthropological, psychoanalytic, or political—are also subject to the tacit conventions and interpretative practices of literary studies. The transcendence of disciplinarity announced by the course in theory turns out to be more apparent than real.

While literary critics, for example, are often expected to position themselves in terms of gender, race, or sexuality, scant attention is paid to disciplinary location, surely the most salient influence on how we write and read. Only when we venture abroad are we forced into a realization of the sheer contingency and strangeness of our mother tongue. Literature scholars recruited to serve on interdisciplinary hiring committees soon discover how puzzling their working assumptions can seem to scholars in other fields. These methodological differences are modified but far from dissipated by the spread of interdisciplinary work. Victorianists may pride themselves on stretching the boundaries of their field by writing on drains or Darwin, yet to outsiders their arguments, interpretations, and use of evidence unequivocally proclaim their English department training. Disciplines, in other words, are defined less by subject matter than by method. Hence the often noted irritation of cultural studies scholars when English professors appropriated the term *cultural studies* to characterize their own fine-grained exegeses of movies and soap operas, while ignoring the methodological history of cultural studies, including its thoroughgoing questioning of the evidentiary value of close reading.

A course on critical method, then, allows teachers and students to reflect on the often invisible conventions and interpretative routines of literary studies as they intermesh with, and are shaped by, intellectual innovations and transformations in the humanities. Its role is neither to police scholarship by insisting on a narrow and limited definition of what constitutes an academic field (as evidenced in recent reclamations of close reading as the sine qua non of literary studies) nor to endorse the questionable ideal of shrugging off the shackles of disciplinarity, as if we could somehow, by a supreme effort of the will, achieve a god's-eye view of knowledge unblemished by any trace of particularity. Rather, such a course allows us to explore both the transformations and continuities in the field of literary studies as they shape current forms of debate and argument.

My perspective thus diverges from Stanley Fish's well-known defense of disciplinary autonomy against the inroads of political criticism and cultural studies. While I share Fish's view that the claims made for the political effects of scholarly work are often exaggerated, I am not convinced that we must safeguard the disciplinary distinctiveness of literary studies by protecting it from politically informed arguments. Fish imputes an imagined essence to literary scholarship derived from the moment of New Criticism, an essence contravened by the sheer eclecticism of interpretative methods espoused by literary scholars of different stripes not just in recent years but throughout the twentieth century. This eclecticism was memorably if ungenerously described by Monroe Beardsley as a "mishmash of philology, biography, moral admonition, textual exegesis, social history, and sheer burbling" (188). Literary studies has always been a mishmash, never a unified or purified field. The aim of a course on critical method is not to focus on text-immanent interpretation at the expense of theory or politics but to investigate how a spectrum of themes, frameworks, and intellectual projects are translated into the distinctive yet varied idioms of literary studies.

My own course begins with a reappraisal of the venerable categories of author, reader, and genre, examining how the deployment of such categories is inflected by the specifics of interpretative method. A view of readership derived from the phenomenology of Wolfgang Iser, for example, generates a style of argument very different from the materialist, historicist perspective of Roger Chartier. The course subsequently canvasses conflicting models of the relation between literature and history, presenting it not as a self-evident actuality but as a series of unresolved questions and a methodological can of worms. Over several weeks, the class considers the merits of reflection theory, symptomatic interpretation, models of containment and transgression, and the method of articulation developed in cultural studies. A final session on anti-antimimesis introduces students to recent rebuttals of the antimimetic orthodoxy that held sway during my graduate education. The concluding section of the course engages with diverse critiques of historicism alongside efforts to imagine alternatives to ideology critique and the hermeneutics of suspicion. After pondering the many varieties of formalism, we examine contrasting conceptions of literature and ethics, ranging from Martha Nussbaum to Emmanuel Levinas, and conclude with an investigation of the recent surge of interest in affect, feeling, wonder, and enchantment. The overall goal of the course is to infuse students with an awareness of the variety and complexity of methodological choices, in a manner that allows them to better refine, defend, and justify their own styles of interpretation and argument.

A unit that often attracts interest is the one dealing with symptomatic reading. Many students have unconsciously absorbed the conventions of this interpretative method during their undergraduate career, often without being aware of either its name or its history. Materials for this unit include Catherine Belsey's well-known analysis of Sherlock Holmes, a chapter from Terry Eagleton's *Criticism and Ideology*, Annette Kuhn's account of symptomatic interpretation in feminist film theory, and a critique of symptomatic reading by David Bordwell. Compared with what students do in a traditional course in literary theory, we spend less time parsing the details of Althusserian Marxism or clarifying the differences between Freud and Lacan and more on analyzing the guiding assumptions, formative metaphors, and interpretative techniques underpinning the critical argument. Why is a text imagined as containing ruptures, contradictions, or fissures? What is the relation between the symptomatic reading of a trained critic and the interpretation of an ordinary reader? Is symptomatic reading equally appropriate for all texts or more likely to be applied to some works over others? What is the rationale for referring to implicit meaning as repressed meaning, and what are the pros and cons of such a claim? How do the assumptions underlying symptomatic reading differ from those at work in other forms of politically invested interpretation (reflection theory, models of containment and transgression, articulation)? Instead of treating interpretative method as either self-evident or as a vehicle for delivering theoretical or political propositions, in other words, we place it at the very heart of our discussion.

One advantage of such an approach is that, by cutting across predictable alliances and entrenchments, it can alleviate the often noted specialization and fragmentation of literary studies. An avowedly apolitical student interested in working on poetic form will soon discover that Marxist criticism, in many of its variants, is highly formalist in orientation. A queer theorist working on transgression in the Renaissance can pick up useful insights from debates about the merits of transgression in postcolonial studies. Scholars with contrasting, even clashing, affiliations or working in different historical periods can, it turns out, learn much from one another's work. Such intellectual cross-fertilization also guards against reinventing the methodological wheel with each new style of criticism. If the belief that literature reflects society turns out to be an intellectually shaky premise, it remains shaky no matter whether the writer is a Marxist, a feminist critic, or a scholar working in disability studies. The political stakes may vary, but the methodological issues are similar in kind.

How does such a course shape what students learn? First of all, participants gain a systematic introduction to a wide range of critical methodologies, including ones to which they have not been previously exposed. Second, they acquire fluency and confidence in applying such methodologies, gaining a firm grasp of the guiding assumptions and interpretative moves that characterize particular ways of reading, arguing, and drawing conclusions; they also gain the ability to justify their evidentiary claims against skeptical or hostile criticism. Finally, they acquire a map of how these differing methods fit into the history of literary studies, including the ways in which styles of reading are shaped by theoretical developments, political changes, and the vagaries of intellectual fashion. The goal of a course on critical method is thus to make explicit what is often left implicit and to make students more aware of interpretative choices that they often make unknowingly and unconsciously.

A course on method signals a shift from the macrolevel to the microlevel of intellectual argument, a move from big pictures—theories of sexuality, postmodernism, power-discourse relations—to reflections on how those pictures are translated into the working assumptions and routines of particular disciplinary fields. Some readers may view this reorientation as a diminishment, a muting or taming, of theory's radical claims, but this reaction testifies to the deep-rooted allegiance of literary studies to modernist ideals of defamiliarization, novelty, and transgression and its concomitant inability to conceive of habitual structures in anything but negative terms. Such structures, however, are not simply constraining but also constitutive and enabling, even as the significance of theory cannot be assessed in abstract or absolute terms but only in relation to the needs and interests of a specific context. Knowledge is always shaped by a pragmatic horizon—the milieu and the larger set of purposes that frame individual acts of thinking, reading, and writing. In this case, the pragmatic horizon is provided by the tacit protocols and defining assumptions of literary studies as they play themselves out in the context of the dissertation, the journal article, or the classroom. We need to think more carefully and more amply about how disciplinary training, however much we may struggle to resist or deny it, shapes what we know and how we know it.

NOTES ══

I would like to thank James English and Allan Megill for their helpful comments.
  1. For a recent overview of such courses, see Howard.
  2. Bordwell offers an excellent discussion of this question.

WORKS CITED ══════════════════════════════════════

Beardsley, Monroe C. "Intentions and Interpretations: A Fallacy Revived." *The Aesthetic Point of View: Selected Essays.* Ed. Michael J. Wreen and Donald M. Callen. Ithaca: Cornell UP, 1982. 188–207. Print.

Belsey, Catherine. "Deconstructing the Text: Sherlock Holmes." *Sherlock Holmes: The Major Stories with Contemporary Critical Essays.* Ed. John A. Hodgson. Boston: Bedford–St. Martin's, 1994. 381–88. Print.

Bordwell, David. *Making Meaning: Inference and Rhetoric in the Interpretation of Cinema.* Cambridge: Harvard UP, 1991. Print.

Eagleton, Terry. *Criticism and Ideology: A Study in Marxist Literary Theory.* New ed. London: Verso, 2006. Print.

Fish, Stanley. *Professional Correctness: Literary Studies and Political Change.* Oxford: Oxford UP, 1995. Print.

Howard, Jennifer. "The Fragmentation of Literary Theory." *Chronicle of Higher Education* 16 Dec. 2005: A12. Print.

Kuhn, Annette. *Women's Pictures: Feminism and Cinema.* 2nd ed. London: Verso, 1994. Print.

Selden, Raman, and Peter Widdowson. *A Reader's Guide to Contemporary Literary Theory.* 3rd ed. Lexington: UP of Kentucky, 1993. Print.

Do We Teach Disciplines or Do We Teach Students? What Difference Does It Make?

MARSHALL GREGORY

During my time as a graduate student at the University of Chicago, the professors running the graduate program never hinted at my true destiny, by which I mean my destiny as a teacher. In an *ADE Bulletin* of 1994, I characterized the way my generation of graduate students was socialized into academe, and what I said then seems a good entry into my topic now.

> As a student deeply immersed in nineteenth-century British studies and literary criticism, I certainly expected at the end of my doctoral labors to be effortlessly translated, like Enoch, into a higher kind of academic heaven-haven, levitated up and out of my library carrel at Chicago, hurtled toward success down [an] acoustically lined tube, and gently lowered into another library carrel at good old Research U, presumably in a beautiful city with a good symphony and affordable housing, where I would be a faculty member adored by a handful of student researchers who would hang breathlessly on each of my well-polished, professionally impeccable words. (20)

The only use I can now think to make of this absurd vision of an academic career is to offer it up for ridicule on *Saturday Night Live* or *The Daily Show* or maybe offer it to the shade of Aristophanes for a brisk send-up. In partial justification for my naïveté, however, I can truthfully report that my revered professors at the University of Chicago actually encouraged

The author is Harry Ice Professor of English, Liberal Education, and Pedagogy at Butler University. A version of this article appeared in the Winter-Spring 2007 issue of the ADE *Bulletin.*

117

PROFESSION 2008

this absurd vision, and none of them ever alluded to the fact that my real destiny, like Adam's, was to be driven from the paradise of my carrel by an angel with a flaming sword. When the sword angel finally dragged me by the heels out of my fifth-floor library paradise, my fingernails making long, agonized scratches on the concrete floor, he did not send me, as he sent Adam, to toil in the real-world dirt of Mesopotamia. He sent me to toil in real-world classrooms in Milwaukee instead.

That I did not expect this fate was—and is—irrelevant. If there is one thing literary study teaches us, it's that we all fulfill our destinies whether we're talking about Achilles or Frodo. Accordingly, I found myself standing one day, feeling awkward and dazed, in front of my first 8:00 a.m. freshman composition class (yes, in Milwaukee), realizing with the mounting panic of a prisoner walking up the steps to the gallows that I knew a lot about literature—at least I thought I knew a lot about literature—but that I did not know one blessed thing about composition, about teaching composition, about teaching literature, or about teaching in general. This was the first moment I really understood—and I understood it viscerally—that there was a huge unspanned chasm between what graduate school had trained me to do and what my job required me to do.

It got my attention. Some academics of my generation took their version of this experience as a good reason to bypass classrooms as much as possible in favor of doing library or laboratory research. Others of us, however, once over the shock of finding that we were totally unprepared, became fascinated by the complex dynamics of this unexpected classroom dimension to our careers. Professors like me chose a career path directed straight toward the heart of classroom experience. I have been deeply interested in teaching, both as practice and as scholarship, ever since, and I still think teaching is the most interesting and challenging game in town. Few graduate programs today leave students as unprepared for teaching as the graduate program I enrolled in in the 1960s—I walked into my first class with not even five minutes of teaching experience and with not even five seconds of teaching talk as part of my graduate education. But the fact that today's graduate students are not totally unprepared for teaching does not mean that they are well prepared for teaching.

The single most difficult notion for graduate students and new professors to grasp about teaching—and, indeed, many experienced teachers never grasp this point either—is that successful teaching to undergraduates has little to do with the degree of one's mastery of disciplinary knowledge. I am not making the well-rehearsed point that there is a big difference between knowing disciplinary information and knowing how to teach it. I am making a different point and, I hope, a deeper one. Allow me to illustrate my point, like Socrates, starting with my own ignorance. After diligent study in my field that began with voracious childhood reading, followed by a college English major and a PhD in English, I think that by now, at age sixty-six, I may know about ten percent of all the disciplinary knowledge available to me. Actually, that's an optimistic estimate, but for purposes of argument and diminishment of embarrassment, let's assume that it's true. (It's hard to keep up with the output of Harold Bloom alone, much less find the time to fill in my chagrined ignorance of Schiller, Rabelais, Henry Gates, the spasmodic poets, and David Foster Wallace.) If you are like me, every time you look at your must-read list, you feel the onset of heart attack symptoms. Your should-read list could stretch to Tokyo. But my students are even worse off. They probably learn no more than ten percent of the disciplinary knowledge that I introduce to them in my classes, and if you think they remember ten percent of that ten percent six months after they leave my classes, you're the kind of person who buys ten lottery tickets every single day on the grounds that someone has to win.

The point I am making is that given all there is to learn in any field, we are all pikers, stumblers, and terminal beginners. But while I am aware of the huge blank spaces of ignorance in my learning, my students are not aware of those blank spaces, and they nibble like mice around the edges of what I don't know and often mistake me for a vastly learned man. They say so in their course evaluation forms. "Dr. Gregory knows everything about literature and literary criticism." "Yeah?," I want to say, "and you would be measuring my knowledge against what standard?" In undergraduate teaching, we are all doing no more than dabbling around the edges of a vast pool of knowledge and information that not even we as experts claim to digest, an observation that invites the following conclusion. If we are all getting so little disciplinary work done and if undergraduate teaching does actually work a fair amount of the time, it cannot be because we are all doing a box office business expanding the boundaries of our students' disciplinary knowledge. It has to be working for reasons other than disciplinary reasons.

I will tell you why and when teaching works, and doing so will bring me back to my claim that good undergraduate teaching correlates poorly with anyone's having mastered massive amounts of disciplinary information. When undergraduate teaching works, it works because the disciplinary material we teach—the same material that inevitably gets forgotten—endures a better fate than getting remembered. (Remember that I am only talking here about good teaching, teaching that works, not about teaching that fails.) A thing's merely getting remembered is not a good criterion of its value because, if we stop to think about it, we all remember, for reasons we can never explain, a whole attic full of useful rubbish. A better fate than a thing's getting remembered is its getting absorbed. When a thing gets absorbed, it may not be recallable later as stored information, any more than the toast you had for breakfast this morning is recallable as toast, but the nutritional value of the toast makes its contribution to your life even when it is no longer toast, and the things that our students forget but absorb from our classes also become transformed. Knowledge that gets absorbed shows up not as knowledge but as features of mind and character that are much more valuable than mere information. Information we can always look up, but when a thing gets absorbed it turns into ideas and skills, and it turns into forms of socialization and cognition that shape students' intuitions and that strengthen their powers of language, imagination, judgment, and reasoning.

In short, when teaching works, it forms ethos, for what else *is* ethos if not the particular configuration of anyone's intuitions and our powers of language, imagination, judgment, and reasoning? Students absorb from us ideas, imaginings, judgments, and forms of reasoning because we model how these components of ethos may be used. Talking about imagination does not teach anyone how to jump-start his or her imaginative powers. But as we model in our teaching how imagination may be used, we do teach others how to use their imagination with greater fecundity and vividness. The literature classroom is our exercise field for demonstrating how to use ideas, how to develop imagination, how to construct judgments, and how to argue using reason.

For reasons we can all understand and sympathize with, these are not the kinds of thoughts waving for attention in the foreground of graduate students' and new professors' minds. At the beginning point of their careers, most teachers are insecure about their mastery of content, about their authority in front of a classroom full of adolescents, and about how to fill each class period with content that is well informed and well developed. They are not thinking about student ethos; they are wondering how to explain Coleridge's notion of multiety in unity or Eliot's notion of tradition or Foucault's notion of the episteme. In short, the training of graduate students and new professors is pretty much guaranteed to produce teachers who think it is their duty to teach undergraduates the way their graduate professors have taught them. This is the kind of teaching that graduate students themselves have been experiencing, many of them for seven or eight years. Why would this kind of teaching not seem the natural model for graduate students' or new professors' teaching?

Two things need to be said about this "natural" model, however. First, it is a model for training apprentices to become professional colleagues, not for educating undergraduates in the liberal arts. Second, it is a model that could hardly be more dysfunctional for undergraduate education. Most of the undergraduates we face wind up occupying professional worlds far removed from academe, but even when new teachers do pause to consider that few of their students are headed for academic careers, they tend to approach teaching as disciplinary apprenticeship anyway. Given their own recent and protracted graduate education, this is the only approach to teaching that they are intimately familiar with. "How can I not be a good teacher if I really know my stuff?" they are inclined to think, and they are even more inclined toward the obverse version of this claim, thinking that "surely, knowing my stuff really well will at least protect me from being a bad teacher." And they will persist in their inclination toward these beliefs even though everyone in his or her education encounters at least one— and sometimes, unfortunately, more than one—professor who is a true expert in his or her field but who may as well be a penguin when it comes to teaching effectively.

All this means that before graduate students become new assistant professors, they need to think about several salient considerations deriving from the powerful instinct to conflate good teaching and a maximum coverage of disciplinary knowledge. The confused notion that most of teaching is wrapped up in how well one knows one's material is a pernicious influence on undergraduate education, and new teachers need to become unconfused about it before they can become effective. Let me try to demonstrate how serious this issue is.

When anyone asks an academic, "What do you teach?," the academic invariably gives a disciplinary answer. "What do I teach, you ask? I teach nineteenth-century British literature," or "I teach ancient philosophy," or "I teach calculus." The disciplinary answer about what one teaches is overwhelmingly familiar, but, in fact, its familiarity masks the fact that, measured logically, it's a very strange answer. Decades ago in our discipline we learned how to deconstruct and how to ferret out the biases in the language that we use in scholarship and criticism, but it is equally important to learn how to deconstruct the langue of our pedagogy, and, frankly, we are a long way from doing this well. It was once not strange to explain the causes of mental or emotional disorders as demonic possession, but the discovery of viruses and bacteria and brain chemicals made demonic explanations disappear. There's a parallelism here. The mindset indicated by "I teach literature" or "I teach discipline X" is as strange in its way as the claim that demons cause fever because, in fact, we know as certainly as we know that demons don't cause fever that teachers do not teach disciplines. Teachers teach students, not disciplines, and the difference to a teacher, not to mention the difference to students, of describing his or her function in either of these ways is the difference between two orientations toward teaching.

I am not stretching to make an arcane point. If it seems that I am obtusely or falsely dramatizing a trivial matter of social rhetoric, let me remind everyone that it was our discipline that first taught other disciplines to understand that conventions of social rhetoric often mask large subterranean structures of value and belief, the power of which goes unchallenged as long as the structures lie mostly unseen. It was disciplinarians in English who taught everyone else how to analyze the structures of patriarchal privilege buried in what used to be taken as mere social rhetoric, such as the erasure of women's individuality that occurs inside the convention of sending formal invitations to married couples using only the husband's name—my wife and I still occasionally get wedding invitations addressed to "Dr. and Mrs. Marshall Gregory," as if my in-laws had been too thoughtless to give their daughter a name—or the dismissal of the female point of view accomplished by the long-standing social convention, the loss of which is still lamented by many, of using *man* as a synonym for *human being*.

On critical examination, it turned out that these mere conventions of social rhetoric were in fact not mere, and not innocent, either. Those who objected to placing these conventions under critical scrutiny always had a typical ploy of resistance. It went without saying, they asserted, that a wife had her own personhood, despite the erasure of it by certain forms of address, and it likewise went without saying, they continued, that *man* as a synonym for *human being* covered women as well. However, we have learned by now, or should have learned by now, that whatever meanings are asserted as so obvious that they can "go without saying" are exactly the meanings that need to be said.

Thus when I criticize the social convention of teachers saying "I teach philosophy" or "I teach English," it does not strike me as a plausible rejoinder—nor does it convince me of the innocence of such descriptive locutions—to respond that it goes without saying that all teaching is as concerned with students as it is with disciplines. The subterranean value structure of "I teach English" describes a classroom mindset that is focused primarily on the discipline—in a way that probably seems defensible to the teacher as mere common sense or as mere shorthand—rather than on students. Academics are not generally hypocrites on this front. They do not say "I teach English" rather than "I teach students" because they are trying to pull the wool over anyone's eyes. They say "I teach English" because no one has yet helped them think through their teaching mission. In this sense their professional self-description *is* a bit innocent, but it is certainly no more innocent than the innocence of the patriarch to whom it never occurred that using *man* as a synonym for *human being* might constitute a teensy privileging of the male perspective.

So what difference does it make if grad students and new professors think of themselves as teaching students first and disciplines second? If it didn't make a difference, talking about it would be more of a bother than a help, but it makes a world of difference in the teacher's entire orientation to the classroom. The classroom world in which teachers think of themselves as primarily teaching students is a different classroom world from the one in which teachers think of themselves as primarily teaching disciplines.

When teachers think of themselves as teaching students first, they are more prepared to understand both the intellectual rationale for and the everyday utility of meeting students where they are rather than endlessly whining about students not being adequately prepared. One of the commonest and silliest themes of informal academic discourse is teachers' glazed-eyed cliché about how terrible it is that students today are not prepared for college-level work. It is egregious nonsense that so many teachers derive a kind of self-back-patting comfort or construct a kind of bogus self-satisfaction by characterizing students as inadequately prepared, especially since the very people with whom we often enjoy contrasting ourselves, the denizens of market-focused boardrooms whom we often scorn as having no life of the mind, are at least intelligent enough not to avail themselves of this flimsy excuse.

Corporate moguls driven by market values do not criticize their customers for not being adequately prepared. They study hard how to meet their customers' needs or how to educate their customers about needs that they as market agents would like to meet. Then, beginning where the customer is, they undertake to move the customer to look desirously, appreciatively, or admiringly at the goods they offer. Only teachers awash in delusions of superiority to their students have the effrontery to walk into their classrooms and think it a shameful injury to themselves that students aren't ready to join them in disciplinary high jinks right off the bat. If more professors would pat themselves less and start looking in a hard-headed, clear-eyed, empirical manner at their students' needs, they might see that they are the ones starting off on the wrong mark, not their students.

I am making a strong argument about this point because there is no community more toxic to the professional socialization of graduate students and new professors than the community of professors bonded together by the belief that students are not adequately prepared. This community is toxic because new professors seduced by its appeal inoculate themselves against either self-inquiry or student criticism for the rest of their careers. Just as Wonder Woman deflects a volley of bullets with her magic bracelets, the professor who begins a teaching career with the expectation that few students will be prepared arms himself or herself with a magical deflection of all self-blame for any teaching failures. All problems with teaching will always be the fault of the unprepared student.

A second difference it makes when teachers think of themselves as teaching students first is that they become much more receptive to the crucial fact that the most important cluster of variables affecting students' learning in the classroom are ethical and social variables, not intellectual or professional variables. Teaching consists of a lot of activities that most teachers focus on diligently, such as description, exposition, explanation, time management, use of technology, testing, evaluation, and so on. But there is an additional cluster of variables more important than any of these that many teachers hardly think about at all. Whatever else teaching is, it is also an ethical and social relationship, and if teachers do not know how to tend to the social and ethical dimensions of teaching, they can, sadly, undermine their own best intentions and efforts.

On the ethical front, students evaluate every teacher from nearly the first moment he or she walks through the classroom door on the first day of any semester. This evaluation kicks into gear on four fronts that have nothing to do with how well the teacher knows his or her disciplinary content. Students evaluate teachers on fairness, respect, charity, and civility, and the teacher who fails on any of these fronts, especially fairness, will be fighting an uphill battle all the way because he or she will be working against an ethical deficit of discredit. That a teacher whom students evaluate low on ethical fronts may be a true expert in the field will never erase students' low opinion. Ethical assessment precedes and trumps academic and intellectual assessment.

On the social front, every graduate student and every new teacher needs to keep in mind that students may remember little content from class but are likely to remember a lot about the teacher as a personality and as a social agent. Teachers may think that the classes they teach are about chemistry or literature, and they are, but teachers need to remember that every class is also about the teacher—or at least about the teacher's embodiment of certain values—and any teacher who fails to realize this is not a full participant even in his or her own classroom. I have spoken to hundreds of former students who, when they talk about their former teachers, never mention anything they learned in *any* class. That always shocks me, but it never varies. Decades after taking a class, however, many students will remember their teachers' temperaments, habits, manner of speaking, passions, enthusiasms (or lack thereof), and personal interactions. All graduate students and new professors need to consider that who they are as persons is a whole dimension of teaching in itself and is perhaps the most important influence on student learning.

A third difference it makes when teachers think of themselves as teaching students first is that they become amenable to the reality that while most of the content they teach will be forgotten (just as most of the content that everyone learns is forgotten), the effects of learning do not merely evaporate. An old but true adage about education says that education is what remains when everything you learned has been forgotten. The truth of this adage helps us focus on the reality that I now want to probe more deeply: the reality that when content is really learned, it gets absorbed, not stored. We only remember stored information when we continue to use it and thus reinforce it. We remember absorbed information all our lives because what gets absorbed does not have to be recalled. Instead of being carried about as part of the mind's burden, it changes the interior architecture of thinking itself, which means that it becomes part of the mind's structure.

The lists that you, I, and our students have learned over the years in order to make ourselves look smart on tests and papers are rigged with built-in self-destruct mechanisms just like the destruction mechanisms that destroy each list of tasks at the beginning of *Mission: Impossible* episodes. Sure, I still remember from elementary and high school classes that the sun is ninety-three million miles from the earth, that the speed of light is 186,000 miles per second, and that Milton was forty-two when he went blind, but such an array of random facts is more like a neural accident than useful memory. No one has ever asked me if I know the speed of light or how old Milton was when he lost his sight. We all have facts like these stuck in our heads, and the same is true of our students. Later in students' lives (like next semester), after they have taken our classes, the course content they studied with us may no longer be recallable as information. But if the class provided a real learning experience, the students' struggle with our assigned content will have turned into something deeper than information. It will have turned into new habits of reasoning, speaking, writing, and imagining.

A fourth difference it makes when teachers think of themselves as teaching students first is that they are more likely to see that what is interesting to them will almost always be separated from what is important to their students by a large gulf of mutual incomprehension that only grows wider as teachers grow older. Many teachers focused primarily on their disciplines never see the difference between what is interesting to them and what is important to their students. It's a bit narcissistic not to see this, but, as the Duke says in *Amadeus*, "there it is." Teachers who are actively and empirically engaged with their students, however, will realize, eventually, that if they want what is interesting to them to become important to their students, they have to explain to them why it's important and they have to do so in concrete terms and in the present tense, not in some vague future that students can hardly imagine.

A fifth difference that surfaces when teachers think of themselves as teaching students first is that they find it easier to understand the coded nature of students' complaints about course content. The teacher focused on disciplinary content gets frustrated and sometimes offended when students express what sounds like hostile resistance or contempt for the teacher's beloved content. Teachers who are empirically trying to judge where their students are in their learning stages, however, more easily keep in mind that when students complain about a classroom assignment, saying, "this is stupid," what they generally mean is, "this makes me feel stupid." "This is stupid" or "this is boring" is code for "I'm afraid I can't do this. Can you help me understand this assignment in a way that will allow me to do well on it?" The teacher's job is to support students' efforts to acquire the confidence they need to take risks.

A sixth difference that occurs when teachers think of themselves as teaching students first is that they are better at modeling good learning for their students than are teachers whose attention is riveted by content. What teachers are likely to think of as modeling good learning for their students is probably not, because, typically, teachers are profoundly averse to modeling for students the messy, ragged parts of learning—the parts where we once made fools of ourselves or failed the statistics course or were rejected by an editor or were jealous of others or just said something plainly stupid. All of us are tempted to present an airbrushed, marketer's image of ourselves as flawless learners, but teachers who spend more time looking hard at students than at disciplinary content will be more likely to see that such a presentation of themselves is one of the most discouraging and diminishing things they can do to their students. We owe students the truth. In the pursuit of real learning, failure is an off-and-on certainty for everyone but is seldom fatal for anyone.

Teaching, as Bartlett Giamatti has said, "is an instinctual art, mindful of potential, craving of realizations" (194). Such an art does not allow for rules or directions that work with mechanistic certitude: "Use a torque wrench at 65 pounds of pressure to bolt Idea A into Student B's brain." Directing regular teaching seminars over many years at my home institution,

Butler University, and at my second academic home, Emory University, has forced on me the truth of my three concluding points. First, talking to many teachers in intense conversations has made me realize the extent to which teachers are often too busy teaching to engage in sustained thinking about it. This is why we all need to gather round our watering holes and talk about teaching as much as we talk about scholarship. Second, directing teaching seminars has also made me optimistic about how readily we may all improve what we do by sharing what we know. Many college professors get frustrated with teaching, but only a few descend to terminal cynicism. Given genuine support for thinking afresh about teaching, especially in the company of peers, most teachers not only seize the opportunity but run with it.

Third, and finally, I would like the chance to tell all graduate students and new professors that a career devoted to teaching can be a noble, sustaining, and deeply satisfying life choice, not merely a utilitarian maximization, as some economists might say, of certain bodies of knowledge and investments of talent. Sentimental and melodramatic clichés about teachers, such as the Mr. Chips stereotype 3 and the Professor Snape stereotype 4—also heroic clichés, such as the music teacher in *Mr. Holland's Opus* or the literature teacher in *Dead Poet's Society*—swirl so thickly in our culture that it is difficult for young teachers to get a fix on who they should be and how they should comport themselves. I would recommend to them that they get their bearings not by focusing on pop culture narrative and certainly not by focusing on personal advancement but by concentrating on the needs of their students. Those needs are great, and teachers are in a position to exert a positive influence, an influence needed now more than ever before.

The need is great because when it comes to the teaching of desire, college and university teachers are being outtaught as if we were the Seem Team playing the Dream Team, and the people outteaching us are corporation marketers. The *Lord of the Rings* and *Harry Potter* movies have recently reanimated wizards in our imagination as figures of great power, but these fictional wizards are pikers compared with today's corporate marketers. What makes them so powerful is that they know how to manipulate their magical spells and incantations in order to make all of us desire not just to have certain consumer products but to be certain kinds of people. Marketers know how to make us want a certain kind of life, and there is nothing more important to the kind of life we actually live than the kind of life we are taught to want. Teachers often have the sense that their teaching lies on the surface, while evidence all around us suggests that the pedagogy of corporate marketers goes right to the core of our students' lives.

It is sad to realize that our college students inhabit a social, moral, and political space that is so deficient in the helpful cues, prompts, exercise, and stimulation that they need for the balanced development of those capacities that lie at the heart of their humanity. In referring to such capacities I do not refer to notions highly theorized or highly scientific. I refer to those basic capacities that seem to belong to human beings as such, primarily derived from the fact that all human beings have a common brain structure and a common evolutionary history and universally live in groups. The human capacities that seem to issue from these three determinants are the capacities for reason, language, imagination, introspection, moral and ethical deliberation, sociability, aesthetic responsiveness, and physicality.

On all these fronts our society fails young people on a massive scale every day. Their imaginations are rendered passive by the ingestion of images that threaten to overwhelm us all, images that are almost hallucinatory in their vividness and intensity and, in movie houses, are nearly the size of Texas. All these images come ready-made, however, and are thus inadequate for the stimulation of an independent, constructive imagination. On the language front, our students' linguistic capacity receives profoundly inadequate stimulation in a society more and more dependent on icons and images rather than arguments and poetry and narration, leaving students less and less aware of the satisfactions and successes, not to mention the nuances and precision, that can be achieved by getting the right words in the right order for purposes of either self-expression or public appeal.

Right down the list of capacities I just enumerated, young people are not simply left alone—far from it; in some senses they would be better off if they were left alone—but more and more manipulated by mass media and market forces. Their sexual energy is exploited and ramped up to sell a vast array of consumer goods; their natural curiosity and desire to learn are short-circuited by educational narratives ranging from *Animal House* to *Harry Potter* to *Paper Chase* to *Buffy the Vampire Slayer* that tell them that school is dull and that teachers are either stupid, mean, or come from hell; and their desire to be mature is infantilized by a television culture that tells them that the unflappable, ironic, David Letterman and Jon Stewart version of cool is the only kind of maturity that counts. Worst of all, market forces have mastered the rhetoric of autonomy and freedom that we would like to use with our students but that is difficult for us to redeem from the corruptions of language that conflate autonomy with mindless partisanship and freedom with nothing more than the power to purchase a wide range of consumer goods.

Where are the contexts, the social spaces, where students are likely to find models of people who know how to bring trained intelligence, intellectual honesty, clear expression, aesthetic sensitivity, and ethical responsibility to the solution of problems both personal and social? Where are the social sites today where young people are likely to find serious people asking questions about serious issues, yet conducting their pursuit of these issues by means of companionable, civilized, and respectful discourse? Such contexts are few indeed, but our university and college classrooms can be such places because we can choose to make them so. I would like the chance to tell every graduate student and every new professor that when they walk to the door of their classroom on any given day, close it, and turn to their class of students, no one in the world has more unfettered power for the next fifty or seventy-five minutes than *they* do for speaking directly to students' minds and hearts in ways that can potentially influence how those students think, feel, and judge for the rest of their lives. Every day I feel the thrill and the responsibility of this challenge. It is a job worth getting up for every day. It is a job worth doing as long as one can do it well.

I want to tell graduate students and new professors that the real aim of teaching is not helping students rivet the juggernaut of careerism onto the framework of their young lives. The real aim of teaching is helping students acquire such capacities of mind and heart as will assist them in living lives that are autonomous, personally enriched, socially responsible, intellectually perspicuous, and morally defensible. This is not an aim that pays well, but it is a noble and sustaining activity. It is a task to which a man or woman can dedicate an entire life and not feel hoodwinked at the end. However, the only way we veterans in the profession empower our graduate students and young professors to turn around and empower their students to live these kinds of lives is to live them ourselves, especially inside the domain of education, where we should exert our best efforts to think clearly about not only what we do but what we want.

WORKS CITED

Giamatti, Bartlett. *A Free and Ordered Space*. New York: Norton, 1990. Print.

Gregory, Marshall. "From PhD Program to BA College; or, The Sometimes Hard Journey from Life in the Carrel to Life in the World." *ADE Bulletin* 107 (1994): 20–24. Print.

"Speak German or Sweep the Schoolyard": Linguistic Human Rights in Germany

LUCINDA MARTIN

A BERLIN school has unwittingly put itself at the center of an ongoing controversy in Germany about language policy.[1] The Hoover School introduced a German-only rule, not only in the classroom but also for class trips and breaks in the school day. Germany's minister for migration issues, Maria Böhmer, quickly endorsed the policy for other schools, saying that "language is the key to integration."[2]

Germany's largest immigrant group is Turkish (Berlin is famously, in terms of population, the second largest Turkish city after Istanbul)[3] and representatives of the Turkish community did not waste any time in condemning the policy as racist, counterproductive, and ultimately futile. The Federation of Turkish Parents in Germany sharply criticized the forbidding of any language, and a Turkish member of the Green Party, Representative Özcan Mutlu, spoke of "a break with the constitution" (Küpper 5).

To many, the school's German-only policy smacked of cultural imperialism, yet the policy became harder to criticize as new details emerged. Over ninety percent of the Hoover School's pupils have a migrant background, and classrooms often serve native speakers of up to ten different languages. Furthermore, a committee composed of the administration,

---

The author holds a postdoctoral position in the Exzellenznetzwerk Aufklärung—Religion— Wissen at the Martin-Luther-Universität Halle-Wittenberg in Halle, Germany. A version of this article appeared in the Winter-Spring 2008 issue of the ADFL Bulletin.

---

teachers, parents, and students had worked together to formulate the policy (Lau, *Man spricht Deutsch*). Most compellingly, administrators claimed that they designed the policy not only to help students learn to function in German society but also to avoid instances of bullying by some groups of migrant youngsters (Monch).

Emboldened by these new revelations, the vice president of parliament, Wolfgang Thierse of the left-wing Social Democratic Party, urged adoption of the policy by all schools in Germany. Meanwhile, Robert Heinemann, an education expert for Angela Merkel's Christian Democrats, stirred outrage in minority communities by calling for punishments for students who break such *Deutsch*-only rules. Specifically, Heinemann suggested that students who don't speak German "should sweep the schoolyard" (Köpke, Selonke, and Wüllner). For her part, Böhmer remained steadfast in supporting the Hoover School's policy. In a radio interview, she stressed the importance of trying out different techniques and learning from others' experience, a model she referred to by using the English phrase "best practice."[4] Best practice? No word yet on whether or not Böhmer was asked after the interview to do any sweeping.

GERMAN IDENTITY

The Hoover School controversy is just one more episode in an ongoing public debate about the role of minorities in German society. Emphasizing the connections among language, education, and minority issues, Germany's best-known education expert, Peter Struck, saw events at the Hoover School as more evidence that "the multicultural model has failed" (1).

Multikulti, as it's called in Germany, is shorthand for the notion that many cultures can coexist, each retaining its uniqueness. The alternative model being discussed is *Leitkultur*, or "lead culture," in which traditional German culture leads other ethnic groups in German society. According to *Leitkultur* advocates, members of minority groups could carry on their usual practices, so long as they do not contradict German lead-culture values.[5]

Advocates of lead culture fear parallel societies of foreigners with high rates of unemployment who cling to practices such as forced marriage or honor killing, which in their opinion have no place in a democratic society. Lead-culture proponents see language as the key to getting foreigners out of ghettos and into mainstream society. Those who promote the alternative multicultural model argue that attempts to destroy cultural difference only lead to further marginalization, not to integration. Members of minority groups argue that lead-culture models that forbid the wearing of veils by Muslim women or even the use of non-German languages essentially shut minorities out of the public sphere.

Nearly every European country is engaged in a similar debate about cultural identity, but in Germany the discussion is, like nearly all major issues, informed by Germany's Nazi past. Germans want at all costs to avoid charges of racism. Yet race- or ethnic-based understandings of nationality persist. People with German parents who grew up in South America are seen as German, while people of Greek ancestry who have lived their entire life in Germany are seen as Greek.

A recent media campaign illustrates the complexity of cultural identity in modern Germany. In an effort to battle rampant negativity in Germany and to promote an understanding of nation not tied to race, ethnicity, or origin, a consortium of leading media companies launched the You Are Germany campaign. In television and print media spots, popular celebrities, regular Germans, and persons from Germany's history appear next to the message *Du bist Deutschland* ("You are Germany"). The spots encourage Germans to not let hard times get them down, to take responsibility, and to get to work at doing whatever they can for Germany. Echoing JFK, the spots urge, "Don't ask what the others do for you. You are the others" ("Manifest").[6]

Significantly, You Are Germany features a mix of men and women of all ages and from various cultural and racial backgrounds. Yet critics immediately denounced the campaign as nationalistic for its attempts to create out of many groups one German *Volk*, or "people," as Hitler wanted to do with the various "Aryan" peoples. Critics were even able to point out that Hitler sometimes used the phrase, "because you are Germany," a fact that the creators of the media campaign obviously did not know.[7] In its spots, the campaign also presented images of former Nazis, such as the industrialist Ferdinand Porsche, who used Jewish slave laborers in his factories and who developed weapons for the regime. Critics also lambasted the You Are Germany campaign's appropriation of Albert Einstein, a staunch critic of Nazi Germany who, after the Nazi takeover in 1933, lived in exile in the United States.[8]

The problematic juxtaposition of Porsche's and Einstein's likenesses in the same collage of German greats embodies modern Germany's identity crisis. The controversy surrounding You Are Germany reveals just how entwined Germany's present is with its Nazi past and how difficult it is for Germans to define their identity without reference to that past. Everyday symbols of Germanness, such as folk songs or traditional German clothing, become in certain contexts reminders of the Nazi era, particularly because the Nazis exploited traditional culture for propaganda purposes.

An incident at the Berlin Hoover School, where the German-only controversy exploded, illustrates this legacy of a culture corrupted. A team of Turkish television reporters was scheduled to appear at the school one day to do a piece on the story. As she got ready for work that morning, the school's principal, Jutta Steinkamp, started to put on her favorite jacket, a traditional Tyrolean-style cardigan, but then she thought to herself, "With this German-to-the-core jacket, you've lost before you even get started." The next thing that went through her mind was "Has everyone gone mad?" (Lau, "Deutschstunden" 62).

Germans constantly struggle with defining themselves in some way that doesn't refer to their Nazi past. In fact, public debates like the one surrounding You Are Germany pop up on a regular basis. A few years ago, the German media obsessed over the question, Are you proud of being German?, and all the most important German politicians ended up having to answer the question (both yes and no were wrong answers). Germany is engaged in a quest to find its identity or else to forge a new one, and language—as both a key component of identity and the tool for articulating identity—is at the nexus of the problem.

LANGUAGE POLICY IN "OLD EUROPE"

Although discussions of ethnic difference are particularly problematic in Germany because of its Nazi past, nearly all Europe is dealing with minority issues similar to those in Germany. Recent events like the subway bombings in London, the riots in the Paris slums, and the controversy set off by the Danish Muhammad cartoons have brought these countries' treatment of their minorities into the spotlight. "Old Europe" in general is having to face the problems of an increasingly diverse population. Western countries are trying to find ways to cope with the legacy of their colonialist past, not to mention cope with the steady influx of economic refugees and asylum seekers.

Thus in the same week that the Hoover School controversy erupted in Germany, a similar debate erupted in the Netherlands. Rita Verdonk, the Dutch minister for integration and immigration, proposed that only Dutch should be spoken in public, and a majority of the parliament supported her idea. Rotterdam, in which half the population is non-Dutch, has already adopted such a policy. At the same time, the Dutch government has initiated an obligatory language and culture test for asylum seekers, and it is reportedly outrageously difficult and prohibitively expensive, at 350 euros ("'Dutch-Only'"). Following the Netherlands' example, several German states have proposed similar tests.

In the Netherlands, Germany, and elsewhere, politicians justify such policies by pointing to instances of violence committed by minority groups. They believe that only by breaking links between a member of a minority group and that person's native culture and language can such violence be quelled. In the Netherlands, this argument surfaced strongly after the Islamist murder of the filmmaker Theo van Gogh. Perhaps more to the point, Minister Verdonk explained to a congress of her party that ordinary Dutch feel ill at ease hearing other languages on the street. Unable to find a fitting Dutch word for the concept ill at ease, she said that Dutch people who hear other languages in public feel "unheimisch"—she apparently meant the German word *unheimlich* (Spieker; "'Dutch-Only'").

At the same time that Europeans are trying to come to grips with a multitude of immigrant languages, they are also having to face the hegemony of English. Germans, for example, expected that their language (and their voice in international affairs) would gain influence at the end of the cold war. They foresaw German growing into a lingua franca, binding Western Europe to former Soviet countries, like Poland and the Czech Republic, where German is widely spoken. In fact, Germany has lost prestige on the world stage, which is increasingly dominated by Asia and, of course, the United States. English is the lingua franca of Europe, with French, not German, in second place.

Moreover, Germans constantly complain about the steady influx of English words into *Deutsch*, creating what some have dubbed Denglish. Germany, which has long defined itself as the land of poets and thinkers, fears losing its rich cultural heritage, often subsumed under the phrase "Goethe's German." Yet many Germans grudgingly admit that English, not German, is the key to success in a global world.

Thus even as a few schools in Germany tentatively experiment with Turkish classes, many more are initiating German-English bilingual education and are doing so with younger and younger children. In the tiny state of Schleswig-Holstein, there are at least thirteen German-English kindergartens and two German-English elementary schools (Mikuteit). Besides which, nearly all German schools require children to study English starting in the third grade. One north German school is even trying an English-immersion first grade in which children learn all subjects in English—regardless of whether they speak German, Turkish, Polish, or Russian at home.[9] In the charged climate of what some are calling a *Kulturkampf* ("cultural war"), this solution may be the most acceptable to all concerned. It neatly avoids serious debate about language and the tricky related issues of education and immigration. But is surrendering all linguistic difference in favor of English really the answer?

The National Minorities

In the light of European countries' ambivalence over linguistic difference, it may seem strange that some American language experts have called on policy makers in the United States to look to Europe as a model (Stanton 72). In fact, many European countries do offer progressive linguistic rights for so-called national minorities. The Council of Europe's 1995 Framework Convention for the Protection of National Minorities (signed by Germany in 1997) includes key provisions regarding the language and culture of certain—but not all—minorities.[10]

The Framework Convention has granted these national minorities a number of important protections. Article 5 guarantees them the right to maintain and develop their cultural heritage, including their religion and language, and forbids coerced assimilation. Article 14 guarantees every member of a recognized national minority the right to learn his or her language. It also requires the signatories to provide language instruction or general instruction in the minority language if the minority desires it.

These are powerful legal protections, and, not surprisingly, they have not been granted across the board to all linguistic minorities. Indeed, individual European countries have narrowly defined what constitutes a national minority and thus who is eligible for the protections.[11] Germany, along with several other countries, adopted a definition much more conservative than the Framework Convention foresaw. Germany's definition stresses that national minorities must have strong historical ties to the state, must be linked to a traditional area of settlement, and must be citizens of the state. Germany recognizes four such national minorities: the Danish-speaking minority living near the German-Danish border; the Frisian minority in the North Sea coastal regions; the Sinti and Roma, who live throughout Germany (and are thus an exception to the territorial clause); and the Sorbs (or Wends), who live mainly in the east German states of Brandenburg and Saxony (see fig.). These protected minorities receive federal and state funding for language and cultural maintenance programs and are guaranteed some degree of political representation.

Germany's national minority programs have worked best with the Danish minority. Danish Germans live near Denmark, and since many Germans also live in Denmark, it is in the interests of both lands to be mutually hospitable. Moreover, ethnic northern Germans and Danes often look similar, practice the same religion (Protestantism, usually Lutheranism), and have comparable educational levels.

The Germanic Frisians have also had mostly positive relations with the larger German society in recent years. The Frisian language is in danger of dying out, and although an older generation of Frisian speakers are proud to speak their language, fewer and fewer young people do so. Frisian has not been able to hold its own against its numerically stronger neighbors—German, Dutch, and Danish. Nonetheless, it has made a kind of popular comeback since Germany signed the Framework Convention, which, for example, allowed signs to be posted in both German and Frisian.

Although the Slavic Sorbs far outnumber Frisian speakers, they are still a tiny minority. The Sorbian language, which was forbidden at various times in history, most recently in Nazi Germany, seems to be faring well. There are Sorbian-language schools, including one gymnasium (college preparatory high school), as well as radio, television, and newspapers. Like Frisian, Sorbian has benefited from government support programs.

The situation concerning the Roma and Sinti is less clear-cut. Since these groups have never had a homeland, much less one in Germany, technically they do not fit the definition of a national minority. Yet thanks to a new international political activism on the part of Roma and Sinti, they have made huge gains internationally in recent years in terms of winning protections for their communities. One example of such activism was getting European countries to recognize Romani as a nonterritorial language deserving of national minority protection (Gheorghe and Mirga; Rooker).

Sadly, European countries made this exception only in recognition of Europe's, and especially Germany's, long and infamous track record in its treatment of the Roma and Sinti. Centuries of harsh treatment all over the continent culminated in the extermination of 500,000 Roma in Germany's Nazi death camps. Significantly, to date, the only other linguistic group that has achieved an exception to the territorial clause is Yiddish speakers, who, of course, can look back on a similar history of persecution and genocide.[12]

The German recognition of the Roma and Sinti as a national minority is problematic in other ways as well. The policy applies only to those Roma and Sinti who are German citizens with a long ancestral history in Germany and not to the thousands of stateless Roma and Sinti and those who are asylum seekers or refugees. The new protections have thus served as a wedge dividing the Roma and Sinti communities, since some Roma and Sinti now get better treatment than others. Furthermore, many Roma and Sinti do not see themselves as European at all and reject the embracing of a European identity in order to be guaranteed linguistic and other human rights, even as other Roma and Sinti have long since adopted a hyphenated identity.

Whether or how Germany's 70,000 Roma and Sinti recognized citizens will ultimately benefit from the new protections is unclear. Roma and Sinti themselves are ambivalent in many ways to their new rights in Germany. They see education, for example, as both the key to raising their low economic status in German society and, at the same time, as the mechanism of assimilation and loss of identity. In fact, experts note that "the overall situation of the Roma in society has not changed much—indeed, it has worsened in recent years—and that reality serves to perpetuate majority prejudices and discrimination" (Gheorghe and Mirga).

Germany's *Ausländer*

The situation of Romani and Yiddish speakers points to a looming problem presented by many other minorities. Romani and Yiddish speakers as groups have no ancestral homeland. Living in different countries, either for economic reasons or to flee persecution, these groups were behaving in a global way long before the word *globalization* was coined. Yet modern minorities who behave in similar ways, moving about either because they need to earn a living or because they want to escape war or persecution, are not offered the same protections in modern Europe.

In fact, it is clear that the laws protecting national minorities were formulated less to protect historic minorities than to create a bulwark against more recent immigrant groups. One need only look at the process by which the Framework Convention for the Protection of National Minorities was agreed on. All the documents, including the resolutions of individual nations' ministers, are publicly available (www.coe.int).

Although Recommendation 1201 of the Parliamentary Assembly did not pass, it contained the key wording that countries such as Germany would later adopt on their own to define national minorities (*Recommendation 1201*). Article 1 includes not only the citizenship condition but also the requirement of "longstanding, firm and lasting ties with the state." This wording was specifically aimed at excluding citizens from new immigrant groups. Yet another precursor of the Framework Convention, the 1992 European Charter for Regional or Minority Languages, takes a similar tack: "regional or minority languages" are defined as those "traditionally used within a given territory of a State," with the express exclusion of the "languages of migrants" (*European Charter*). Disturbingly, "languages of migrants" even refers to the languages spoken by second- and third-generation individuals, born in Western countries, many of them citizens of these states.

GERMANY'S NATIONAL MINORITIES AND *AUSLÄNDER*

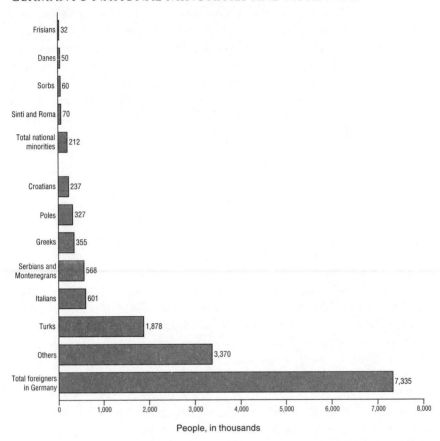

People, in thousands

The statistics give 10,000 North Frisian speakers and 2,000 Sater Frisian speakers; 20,000 others can understand only one of these two dialects. East Frisian is considered a dead language. The figures for Romani speakers give only German citizens. The figures for Sorbs give 20,000 who speak Lower Sorbian and 40,000 who speak Upper Sorbian (*Facts*).

Statistics are from the German Interior Office (*Statisik*). Germany has a total population of 82.5 million. The 7.335 million foreigners make up about 9% of that population.

In October 1993, the Summit of the Council of Europe rejected Recommendation 1201. The Council of Europe countries eventually decided instead to adopt the looser Framework Convention—a compromise that was much weaker than Recommendation 1201. Containing no definition of national minorities and only general recommendations about the cultural and political rights of minorities, the Framework Convention essentially left a great deal up to member countries to decide. The result has been laws protecting autochthonous groups—mostly tiny minorities—that have been largely assimilated (Danish Germans, Frisians) or otherwise subdued (Sorbs, Roma), even as the laws specifically exclude most minority language speakers (see fig.). The German government uses the catchall word *Ausländer* ("foreigners") to describe all its other nonnational minorities, a category that includes second- and third-generation people who may never have set foot in the country of their grandparents' origin. Many of these are the descendants of guest workers, who rebuilt Germany after World War II. The term *Ausländer* is also applied to asylum seekers, many of whom have been waiting up to fifteen years for their cases to be decided. In the meantime, these refugees are forbidden from working and so are their children, even children who have completed an education in German schools.

The plight of asylum seekers in Europe is the result of a competition to see which country can offer the worst conditions for refugees. Far from the ideal of a unified and compassionate Europe, each European country hopes to scare away new asylum seekers and to wear old ones down until they pack up and leave. European countries, in their negotiations over minority language rights, have been equally cynical. In setting up systems in which certain supposedly legitimate or old minorities are protected, they are in fact heading off other, new minorities who might make claims to the same cultural and political protections.

Language, Education, and Human Rights

What linguistic rights Germany's foreigners have is, legally speaking, a gray zone. The German government's efforts have been aimed mainly at getting non-German speakers to speak German, but even here, support has been sorely lacking. Most of the focus has been on public schools. Yet preschool and kindergarten are not obligatory in Germany and require parents to pay for part of the cost. Thus most children with migrant backgrounds arrive at German schools with little or no knowledge of German (Beckermann).

Furthermore, pupils' performance is more closely tied to socioeconomic background in Germany than in any other industrialized country, and the German school system disadvantages children from immigrant families the most (Siegele 8). One reason is that cost plays a role at nearly every level of German education, especially since parents often pay for supplemental tutoring for their children. That most German schools are in session only half the day makes homework much more important than in the whole-day schools typical in British and North American systems. German teachers introduce material, and pupils are expected to practice at home with parents. Even educated parents can meet this need only to a limited extent, which is why *Nachhilfe* ("tutoring") is a big business in Germany.

The main problem, however, is that Germany has never modernized its class-based, three-tier school system. Most German states separate children after the fourth grade into three different kinds of schools, essentially determining much of the rest of a child's life: the *Hauptschule*, for those who plan to do an apprenticeship—in a factory or bakery, for example; the *Realschule*, for mid-level clerks, salespeople, and the like; and the gymnasium, for those who might go to a university. Despite much evidence that the system is grossly unfair to children whose parents are not themselves highly educated or who don't speak good German, most Germans, a tradition-loving people, are not keen on giving up their cherished school system.

The most recent critic of the system, however, has shaken things up a bit. As part of a human rights investigation of schools worldwide, the United Nations sent a special rapporteur, Vernor Muñoz Villalobos, to visit Germany's schools in February 2006. Muñoz's findings were damning, particularly in regard to the education of children whose parents do not speak German. Stressing that education is a "human right," Muñoz urged that all children be given the opportunity to learn German before the first year of school in kindergartens that should be free of charge. He also condemned the practice of separating children into three levels after only four years of school. He noted that four years of half-day school is hardly long enough for a child with any kind of deficit to catch up (Spiewak).

These are not revelations in Germany. Everyone knows the results of sorting children into three levels of potential learning—and ultimately earning—power, and some states have stepped in to try to fill the gaps in the German educational system, particularly for children whose parents do not speak German at home. For example, the state of Nordrhein-Westfalen has created an agency to promote the integration of migrant families. The agency has developed innovative programs in bilingual and early childhood education and even offers language classes for the mothers of migrant children ("Project"). Such programs offer much-needed support to minorities, but they are still few and far between.

The Future of Language Policy in Germany

Despite a host of problems, European language policies provide at least a base to build on. Established minority groups have benefited greatly from Europe's national minority cultural programs. Many of these groups paid a high price—centuries of persecution—and their hard-won protections should not be taken for granted. Yet no effective or moral language policy can ignore the rights of newer, less-established migrant and immigrant populations. By what moral authority, for example, should the tiny but powerful Danish minority have more linguistic and cultural rights than third-generation Turks or Italians, whose forebears rebuilt Germany after World War II as guest workers? What about refugees who have no physical territory, only their cultural and mental territory?

Language policy in Germany and in Europe in general is intimately bound up with issues of education and immigration. Current German language policies do provide important protections for historic minorities. As some people have suggested, these policies might indeed provide a model for the preservation of endangered American Indian languages (Stanton 71–72). But a German language policy that doesn't consider Turkish is just about as useful as a United States language policy that doesn't consider Spanish. Injunctions to keep language and culture private will not do. Any fair—or workable—language policy in either the United States or Germany will have to deal with education and immigration as well as the emotional matter of identity.

German politicians are fond of asserting that it is not too much to expect people living in Germany to speak German. Yet it is too much to expect immigrant populations to do so out of patriotism alone. They will want to speak German only if they are granted the rights and responsibilities that membership in German society brings with it, including the right to work and to a proper education for their children. Asylum seekers who have been languishing in limbo (and poverty) for years should be granted citizenship—especially if there are children involved who have been schooled in Germany. At the very least, the German government must reclassify second- and third-generation *Ausländer* as German citizens.

It is not only the tradition-loving Germans who are struggling with issues of identity in a world that is increasingly multiethnic and multicultural. Minorities deal with similar issues: they want to fit in but also want to retain their cultural uniqueness. They are willing to learn a new language but seldom at the expense of their native tongue. Inclusion, economic as well as cultural, would lead most to be more culturally integrated.

Indeed the German writer Peter Schneider has remarked that the isolation of Turks from the larger German society may have enabled Berlin's Turkish neighborhoods to be more Islamist than Anatolia; even as Turkey has modernized, Turkish ghettos in Germany preserve eighteenth-century peasant values.

Developing an identity based on democratic principles and not on ethnicity is crucial to Germany's future (just as it would have helped Germany avoid its most disastrous mistakes in the past). What is more, the whole debate in Germany between multiculture and lead culture is anachronistic; German society is de facto multicultural: forty percent of school-age children in Germany's western states have at least one parent who is not an ethnic German. The dichotomy between an ethnic German majority and various minorities makes less and less sense.[13] In fact, this outdated construction may be the greatest danger to Germany's future, since Germany, with a birth rate that is among the world's lowest, desperately needs its minorities just to keep the country running.

Germany's future hinges on the success of its immigrants. Whether they will work on the black market or whether they will, as citizens, contribute to state coffers is largely a function of Germany's language policies. By adopting a very strict definition of which minorities are due linguistic rights—that is, national minorities—Germany has tried to protect itself from some of its other minorities instead of pursuing integration in a serious way. In effect, Germany has used language as a tool to keep foreigners from competing, at the same time condemning itself to the burden of parallel societies.

Already saddled with high taxes, Germans are loathe to fund new educational programs, especially those that would primarily benefit others. Yet it is in Germany's financial and social interest to invest in the education of its minority populations. Germany need not open hundreds of Turkish schools to recognize the human rights, including the linguistic rights, of its immigrant populations. But it must at the very least acknowledge that they have the right to proper instruction in German. Currently many migrant children learn neither German nor their parents' native language at a more than superficial level. Germany should follow the urgent advice of the United Nations commissioner Muñoz and implement state-funded kindergartens, where children could learn German before starting school. Head Start programs in the United States, which have been in place for immigrant and poor children since the 1960s, might serve as a model.

Germany and "Old Europe" in general face a number of moral predicaments related to language, immigration, and education policies. Can the West claim social democratic models of government even as it turns away thousands of legitimate asylum seekers and refugees or turns them into a permanent undereducated underclass? How can countries like Germany best deal with the steady influx of newcomers and their needs without betraying their own democratic ideals?

There are no easy answers to these questions. But the search for solutions should focus on individual rights and democratic and legal procedures rather than on historical-cultural reference points. How Germany deals with the challenge of its minority populations not only will determine which languages they speak, it will also articulate that most elusive pursuit, a German moral identity. In negotiations over cultural and political space, Germany cannot allow sentiment for the past to trump human rights. In other words: Goethe and Tyrolean cardigans—yes; class-based schools and language bans—no.

NOTES

1. The policy went into effect in January 2006, and the school has been scrutinized since.

2. All translations from German are mine.

3. Berlin's official statistics office, Statistik Berlin-Brandenburg, confirms the commonplace. Official figures are based only on legally registered persons.

4. "Wir sind in einem Feld, wo es darum geht, nach dem Motto *Best Practise* voneinander zu lernen. . . ." ("We're in a situation where it's all about learning from one another, according to the motto Best Practice.")

5. In general, Britain has served as a model of the multicultural paradigm, while France is said to favor an assimilation approach. Yet neither of these is identical to a German model (Loizos).

6. The original: "Frage dich nicht, was die anderen für dich tun. Du bist die anderen."

7. The phrase appears, for example, in the 1935 Leni Riefenstahl film *Triumph of the Will*, which Hitler commissioned for propaganda purposes.

8. The criticisms are summarized in Cords, Hohhjann, and Schüttler.

9. The school is the Rudolf-Roß-Gesamtschule in Neustadt.

10. The Council of Europe is an organization of forty-six member states extending from Europe into parts of Asia. The organization ratified the European Convention on Human Rights in 1959 and continues to concern itself mainly with human rights issues. The Council of Europe should not be confused with other European institutions such as the Council of the European Union or the European Council.

11. Tanase notes that the openness of the document has left ample room for monitoring bodies to maneuver, and these have been far more liberal than the countries themselves in the application and interpretation of minority rights.

12. The European Charter for Regional and Minority Languages of the Council of Europe (1992) recognized Romani and Yiddish as nonterritorial languages. The charter is printed in Trifunovska 159–71.

13. The Turkish-German politician Lale Akgün has also called this debate anachronistic. I take the 40% figure from her as well.

WORKS CITED

Akgün, Lale. "Das Wir-Gefühl." *Die Zeit* 16 Feb. 2006. Web. 1 Mar. 2008.

Beckermann, Antonia. "Herkunft schlägt Leistung." *Welt am Sonntag* 19 Feb. 2006: 3. Print.

Böhmer, Maria. "Sprache ist der Schlüssel für Integration." Interview with Matthias Hanselmann. *Deutschlandradio Kultur.* 26 Jan. 2006. Web. 8 Mar. 2008.

Cords, Lars-Christian, Olaf Hohhjann, and Kathrin Schüttler. "'Du bist Deutschland': Vorbild für Regierunskommunikation?" *Handbuch Regierungs-PR: Öffentlichkeitsarbeit von Bundesregierungen und deren Beratern.* Wiesbaden: Sozialwissenschaften, 2006. 287–300. Print.

"'Dutch-Only' Bid Stirs Angry Debate." *Deutsche Welle* 25 Jan. 2006: n. pag. Web. 8 Mar. 2008.

European Charter for Regional or Minority Languages. Council of Europe, 5 Nov. 1992. Web. 10 Mar. 2008.

Facts about Germany. Ed. Peter Hintereder. Societäts-Verlag, Frankfurt am Main, for the German Federal Foreign Office, 2006. Web. 2 Mar. 2006.

Gheorghe, Nicolae, and Andrzej Mirga. *The Roma in the Twenty-First Century: A Policy Paper.* Project on Ethnic Relations, May 1997. Web. 23 Sept. 2008.

Köpke, Jörg, Simone Selonke, and Christoph Wüllner. "Deutsch sprechen oder Schulhof fegen!" *Bild Hamburg* 26 Jan. 2006: 3+. Print.

Küpper, Mechthild. "Pausensprache ist Deutsch." *Frankfurter Allgemeine Zeitung* 26 Jan. 2006: 5+. Print.

Lau, Jörg. "Deutschstunden." *Die Zeit* 2 Feb. 2006: 62+. Print.

———. "Man spricht Deutsch." *Die Zeit* 26 Jan. 2006: 13+. Print.

Loizos, Peter. "London ist nicht Paris." *Le monde diplomatique* 9 Dec. 2005: n. pag. Web. 23 Sept. 2008. German ed.

"Das Manifest: 'Du bist Deutschland' im Wortlaut." *Hamburger Abendblatt* 29 Sept. 2005: n. pag. Web. 8 Mar. 2008.

Mikuteit, Hanna-Lotte. "Unterricht auf englisch—please!" *Norddeutsche Zeitung* 23 Feb. 2006: 18+. Print.

Monch, Regina. "Wir sprechen hier Deutsch." *Frankfurter Allgemeine Zeitung* 28 Jan. 2006: 33+. Print.

"Projekt 'Mehr Lehrkräfte mit Zuwanderungsbiographie.'" *Regionale Arbeitsstellen zur Förderung von Kindern und Jugendlichen aus Zuwandererfamilien.* RAA, n.d. Web. 10 Mar. 2008.

Recommendation 1201 (1993): On an Additional Protocol on the Rights of National Minorities to the European Convention on Human Rights. Parliamentary Assembly of the Council of Europe, 1 Feb. 1993. Web. 10 Mar. 2008.

Rooker, Marcia. "Non-territorial Languages: Romany as an Example." Trifunovska 43–54.

Schneider, Peter. "The New Berlin Wall." *New York Times* 4 Dec. 2005. Web. 8 Mar. 2008.

Siegele, Ludwig. "Waiting for a Wunder." *Economist* 11–17 Feb. 2006, spec. report: 1–20. Print.

Spieker, Thomas P. "Holland dem Holländischen." *Stern.de* 25 Jan. 2006. Web. 23 Sept. 2008.

Spiewak, Martin. "Schlechte Noten." *Die Zeit* 21 Feb. 2006. Web. 23 Sept. 2008.

Stanton, Domna C. "On Linguistic Human Rights and the United States 'Foreign' Language Crisis." *Profession* (2005): 64–79. Print.

Statistik. Bundesministerium des Innern, 2005. Web. 10 Mar. 2008.

Struck, Peter. Interview with Jörg Köpke. *Bild Hamburg* 26 Jan. 2006: 1+. Print.

Tanase, Ioana. *Defining National Minorities: Old Criteria and New Minorities.* St. Antony's Coll., U of Oxford. Jan. 2003. Web. 10 Mar. 2008.

Trifunovska, Snezon, ed. *Minority Rights in Europe: European Minorities and Languages.* The Hague: Asser, 2001. Print.

Taking Liberties: Academic Freedom and the Humanities

DOUG STEWARD

*It is absolutely essential that the learned community at the university . . .
contain a faculty that is independent of the government's command with regard to its teachings; one that, having no commands to give, is free to evaluate
everything, and concerns itself with the interests of the sciences, that is, with
truth: one in which reason is authorized to speak out publicly. For without a
faculty of this kind, the truth would not come to light (and this would be to
the government's own detriment); but reason is by its nature free and admits
of no command to hold something as true (no imperative "Believe!" but only
a free "I believe").*

—Immanuel Kant

The Western history of academic freedom begins with Plato's account of
the trial of Socrates, who was executed after spurious charges of his teaching's impiety and corruption of youth scandalized his fellow citizens. More
recently, in 1951, William F. Buckley played Meletus to what he called
"academic freedomites" (146) in *God and Man at Yale: The Superstitions of
"Academic Freedom."* Buckley hailed the 1950s as an era of consumer rule in
higher education, asserting that trustees and alumni have not only the right
but "the *duty* to 'interfere'" when a university does not urge pro-capitalist,
pro-Christian viewpoints on students (115). University faculty members
would necessarily comply since, as Buckley put it, "every citizen in a free

---

*The author is associate director of MLA Programs and the ADE. A version of this article ap-
peared in the Winter–Spring 2007 issue of the ADE Bulletin.*

---

economy, no matter the wares that he plies, must defer to the sovereignty of the consumer" (185). Elaborating on this view, John Chamberlain wrote, "in a democracy, the customer (who pays the bills) must have the right to exercise his free choice when he is out shopping in the market place. The *autonomy* of the customer should hold whether he is buying toothpaste, tennis rackets—or education for his children" (emphasis added). This consumerist attitude did not originate in the 1950s: Kant mocked something like it in 1784 when he wrote, "I need not think, so long as I can pay" ("An Answer" 54). Buckley considered it morally incumbent on the trustees of Yale to direct the economics faculty to promote individualism and free markets, which faculty members' expertise in economics apparently left them reluctant to do voluntarily. He was also displeased by what he considered the lewd content of some courses and by an ambient irreverence toward religion. In short, he objected to the Yale faculty's impiety and corruption of youth and promoted a moralizing view of education as a commodity subject to the sovereignty of consumer whim, a view that has taken root in public discourse in the intervening years. The view is more than half a century old, its roots stretching back well before the culture wars of the 1980s; the feminist, gay, and Chicano/a movements of the 1970s; and the black civil rights movement of the 1960s—moments when certain myopic commentators would have us believe that politics illicitly entered higher education through the machinations of one disruptive minority or another. Sweepingly, we might ask, with Jacques Derrida, "has impiety not always been, and thus still is today, the principal and surest charge against any disquieting thinker?" (*Du droit* 46; my trans.).

Prevarications of the Unfreedomites

After decades of development by a network of funding agencies, think tanks, and activist organizations, consumerist rhetoric is now taken for granted even at the highest levels of government. In a recent interview, Margaret Spellings—the United States Secretary of Education, whose daughter attends Davidson College—referred to herself, off-handedly, as a concerned "customer of a private college" ("Time"). This customer-service mentality's failure to distinguish a substantive difference between purchasing toothpaste at a drugstore and paying tuition to a college is troubling. The implication in Spellings's and Chamberlain's view that they, rather than the students, are the ones being served is unfortunate and symptomatic of class-specific assumptions about money and tuition: my money buys my child the commodity of my class legacy.

Combined with a moralizing political agenda, such as Buckley's, some versions of educational consumerism are ominous. Riled by allegations of impiety and corruption of youth, in March 2006 Arizona legislators put forward a bill that would have required professors at state institutions to provide alternative assignments for students who were offended by content in course materials. Linda Gray (Republican, Phoenix), chair of the Arizona senate's Higher Education Committee, declared, "[Professors] contribute to society accepting immoral behavior." Considering Gray's position on the Higher Education Committee, this is a startling judgment. "(The classroom) is where they get to the mind," she warned (qtd. in Cronin). This bill is only one of many recently inspired by David Horowitz's so-called Academic Bill of Rights, which purports to ensure ideological balance on university faculties by stripping the faculty of the right to choose whom to hire based solely on the person's professional qualifications and the institution's educational goals. Not always articulated in explicitly consumerist terms, this profoundly anti-intellectual politicization of faculty hiring typifies attempts to immolate academic freedom in its own name: by declaring the importance of ensuring an Orwellian "intellectual diversity" even at the cost of the faculty's expert self-determination.

In their worst forms, such anti-intellectual movements seek not merely to exercise the right to critique how universities run their affairs but to put the stopper on controversial scholarship and teaching, to defund the institutions sheltering controversial professors, and to institute a kind of academic unfreedom closely monitored by trustees, governors, alumni, legislators, parents, and affluent think tanks with well-defined agendas. Founded by Lynne Cheney, among others, the American Council of Trustees and Alumni (ACTA) is an especially menacing antifaculty activist organization that has received more than $2 million in grants in the past eight or nine years from such right-wing agencies as the Sarah Scaife, the Earhart, and the Lynde and Harry Bradley Foundations (*Media Transparency*). ACTA takes special interest in the "interpretive" fields of the humanities and social sciences and hastened to profit politically from the attacks on 9/11, publishing an inflammatory pamphlet, *Defending Civilization: How Our Universities Are Failing America and What Can Be Done about It*, on its Web site only two months after the terrorist strikes. In that pamphlet, ACTA's principal employees, Jerry Martin and Anne Neal, applauded United States military action on the basis of the general public's anger and patriotism immediately following 9/11 (1)—not on the basis of military strategy or intelligence community recommendation—and impugned the reputation and character of any professor who wondered aloud about the hijackers' motives, discussed critically the history of United States foreign policy in the Middle East or Latin America, encouraged the study of Islam, or distinguished between proximate and ultimate causes. Throughout the pamphlet, debate on terrorism and 9/11 is cast in the crude terms of those who support the president and oppose terrorism and those who oppose the president and support terrorism, those who "[call] evil by its rightful name" and those who "BLAME AMERICA FIRST" (1, 3). *Defending Civilization* is essentially a compilation of professors' (sometimes intemperate) remarks taken out of context and as such was widely understood to be a kind of blacklist. The pamphlet prompted Senator Joseph Lieberman to write to ACTA to object to it and its unauthorized insinuation of his support and to ask that his name be removed from ACTA's Web site as a cofounder. The council then added an acknowledgment that no public figure, including Lynne Cheney and Lieberman, "had endorsed or been asked to endorse" the pamphlet. This devious maneuver allowed the council to maintain its pretense of bipartisanship, appeared to lift the pamphlet above the fray of politics, and concealed the fact that Lieberman had explicitly denounced it.

ACTA has never said anything about the innumerable xenophobic responses to 9/11, but in a series of documents stretching back a decade, such as *The Shakespeare File* (Martin, Neal, and Nadel), it has argued that the faculty has forfeited its right to academic freedom because of its moral relativism, classroom politicking, and low standards and because it has eschewed the concomitant responsibilities, principally respect for the political views of right-wing students when they differ from professors'. For their part, literature professors are allegedly teaching everything but literature (Martin, Neal, and Nadel 8–9; ACTA, *How Many* 7). ACTA never establishes that faculty members do not teach (classic) literature, only that they often have recourse to fields other than literature in their teaching. Literature has not been removed from language and literature curricula, but most folks nowadays do consider formalist criticism only one set of tools and agree with Theodor Adorno's view that "if you attempt to understand a thing purely on its own terms, then you will understand nothing" (13). As a result, the study of literature and its contexts is broadly conceived, often in interdisciplinary ways.

In fact, interdisciplinary work and ethnic studies in particular figure importantly in ACTA's latest salvo, provocatively titled *How Many Ward Churchills?*, which is again largely a compilation of quotations with minimal exposition of argument. The title's question is rhetorical and leads to the further rhetorical questions, "Do professors in their classrooms ensure a robust exchange of ideas designed to help students to think for themselves? Or do they use their classrooms as platforms for propaganda, sites of sensitivity training, and launching pads for political activism?" (foreword). ACTA President Anne Neal is promptly quoted assuring us that she supports academic freedom but intoning that it ends where professors "abuse the special trust they are given to respect students' academic freedom to learn." Even as ACTA admits that "Churchill has followed an exceptional path to academic prominence," it claims that "he is not at all unusual," stating explicitly that he represents faculty members' political radicalism, especially where 9/11 is concerned. More subtly, ACTA's logic of guilt by association suggests Churchill represents faculty members' lack of rigor, since his scholarship was under investigation by an ad hoc committee. The pamphlet pretends to tell us what professors are doing in classrooms, but there is no evidence that anyone from ACTA visited a single classroom in preparing the hefty pamphlet, which relies exclusively on material available on the Internet, such as course descriptions.

I'll only highlight a couple of telltale moments in *How Many Ward Churchills?* (There is so much so fundamentally wrong with ACTA's pamphlets that one must take them sentence by sentence.) Let me underscore at the outset that this pamphlet connects Churchill's exceptionally ill-considered comments on 9/11 to all manner of academic study that has no connection whatsoever to 9/11. ACTA begins with a number of courses that treat questions of race and ethnicity, taking these as the exemplary evil of what it calls "the politicized liberal arts curriculum" (6). In a sense, the tract is an objective description: although it takes a sententious, patronizing tone and imputes traitorous motives to professors, ACTA does not seem to distort the actual course descriptions it cherry-picks from the Web. Instead, it operates by unarticulated argument, as when it declares of several courses on race and ethnicity, "The rationale for such courses stems from the belief that it is the professor's job to challenge students' unexamined assumptions" (6). In context, this observation is meant, prima facie, to horripilate readers who never suspected such perfidy in an American classroom. But in fact it is the professor's job to challenge students' unexamined assumptions—especially on questions of particular obfuscation in the arena of popular opinion, such as race. Questioning unexamined assumptions has been the professor's job since ancient Greece; it epitomizes the Socratic method. As Gary Pavela concisely explains, students' own academic freedom is embedded within the maieutic practice:

> [A teacher] asserts a belief or hypothesis to *invite* refutation. The teacher may have superior knowledge and experience but encourages students to raise doubts and fresh perspectives to define truth anew—a method

rooted in a synthesis of free inquiry and collaboration that could be regarded as the beginning of the scientific method.

The general model of learning as dialogue is the dominant one today in
many disciplines, having replaced the lecture from on high some time ago.
ACTA pretends to defend the Western tradition. Instead, it is not only ignorant of the most basic and ancient pedagogical practice of that tradition
but actually gets pedagogy dead wrong and thus misrepresents courses on
race and ethnicity.

Another example involving race and ethnicity, this time in reference to
a course on the Third World and the West at Duke University, further illustrates ACTA's mode of argument by association. Of the course ACTA's
concluding sentence remarks, "Assigned texts include Ward Churchill's *A
Little Matter of Genocide*—a book whose claims about the U.S. Army's treatment of Native Americans are implicated in the University of Colorado's
investigation of whether Churchill has committed academic fraud" (*How
Many* 6). This rhetorical legerdemain epitomizes the insinuation of guilt
that ACTA specializes in. Although Churchill's scholarship was at the time
under review, ACTA, without (to all appearances) picking up a single one
of his books, not to mention having no one on staff with expertise in Native studies, effectively renders judgment on Churchill's work. At the same
time, without committing itself to any positive statement, ACTA implies
that a course with Churchill on the syllabus is by definition a bad course
and—most remarkably—that the United States Army probably treated
Native Americans just fine (since Churchill, who asserted otherwise, was
under investigation for academic fraud . . .). In terms of evidence this argument by insinuation is null, but it is efficient sophistry nonetheless.

Like Horowitz, ACTA sometimes declares its position to be politically
neutral; at other times, it promotes "intellectual diversity," which means
conservative professors who teach from a conservative viewpoint. ACTA
never says which conservative courses would provide for intellectual diversity; it only fingers the courses that it finds objectionably uniform in
their leftist slant. But we do know exactly what those courses "homoge-
neously" opposed—social injustice, domestic violence, monolingualism,
white power, jingoism, xenophobia, male supremacy, slavery, racism, poverty, homophobia, misogyny, orientalism, genocide, spread-eagle foreign
policy, and Third World exploitation. (ACTA examined only the humanities and social sciences, the disciplines most likely to be concerned with
human rights and wrongs. The natural sciences, not to mention schools of
business, engineering, medicine, and so on, are wholly absent.) Here too
ACTA follows the example of Buckley, who came very close to condemning

Yale for not employing any professors with "anti-Semitic, anti-negroid prejudices" who would espouse "the anthropological superiority of the Aryan," since these were "value-judgments . . . upheld by various scholars not only in the past but in the present day [1951] as well" (148). Buckley and ACTA reproach humanists for their moral relativism, but what they mean is that they don't approve of humanists' moral vision. Indeed, it is not nihilistic moral relativism to take well-reasoned positions on questions of human rights and responsibilities, as professors routinely do; it is nihilistic moral relativism, or something worse, to insinuate that Native Americans were treated well by the United States Army or that Aryanism might legitimately counterbalance antiracism in college curricula since both are "value-judgments." Such is the pedigree of today's push for intellectual diversity.

It will not do to allow insinuation and appeals to prejudice to govern public debate on higher education. Opponents of academic freedom specialize in the prevaricating attack, and their reluctance to advocate for anything more specific than lots of Shakespeare instead of what they attack is a weakness in their assault on the faculty's autonomy. At every opportunity, such critics should be asked to specify the details of their preferred educational program or to specify points on which they dispute a particular work of scholarship. Likewise where they imply that racial and ethnic discrimination no longer exists, or never existed, they should be confronted with evidence to the contrary and required to respond to it. Such critics' ignorance or misrepresentation of the history of the university and of academic freedom should be highlighted. As Toni Morrison reminds us, the people have a right to expose "language that . . . tucks its fascist boots under crinolines of respectability and patriotism as it moves relentlessly toward the bottom line and the bottomed-out mind."

We should also assert that professors in the humanities and social sciences promote certain values over others in the classroom, when they do, because their professional expertise leads them to conclude that some values are not only less desirable but also destructive. These are not questions of mere opinion. Biologists oppose the imposition of "intelligent design" on their curricula because it does not meet relevant standards in biology, not because they are biased. Astronomers hire more astronomers, rather than astrologists, because they share hard-earned scholarly values with the former, not the latter. Intelligent design and astrology are beliefs, not science. Likewise, scholars in the humanities and social sciences do not promote, for example, the beliefs of racism in their courses, because their professional study of the subject matter, to which they dedicate their lives, has led them to conclude that racism is a set of human values and practices worthy of opposition and that students studying, say, *The Tempest* or *La condition humaine* need to know something about colonialism's history in order to understand the meaning of those texts. Humanists, in particular, are trained to make complex judgments about human values and the human creations that give them form. That's what humanists do, and the critique of "the human" itself is one of the most compelling avenues of contemporary thought.

I stress that ACTA plans to abolish existing due process for hiring and firing professors. To counter what it considers biased teaching—and taking another page from Buckley's *God and Man at Yale*—ACTA promotes the hierarchical takeover of higher education faculties through strong, hands-on lay governance by trustees; gubernatorial and legislative intervention; and strategized alumni giving that places strict limitations on how funds can be used, effectively installing donors as curriculum planners. These are not ACTA's hypothetical remedies to be implemented only if the reforms that ACTA advocates are not undertaken through more traditional means. According to Neal's think-tank mantra for state legislatures, strong lay governance is a sine qua non of higher education in a democracy, but Neal's oft-repeated statement is false. Lay governance did not spring from the soil of democracy as such. The lay board of governance is a quirk of American higher education that arose not at all from democracy per se but from the necessity of denominationally affiliated institutions' ability to survive in the United States' religiously plural society: to temper sectarian dogmatism (Hofstadter 122–23). Ironically, ACTA's promotion of strong lay governance by trustees is today designed to do the opposite: to govern *by* dogmatism. In doing so, ACTA would subordinate the systematic pursuit of truth and knowledge by thousands of highly trained and certified experts to the personal opinion of a tiny number of wealthy persons who are more likely to have a business background than an academic one and among whom women and people of color are grossly underrepresented (Fain). As Richard Hofstadter noted in the 1950s, the "system of lay government has created special problems for free teaching and scholarship in America" (120); it is a legacy that ACTA would like to see made even more problematic by urging trustees to exercise legal powers that they have never before routinely exercised.

It would be a mistake to play the ostrich, hoping all this poppycock will melt into air. It is tempting to think that organizations like ACTA are too extreme to be effective, and it is galling to grant their sophistry the legitimacy of a response. Unfortunately, they are politically effective. For instance, many powerful friends and former colleagues of Cheney's buttress ACTA. The former president of the University of Colorado, Hank Brown, helped found ACTA when it was known as the National Alumni Forum

(McAllister; ACTA, "Alumni"). Brown became the university's president when its previous president, Elizabeth Hoffman, was forced to resign, in good part because of the Churchill controversy that ACTA did so much to hystericize. ACTA's current chairman, Jerry Martin, worked on Brown's staff when he was a Republican senator from Colorado (Florida). A former chair of the philosophy department of the University of Colorado, Boulder, Martin also worked at the NEH when it was headed by Cheney (ACTA, "Jerry L. Martin"), who herself holds a master's degree from the university and is chairman emeritus of ACTA's National Council. Anne Neal, who holds a Harvard law degree, was general counsel to the NEH during Cheney's tenure and has been appointed by the secretary of education to the National Advisory Committee on Institutional Quality and Integrity, the panel responsible for reviewing accrediting agencies (Wilson; Lederman). Like the former Colorado governor Dick Lamm, who is the National Council's vice chairman, the current governor of Colorado, Bill Owens, is active in ACTA (McAllister). According to Emma Pérez, Owens hosted an ACTA conference for state trustees and appointed an ACTA coordinator to the board of trustees for Mesa State College when the board was restructured. (ACTA invites appointing committees for trusteeships to consult them for the names of ACTA-approved nominees.) This is only what I happen to know about the accomplishments of ACTA, which is only one such right-wing agency, in only one of its target states. ACTA's Web site lists accomplishments that it takes public credit for in other target states. The site includes a description of the Governor's Project, in which the council notes that its most effective work is done in behind-the-scenes networking—exactly the way it has operated in Colorado. Besides Brown, ACTA claims special success with "Virginia Governor Jim Gilmore, Governor George Pataki and Mayor Rudolph Giuliani . . . , and Florida Governor Jeb Bush" ("Governor's Project").

ACTA is but one organization stumping for external control of higher education faculties. Funding for the National Association of Scholars (NAS) dwarfs ACTA's and comes from the very same sources (*Media Transparency*). In fact, NAS President Stephen Balch is also a director at ACTA, a fact that neither not-for-profit organization's IRS Form 990 indicates on line 80, where one might expect to see it. In 2001 the Colorado Commission on Higher Education paid NAS $25,000 to review the University of Colorado's education program. Drawing on NAS's review, the commission voted to approve only eleven of the university's fifty-five academic majors for elementary education students. The *Colorado Springs Independent* reported, "Some of the majors disallowed by the Commission included American studies, astronomy, chemistry, fine arts, geology, business, music,

philosophy, political science, psychology, sociology, classics, religious studies, women's studies, environmental studies, ethnic studies, Asian studies
and all foreign languages" (Campbell). The NAS first made a name for itself in Texas in 1990, at the University of Texas, Austin, when it successfully
blocked an English course on civil rights readings that had been proposed
in response to increased incidents of racial and sexual harassment (People,
Buying 15). Blocking one English course may not seem serious from one
perspective; from another, this external interference was a grave breach of
academic freedom.

Organizations like NAS and ACTA do not present well-reasoned arguments backed by good evidence, but they don't need to. Their objective
is not to win a legitimate debate but to incite fear, muddy the water, and
activate prejudice. At the end of the day, these objectives are adequate as
long as their audience doesn't have the critical-thinking skills that liberal
arts programs should be teaching students. We need to know what kind of
arguments groups like ACTA make, but it should not be educators' goal to
rebut ACTA itself (or Horowitz, the NAS, etc.). Instead, our goal should
be to persuade various publics of the nullity of ACTA's arguments and to
suffuse classrooms, campuses, and local and national media and legislatures with a deep understanding of traditional academic freedom's value
to professors, students, and society and of the ways in which our curricula
produce literate and culturally sophisticated graduates who contribute not
only to the labor force but also to the nation's enjoyment and livability, its
cultural life and vitality. It is especially critical that we articulate the value
of academic freedom for students. Professors might include in their syllabi a statement on academic freedom—perhaps their university's official
statement or that of the Global Colloquium of University Presidents—
and discuss it in class so that students understand how academic freedom
assures them the best education professors can provide them with. It is a
violation of all students' academic freedom to coerce professors to down-
grade course work to appease philistine political interests, even if the coercion originates from the transient discomfort of an individual student who,
for whatever reason, objects to course work. Individual students do not
have a right to be free from discomfiture in the classroom; all students do
have a right to professors' best educational judgment. Students with objections are perfectly free to enter grievance procedures or, on the consumer-
choice model they may prefer, to buy a degree from a for-profit institution
that will cater to their whims.

Students are key to the current debate over academic freedom, for today's opponents of academic freedom take a theological view of American patriotism, fearing that students will be led to doubt by professors'

questions about the Western tradition and United States history. Such opponents play to parents' fear that their children will be corrupted or otherwise hurt and, to protect patriotic orthodoxy, do not scruple to make the most frenzied charges they can work themselves up to in the hope that some little bit of the mud thus slung will stick. In an introductory segment to an interview with Horowitz on the *700 Club*, Pat Robertson called professors

> termites that have worked their way into our academic society, and it's APPALLING. . . . They are racists, murderers, sexual deviants and supporters of Al-Qaeda—and they could be teaching your kids! . . . These guys are out and out communists, they are radicals, they are, you know, some of them killers, and they are propagandists of the first order. . . . [Y]ou don't want your child to be brainwashed by these radicals, you just don't want it to happen. Not only brainwashed but beat up, they beat these people up, cower them into submission. AGGGHHH!!!!
>
> (People, "Pat Robertson")[1]

The accusation of racism will no doubt surprise those who are also criticized for teaching antiracist courses. If it were only Robertson raving, the incident would not merit mention, and one might think that even Horowitz would not stoop this low. In fact, the man who has succeeded in putting Academic Bill of Rights legislation on the agenda in numerous states—the man whose Los Angeles–based not-for-profit Freedom Center (formerly the Center for the Study of Popular Culture) reported $4.56 million in revenue in 2006 (David Horowitz)—concurred with Robertson, denounced the academy's alleged political bias as a bigger scandal than Enron, and estimated that fifty thousand to sixty thousand professors support terrorism. Horowitz expressed dismay at professors' supposedly enormous six-figure salaries and six-hour work week, and he wanted the audience to know that professors in the humanities generally do have salaries on the order of $300,000 and work six hours a week, eight months a year. He routinely blames professors' Brobdingnagian salaries for the rise in college costs, ignoring such real-world factors as state legislatures that slash funding for higher education and, in states such as Colorado, push through taxpayer bill-of-rights legislation to forestall future efforts to restore funding. In reality, about sixty-five percent of the nation's higher education faculty members are now contingent or part-time and may cobble together as many as twelve courses a year to earn a livable income, the equivalent of teaching a full course's worth of material every month. By one estimate, "median hourly wages for part-time faculty in 2003 range[d] from a low of $11.19 at public two-year colleges to a high of $20.24 at private doctoral universities" (AAUP, *Devaluing* 33). The average salary of all disciplines' full professors, a minority in the teaching corps, was $94,738 in 2005–06 (Survey Report Table 4). Full professors, of course, have spent decades studying for the doctorate, competing for jobs, teaching thousands of students, and publishing research. As senior members of the profession, they naturally earn higher average salaries. But, among them, professors in the humanities are not known for earning the highest salaries. In this context, it is not hard to guess why Horowitz failed to mention his own 2006 salary of $509,000 while railing against the salaries of humanities professors (David Horowitz).

Academic freedom's opponents refuse civil discourse itself and, as Michael Bérubé notes, reject procedural liberalism, too, "the idea that no one political faction should control every facet of a society." What I hope for is not a solid, rational critique that will persuade Robertson and Horowitz that their goals are double-plus ungood. Instead, I hope for classrooms, campuses, and communities full of students who will themselves understand the condescending paternalism of efforts to "protect" them from controversy. To convey to students a deep sense of what traditional academic freedom is and is good for, we need to have a deep sense of what its fault lines are.

THE PARADOX OF ACADEMIC FREEDOM

With that goal I turn to what Domna Stanton calls "the paradox of academic freedom." We immediately encounter problems clearly presenting academic freedom's value, because academic freedom is, to borrow Michel Foucault's phrase from another context, an "utterly confused category" for freedomites and unfreedomites alike (101). Joan Scott and Judith Butler have each explored the ways in which disciplinary norms act not only to ensure the quality of academic work but also to enforce uniformity. About Glenn Morrow's 1968 definition, Scott writes:

> [A]cademic freedom rests on the protection afforded individuals by their disciplines against "incompetent outside authorities." What is ignored is the possible conflict between "mutual criticism" and the selection of new members "through disciplined and systematic training." Morrow, like Dewey, makes the correction of error, argument about interpretation, and the "approval and disapproval" of peers an entirely positive dimension of scholarly activity. But the inseparable other side of that regulatory and enabling authority is that it secures consensus by exclusion. . . . [D]iscipline is at once productive—it permits the organization of knowledge and it authorizes knowledge producers—and confining—it installs

explicit and tacit normative standards which, when they are understood to be provisional, can serve important mediating functions, but which, when they are taken as dogmatic precepts, become instruments of punishment. The two aspects cannot be disentangled; discipline functions in a necessarily paradoxical way. (169–70)

To this paradox, we can add several more:

the legal question of academic freedom's status as an individual or institutional right, a question introduced in 1957 by the reference in Justice Felix Frankfurter's concurring opinion to "'the four essential freedoms' of a *university*—to determine for itself on academic grounds who may teach, what may be taught, how it shall be taught, and who may be admitted to study" (Sweezy 263; emphasis added);

the curious United States arrangement of trustees being, legally, the institution itself, which vests academic freedom in persons who may have no academic credentials and who may, legally, dismiss faculty members on any grounds or none unless otherwise bound by contract or curbed by the First Amendment at public institutions;

the supposed conflict between faculty members' and students' academic freedom; and

the irony that some of the strongest statements in academic freedom's favor have entered the legal lexicon through dissenting opinions, including those of the Great Dissenter himself, Oliver Wendell Holmes, whose dissenting opinion in *Abrams v. United States* introduced the notion of a marketplace of ideas as the best test of truth.

Other contradictions, ironies, and paradoxes could be extracted from academic freedom's messy history in academe, scholarly associations, and the courts, in the United States and abroad. These internal fissures threaten to undermine academic freedom in a time when adjunct labor without the protection of tenure constitutes an increasing percentage of the faculty (Laurence; AAUP, *Contingent*), when funding for higher education is increasingly privatized (Doumani, "Between Coercion"; Frydl; "Report of the ADE Ad Hoc Committee"), and when state and federal officials invoke terrorism to abridge constitutionally guaranteed civil rights. (On legal definitions of academic freedom, see Byrne; Van Alstyne.)

I stress these conditions—reliance on adjunct labor, privatization of higher education, and post-9/11 state surveillance—because in this article I can only address one brief point about each.

1. The AAUP has long defined academic freedom hand-in-glove with tenure, a protection against illegitimate dismissal. The public, notes Richard Mulcahy, is today suspicious of this "job security," and we cannot count on support for it without a major enlightenment campaign (156). To the extent that the tenure-

stream faculty, bribed by lower teaching loads or exclusively upper-division and graduate courses, is complicit in allowing adjunct labor to become the norm in higher education, tenure and academic freedom with it will have been eliminated, not with a bang but with the whimper of underemployed PhDs.

2. Kathleen Frydl argues, "Privatization is the most far-reaching answer to the critical challenge posed by the research university: who shall exercise sovereignty over it, and by what logic? This—and not speech outside the classroom—is the front line of academic freedom" (179). She predicts that "the future of academic freedom will be not in the courts but in budgets" (195).

3. Post-9/11 abridgments of civil rights and cutbacks in funding certain subjects threaten to chill or starve research, notably area studies. Beshara Doumani's *Academic Freedom after September 11* includes several essays that ask trenchant and disquieting questions about research in such an atmosphere of state surveillance (Doumani, "Between Coercion"; Butler; Newhall; Beinin). Librarians vigorously resisted such surveillance. As a result, an outlandish smear campaign accused them of supporting terrorism (Ballon; Kaplan; Walfield). An anecdote of particular hilarity involved the Patriot Act's provision that libraries might be required to secretly hand over patron records. Consequently, some librarians chose to post signs that were legal under the letter if not the spirit of the law, such as one that said in large type "The FBI has not been here" and in small type "*[watch very closely for the removal of this sign]*" (Talbot; FBI).

We find none of this levity in Robert Post's stern analysis of the faculty's lackadaisical defense and understanding of academic freedom. Post fears that

> [t]he triumph of the [AAUP's] "1915 Declaration" has been so complete that we have grown soft and complacent. We have come all too easily to assume academic freedom as our "God-given right" and have become oblivious to its distinct justifications and limitations. We have lost touch with the many ways in which the academic freedom we ... enjoy is rooted in progressive-era ideas about the function of the university, the role of professional expertise and self-regulation, and the preconditions for the production of knowledge. (88)

We no longer live in the progressive era, Post reminds us, and we cannot afford to forget it. In this respect, John Dewey's 1902 essay "Academic Freedom" poses useful historical cautions as well as possible keys to our current situation. Dewey confidently assures us, "The university function is the truth-function" (55). What this meant for Dewey surely is not what academics might take it to mean today. We rely less than Dewey on a notion of science as inevitable progress toward absolute certainty, in which some fields are said to be emerging, partial sciences that will eventually achieve the unquestionable certainty of "mathematics, astronomy, physics, or chemistry," against which "there is no leverage . . . to direct an attack upon academic freedom" (55–56). Bear in mind that Dewey wrote this in 1902. Anyone familiar with the course of physics since 1905, in even a superficial lay capacity, will find this statement extraordinary, and the difference that it marks from today is one instance of the very difference to which Post refers. Nor did Dewey's prediction prove accurate that biology would quickly free itself from the opposition of anti-Darwinist superstition, which nowadays goose-steps under the banner of intelligent design.

When the pursuit of truth and knowledge is no longer understood as an inevitable approach to absolute certainty, the concept and foundation of academic freedom must change. It must become not only more complex but also paradoxical. (This is not, as Gertrude Himmelfarb foolishly suggests, to deny "that there is any such thing as knowledge, truth, reason, or objectivity" [97].) To what authority does academic freedom appeal, if not to that of "definitive method" and "verified fact" (Dewey 56)? Post describes the kind of bind that the situation places us in:

> Professional norms are needed to constrain the exercise of academic freedom so as to connect that freedom to the production of knowledge, and yet professional norms are also themselves forms of knowledge that are best advanced when debated with the kind of dissent that requires academic freedom. Academic freedom thus appears to be simultaneously limited by and independent of professional norms. (75)

Worse, professional judgment itself is amenable to enduring difference of opinion (even in physics), exposing it to "suspicion and distrust" (Post 77). Academic freedom's opponents exploit this weakness for all it's worth: contemporary academics are all politicized relativists who have no standards, they declare; "academic freedom" (still in Buckley's 1951 scare quotes) is merely a screen behind which professors do as they please in the classroom, unconstrained by fidelity to rigorous standards of truth.

A redoubtable defendant of academic freedom, Post is acutely aware of the danger involved in allowing such ideas to flourish, and he believes them to be nourished by popular and legal understandings of academic freedom as an individual right derivative of, or "a special concern of," the First Amendment, as certain key judicial decisions suggest (Keyishian 603). Despite these prominent legal rulings and popular understandings of academic freedom as inhering in individual professors, Post observes that "no university currently deals with its faculty as if academic freedom were an individual right"; instead, faculty members are subject to disciplinary review (78). At every stage in scholars' careers, their practices—including teaching and student learning—are subject to "a normative account of the kind and nature of relevant professional knowledge." In Post's view, the necessity of a professional judgment of relevance "strongly suggests that the distinction between education and indoctrination is largely internal to academic standards" and that it must therefore remain a corporate responsibility of the faculty, not the purview of an individual (81). Post is not innovating here. "The *university* would have a certain autonomy (since only scholars can pass judgment on scholars as such)," wrote Kant in 1794, "and accordingly *it* would be authorized to perform certain functions *through* its faculties" (*Conflict* 23; emphasis modified).

This corporate responsibility can provide powerful protection to faculty members who undertake controversial work, as scholars had already discovered in the medieval European university (Hofstadter 3–11). On the other hand, such responsibility might also be construed, Scott reminds us, to imply "that in order to protect the autonomy of the teaching establishment from 'outside' interference, it had to clean its own house by purging politically suspect teachers. On this definition, the greater good of the profession required the sacrifice of its most unconventional or troublesome members" (164). This is precisely what activist groups like ACTA hope to instill in faculty members: a sense that they must, if they wish to protect their freedom, rid the academy of those who attract unwanted attention. In this vein, the "Report of the Investigative Committee" on Ward Churchill wrote that "public figures who choose to speak out on controversial matters of public concern naturally attract more controversy and attention to their background and work than scholars quietly writing about more esoteric matters that are not the subject of political debate" (4). In saying so, the committee meant to answer Churchill's allegation that he was being inappropriately targeted, but the mere fact that controversy does attract attention does not mean that controversy does not attract reprisal. The principle of academic freedom protects against reprisal (the subject of Churchill's claim), not against heightened scrutiny (the subject of the committee's response). I have no position on the committee's recommendations or the quality of Churchill's scholarship; however, I do find the committee's cautionary note on attracting controversy discomforting. It is easy to discern in it the possible message that unpopular scholarship or public speech is undertaken at the individual scholar's risk without benefit of the corporate faculty's protection. There is advantage here in Post's corporate-traditionalist (rather than individualist–First Amendment) argument for understanding and protecting academic freedom.

Churchill's case also raises the tortuous question of intramural versus extramural speech. Advocacy groups such as ACTA and Horowitz's Freedom Center most commonly state objections to professors' influence over students in the classroom—intramural speech that has typically been constrained only by consideration of students' maturity (AAUP, "General Report" 35), the professor's expertise, and the material's relevance to course work. By contrast, extramural speech has traditionally had weaker protection and in Kant's view carried no protection whatsoever. Tellingly, ACTA and Horowitz are actually more likely to quote professors' so-called extramural speech than their intramural speech. Now, I take popular faculty opinion to be that academic freedom ensures faculty members the right to express whatever controversial notion comes into their heads, inside or outside the classroom, regardless of how tenuous or tendentious the notion might be. But in reality academic freedom affords faculty members, in Post's words, "*less* liberty than that enjoyed by ordinary citizens" in expressing opinions publicly because of the obligations their profession imposes on them to be circumspect, accurate, respectful, and so on, obligations the lay citizen does not bear (85). At state institutions, faculty members nevertheless have—over and above the protection of academic freedom—the full protection of the First Amendment from administrative reprisal against extramural speech. However, faculty members at private institutions do not have First Amendment protection against administrative reprisal—a distinction too often forgotten and one that seriously throws into disarray recourse to the First Amendment as a basis for academic freedom, unless we are willing to say that faculty members at private institutions have no claim to it or have only a metaphorical claim to it. Moreover, Derrida reminds us in "The University without Condition" that the "transformation under way in public cyberspace, which is public on a worldwide scale, beyond state-national frontiers" makes the intramural-extramural distinction "more archaic and imaginary than ever" (220). In any event, the AAUP's 1940 statement dropped a 1925 clause requiring a committee to evaluate "doubtful extramural utterances" because it was impossible to enforce (Metzger, *Age* 490), and the 1940 statement is generally cagey on the question of extramural speech, committing itself to very little. Although an adherence to something like an intramural-extramural distinction comes down to us from Kant, we can only conclude with Derrida that the distinction "has never been . . . either tenable or respectable, in fact or by law" ("University" 220). It may be that this wall's effective absence means that professors are professionally accountable for their speech in most circumstances.

Academic freedom, then, should be understood in terms of the corporate faculty's right and in terms of a professional expertise that is as carefully delimited as possible. Examining actual university practices shows immediately that the academy locates the authority that bestows the right of academic freedom in a complex network of disciplinary apparatuses.

These extend from graduate admissions committees through course work, teaching assistants' training, comprehensive exams, professionalization activities, the dissertation, conference presentations, peer review for publication, job interviews, tenure reviews, book reviews, promotion procedures, annual reviews, student evaluations, and service on professional committees and in regional, national, and international associations. Where any one of these controls has weakened, institutions are well advised to redress the weakness to maintain their credibility and accountability. The system is far from perfect, but it does include an extensive battery of controls to enforce the norms of academic inquiry on individuals at the same time that it lends them a special autonomy: it imposes duties in exchange for rights. Indeed, Thomas L. Haskell suggests that professors' work is subjected to "competition more severe than would be thought acceptable in ordinary human communities," not "sheltered" as academic freedom's detractors suggest (47). The basic unit in this competitive system is the department, which is in turn an imprecise administrative embodiment of the more abstract discipline, to which faculty members answer in principle. "Academic freedom, as it is now structured," argues Louis Menand,

> depends crucially on the autonomy and integrity of the disciplines. For it is the departments, and the disciplines to which they belong, that constitute the spaces in which rival scholarly and pedagogical positions are negotiated. Academic freedom not only protects sociology professors from the interference of trustees and public officials in the exercise of their jobs as teachers and scholars; it protects them from physics professors as well. ("Limits" 17)

If the disciplines' autonomy and integrity safeguard the duties and rights of academic freedom, then what do we make of the academy's commitment to interdisciplinary study, which is nowadays trumpeted on every possible occasion? Are we in a pickle if interdisciplinarity is the future of the university at the same time that the future of academic freedom depends on the autonomy and integrity of the disciplines? There are two points to be made here. The first is that interdisciplinarity does pose a challenge to academic freedom when faculty members' research and teaching cross disciplinary lines in ways that set their methodology at odds with one or more of the disciplines that retain the authority to adjudge the merit of that research and teaching. This is not news. Everyone has known for a long time that academic judgment in an interdisciplinary context can treacherously morph into disciplinary "grudgment."

The second point is more interesting. Interdisciplinarity raises in especially salient ways the ever-present question of which academic norms to apply in a given instance and how they should be understood to bear on the work to be evaluated; in fact, it suggests that the appropriate disciplinary norms, as such, do not preexist the work, which takes place in disciplines' interstices. In some forms, interdisciplinarity becomes antidisciplinarity and refuses any existing standards of disciplinarity, subjecting these to a radically heterodox critique. Assuming rigorous standards, such "radical heterodoxy" is exactly what academic freedom should protect (Van Alstyne 123), but how are we to judge the rigor of the standards when the critique takes place outside existing norms, when it refuses what the "autonomy and integrity of the disciplines" admit as norms? Before answering that question, I want to allow space for Menand's caveat:

> Administrators faced with allocating dwindling resources in the period of retrenchment that now seems upon the American university will be delighted to see the disciplines lose their authority, for it means spreading fewer faculty farther, and it gives them far greater control over the creation and elimination of staff positions. ("Limits" 18)

Or, he asks:

> Why support separate medievalists in your history department, your English department, your French department, and your art history department, none of them probably attracting huge enrollments, when you can hire one interdisciplinary super-medievalist and install her in a Medieval Studies program, whose survival can be made to depend on its ability to attract outside funding? ("Marketplace")

As Menand understands it, academic freedom's ability to shelter heterodox interdisciplinarity can grant an orthodoxy to the administrative dismantling of the humanities.

Menand points to a very real danger, but it is not the whole story. As Butler writes, "To question existing norms is not the same as questioning the existence of norms in general or calling for a postnormative mode of academic inquiry" (114). To admit contingency or challenge disciplinary authority is not to dispense with disciplinary authority any more than deconstructing truth is doing away with it. We have seen that even when attacks on academic freedom such as ACTA's aim at individuals—Ward Churchill being the poster boy par excellence—they aim beyond them at the faculty and not only at the faculty of the individuals' interdisciplinary programs but at the humanities and social science faculties as a whole, not only at the University of Colorado but at all United States institutions, public and private. Even while admitting that Churchill is anomalous in sundry ways, they assert him as the norm. In *The Professors: The 101 Most*

Dangerous Academics in America, a book that Cary Nelson exhorts us to ignore, Horowitz admits that "it is a reasonable assumption that a majority of faculty members are professionals and devoted to traditional academic methods and pursuits" (xxvii); nonetheless, he argues that a cherry-picked handful of professors is representative of the nation's faculty as a whole and explicitly attributes the influence that they have to the fact that many of them teach in interdisciplinary areas. "Because activists ensconced in programmatic fields like black studies and women's studies also teach in traditional departments like history and English," Horowitz believes their influence in the academy is dramatically enhanced (xxv). In effect, they are synonymous with the faculty at large even if they are anomalous, since they have metastasized throughout the faculty body through the malignant agency of interdisciplinarity. In this strange view, which ACTA shares, Ward Churchill's work is exceptional but also the very model of a postmodern major in general.

Jingoism and opposition to academic freedom did not begin on September 11, 2001. They did gain new footholds then, however, and have since taken more precise aim at the humanities and social sciences—and at ethnic and area studies in particular, two interdisciplinary fields of special interest to many of us in the modern languages. Many hotheaded people said many intemperate things following 9/11, but only Churchill acquired nationwide iconic status among those seeking to stymie controversial academic work. I attribute Churchill's iconicity to his interdisciplinary location in ethnic studies, his own disputed ethnicity, and long-standing official repression of Native American history. (Again, the issue of Churchill's sketchy scholarship is immaterial here, except insofar as its alleged weakness may have delighted those who exploited it for controversy.) It is unfortunate but not surprising that after 9/11, in Paul Gilroy's words, "[x]enophobia and nationalism are thriving" (2). Colliding with the powerful antiracist critiques of the past centuries, the new xenophobia and nationalism give rise to what Gilroy calls "complex, proteophobic, and ambivalent patterns" of human valuation and devaluation (37). It is easy to see how explosive a figure Churchill is when we consider, as Gilroy asks us to, that

> wherever they were applied, the colonial techniques of indiscriminate mass destruction ended up being closer to the work of extermination than control and settlement. In this bloody sequence, the doctrine of preemptive strikes and the systematic refusal to distinguish combatants from civilians have acquired an elaborate and multinational prehistory.   (47)

These are hard truths to confront, and Gilroy names the inability or refusal to come to terms with them "postcolonial melancholia." His analysis of the sort of ethnic reprisals that have followed 9/11 provides an uncanny diagnosis of the particular focus of current attacks in the United States on ethnic studies. Because academic freedom is authorized by the contingent norms of the disciplines, not individual professors, its opponents must direct an attack not only at individuals but also through and beyond them at higher education as a whole. Interdisciplinary work epitomizes the corporate faculty's responsibility for academic freedom precisely because it transcends the boundaries of the traditional units of disciplinary authority. Meanwhile, "proteophobic" post-9/11 ethnic animosity fuels jingoism. In this way, interdisciplinary programs in ethnic studies afford self-proclaimed patriots like ACTA and Horowitz a privileged location from which to attack the credibility of the corporate faculty.

But the attack typified by *How Many Ward Churchills?* is only the bottom-up prong of the assault on academic freedom. As noted earlier, its opponents are also plotting top-down thrusts. David Rabban warns, "Another terrorist attack on the United States . . . could easily increase pressures on academic and political expression that have mostly been resisted" (xiii). To this danger, we should add that of another economic downturn, since, as Frydl argues, financial interests will increasingly determine the future of academic freedom. Whereas attempts to dictate directly to individual faculty members have "mostly been resisted," top-down efforts like ACTA's to influence governors, trustees, and wealthy alumni donors have been at least partially successful because they primarily take aim not at faculty governance or specific classrooms but at the folks who hold the purse strings, with which they can strangle anyone they care to. For his part, Derrida urged us to consider that, to the extent that the university undertakes its work "absolutely independent" of economic interest, it "is also an exposed, tendered citadel, to be taken, often destined to capitulate without condition, to surrender unconditionally" ("University" 206). He posed the paradox as a question: how can the faculty claim unconditional sovereignty over its work, divorced from economic interest, and not expect that work "to let itself be taken over and bought at any price"? To pose his question more crassly, how can the university faculty defend its intellectual sovereignty, which needs funding, over and against what Buckley named, decades ago, the "sovereignty of the consumer"?

One answer is of course that under the logic of late capitalism nothing, including the principle of academic freedom, remains unpenetrated by commodification, that everything will only be ever more thoroughly commodified, and that in a postindustrial information economy, intellectual work is the premier commodity, not the one form of work preserved from commercial contamination. This would be an immobilizing conclusion if it were all there is left to say, but Derrida's purpose in "The University without Condition" is to marshal an "unconditional resistance" from within the humanities "to all the powers of dogmatic and unjust appropriation . . . to all the powers that limit democracy to come" (204–05). The humanities are the privileged space of academic freedom's defense and definition precisely because the truth as such has been most vigorously debated in the humanities. If academic freedom protects the right to the pursuit of truth and knowledge, it is in the humanities that we learn what we are pursuing. And to the extent that language is the ground of the human figure, the field of language and literature is the epicenter of the humanities. (Think of Diderot's *Rêve de d'Alembert* in which Cardinal de Polignac exclaims to an orangutan in a glass cage, "Speak! And I will baptize you"—an anecdote that is no longer so farfetched as Mlle de Lespinasse must have thought it [675; my trans.].)

To shoulder "truth" and "the human" is a tall order and one that demands disciplinary flexibility in the humanities and the freedom to range into the social sciences, law, the natural sciences, theology, and medicine. It demands the very free range that Kant claims for philosophy in *The Conflict of the Faculties*, where he offers a definition of philosophy that sounds a lot like the humanities at large: "a science of man, of his representations, thoughts and actions" (127). In this vein, we might pastiche Derrida: "there is no outside-the-humanities" ("*Il n'y a pas de hors-texte*" [*De la grammatologie* 227]). The pastiche may seem flippant, but in the age of genocide and terrorism the notion that nothing human could be alien to us as humanists in the world's sole superpower could not be more relevant. This relevance is exactly what many in the humanities have wanted to engage when they have been accused of impertinent politicking in the classroom: to ask if language can be more adequate to the truth; to ask if history has been recounted truthfully; to discern the alien as human; to learn the language and culture of the other; to explore the history of the inhuman/e in the human/e; to demand an expansion of human rights; to interrogate the border rather than the human being at the border; to discover what rhetorics of language and image mobilize a border around who counts as human; to question who is patrolling the border and with what ends. These questions can only be impious.

NOTE

1. I learned of this spine-tingling outburst in Henry Giroux's article. In the body of my essay, I have quoted the version of the interview transcript posted on People for the American Way's Web site, where a video clip is also available ("700"). There is a tamer

transcript of the interview on the CBN News Web site (CBN News). The video clip appears to be a segment introductory to the interview itself. Both Giroux's transcript and that of People for the American Way appear to be of the introductory segment, not the interview itself; however, Giroux cites as his reference the tamer CBN News transcript of the interview itself.

WORKS CITED

Adorno, Theodor. *Kant's* Critique of Pure Reason. 1959. Ed. Rolf Tiedemann. Trans. Rodney Livingstone. Stanford: Stanford UP, 2001. Print.

American Association of University Professors. *AAUP Contingent Faculty Index 2006.* AAUP, Dec. 2006. Web. 12 Dec. 2006.

———. *The Devaluing of Higher Education: The Annual Report on the Economic Status of the Profession, 2005–06.* AAUP, Mar.-Apr. 2006. Web. 30 Nov. 2006.

———. "General Report of the Committee on Academic Freedom and Academic Tenure [1915 Report]." Metzger, *American Concept* 16–43.

American Council of Trustees and Alumni. "Alumni Organize to Preserve Free Speech and Free Thought at Colleges and Universities." ACTA, 17 Mar. 1995. Web. 12 Dec. 2006.

———. "Governor's Project: Reforming Higher Education." ACTA, n.d. Web. 6 June 2007.

———. *How Many Ward Churchills?* ACTA, 2006. Web. 16 Aug. 2006.

———. "Jerry L. Martin." ACTA, n.d. Web. 1 Oct. 2006.

———. "Mission and History." ACTA, n.d. Web. 17 Oct. 2006.

Ballon, Marc. "Library Group Draws Fire over Web Site." *Jewish Journal* 20 Jan. 2006: n. pag. Web. 30 Nov. 2006.

Beinin, Joel. "The New McCarthyism: Policing Thought about the Middle East." Doumani, *Academic Freedom* 237–66.

Bérubé, Michael. "What Does 'Academic Freedom' Mean?" *Academe* Nov.-Dec. 2006: n. pag. Web. 23 Sept 2008.

Buckley, William F. *God and Man at Yale: The Superstitions of "Academic Freedom."* Chicago: Regnery, 1951. Print.

Butler, Judith. "Academic Norms, Contemporary Challenges: A Reply to Robert Post on Academic Freedom." Doumani, *Academic Freedom* 107–42.

Byrne, Peter J. "Academic Freedom: A 'Special Concern of the First Amendment.'" *Yale Law Journal* 99.2 (1989): 251–40. Print.

Campbell, Bob. "State Education Commission Coming under Fire." *Colorado Springs Independent* 24 May 2001: n. pag. Web. 28 Sept. 2006.

CBN News. "The 101 Most Dangerous Professors in America." CBN, n.d. Web. 4 Oct. 2006.

Chamberlain, John. Introduction. Buckley n. pag.

Cronin, Mike. "Conservatives Push to Counter Liberal Professors." *Arizona Republic* 12 Aug. 2006: n. pag. Web. 18 Oct. 2006.

David Horowitz Freedom Center. 2006 Form 990. *GuideStar.* GuideStar, n.d. Web. 23 Sept. 2008.

Derrida, Jacques. *De la grammatologie.* Paris: Minuit, 1967. Print.

———. *Du droit à la philosophie.* Paris: Galilée, 1990. Print.

———. "The University without Condition." *Without Alibi*. Trans. Peggy Kamuf. Stanford: Stanford UP, 2002. 202–37. Print. Trans. of *L'université sans condition*. Paris: Galilée, 2001.

Dewey, John. "Academic Freedom." *1902–1903*. Ed. Jo Ann Boydston. Carbondale: Southern Illinois UP, 1976. 53–66. Print. Vol. 2 of *The Middle Works, 1899–1924*. 15 vols. 1976–83.

Diderot, Denis. *Le rêve de d'Alembert. Philosophie*. Paris: Laffont, 1994. 601–86. Print. Vol. 1 of *Œuvres*.

Doumani, Beshara, ed. *Academic Freedom after September 11*. New York: Zone, 2006. Print.

———. "Between Coercion and Privatization." Doumani, *Academic Freedom* 11–57.

Fain, Paul. "Surveys Find Governing Boards Are Older and Slightly More Diverse." *Chronicle of Higher Education* 1 July 2005: A21. Print.

FBI Sign. N.p., n.d. Web. 9 Oct. 2006.

Florida Department of Education. "Jerry L. Martin." Florida Dept. of Educ., n.d. Web. 1 Oct. 2006.

Foucault, Michel. *An Introduction*. Trans. Robert Hurley. New York: Vintage, 1978. Print. Vol. 1 of *The History of Sexuality*.

Frydl, Kathleen J. "Trust to the Public: Academic Freedom in the Multiversity." Doumani, *Academic Freedom* 175–202.

Gerstmann, Evan, and Matthew J. Streb, eds. *Academic Freedom at the Dawn of a New Century: How Terrorism, Governments, and Culture Wars Impact Free Speech*. Stanford: Stanford UP, 2006. Print.

Gilroy, Paul. *Postcolonial Melancholia*. New York: Columbia UP, 2005. Print.

Giroux, Henry A. "Academic Freedom under Fire: The Case for Critical Pedagogy." *College English* 33.4 (2006): 1–42. Print.

Global Colloquium of University Presidents. "Statement on Academic Freedom." Columbia U, 26 May 2005. Web. 23 Dec. 2006.

Haskell, Thomas L. "Justifying the Rights of Academic Freedom in the Era of 'Power/ Knowledge.'" Menand, *Future* 43–90.

Himmelfarb, Gertrude. "The New Advocacy and the Old." Spacks 96–101.

Hofstadter, Richard. *The Age of the College*. Hofstadter and Metzger 1–274.

Hofstadter, Richard, and Walter P. Metzger. *The Development of Academic Freedom in the United States*. New York: Columbia UP, 1955. Print.

Horowitz, David. *The Professors: The 101 Most Dangerous Academics in America*. Washington: Regnery, 2006. Print.

Kant, Immanuel. "An Answer to the Question: 'What Is Enlightenment?'" *Political Writings*. Ed. Hans Reiss. Trans. H. B. Nisbet. 2nd ed. Cambridge: Cambridge UP, 1991. 54–60. Print.

———. *The Conflict of the Faculties (Der Streit der Facultäten)*. Trans. Mary J. Gregor. Lincoln: U of Nebraska P, 1979. Print.

Kaplan, Lee. "Librarians for Terror." *Front Page Magazine* 24 Aug. 2004: n. pag. Web. 30 Nov. 2006.

"Keyishian et al. v. Board of Regents of the University of the State of New York." 1967. Metzger, *Constitutional Status* 589–629.

Laurence, David. "The Demography of the Faculty, 1993–2004." *ADE Bulletin* 138-139 (2005–06): 3–14. Print.

Lederman, Doug. "Stacking the Deck?" *Inside Higher Ed* 1 May 2007: n. pag. Web. 8 May 2007.

Lieberman, Joe. "Letter to ACTA." *Nation* 17 Jan. 2002: n. pag. Web. 17 Oct. 2006.

Martin, Jerry L., and Anne D. Neal. *Defending Civilization: How Our Universities Are Failing America and What Can Be Done about It.* Rev. ed. ACTA, Feb. 2002. Web. 30 Nov. 2006.

Martin, Jerry L., Anne D. Neal, and Michael S. Nadel. *The Shakespeare File: What English Majors Are Really Studying.* ACTA, Dec. 1996. Web. 30 Nov. 2006.

McAllister, Bill. "Friends in High Places Should Benefit Ex-CU Professor." *Denver Post* 6 Sept. 2000: F1. Print.

Menand, Louis, ed. *The Future of Academic Freedom.* Chicago: U of Chicago P, 1996. Print.

———. "The Limits of Academic Freedom." Menand, *Future* 3–20.

———. "The Marketplace of Ideas." *American Council of Learned Societies.* Occasional Paper 49. ACLS, 2001. Web. 10 Oct. 2006.

Metzger, Walter P. *The Age of the University.* Hofstadter and Metzger 275–506.

———, ed. *The American Concept of Academic Freedom: A Collection of Essays and Reports.* New York: Arno, 1977. Print.

———, ed. *The Constitutional Status of Academic Freedom.* New York: Arno, 1977. Print.

Morrison, Toni. Nobel lecture. *Nobelprize.org.* Nobel Foundation, 7 Dec. 1993. Web. 21 Oct. 2006.

Mulcahy, Richard. "A Full Circle: Advocacy and Academic Freedom in Crisis." Spacks 142–60.

Nelson, Cary. "Ignore This Book." Rev. of *The Professors: The 101 Most Dangerous Academics in America*, by David Horowitz. *Academe* Nov.-Dec. 2006: 81–85. Print.

Newhall, Amy. "The Unraveling of the Devil's Bargain: The History and Politics of Language Acquisition." Doumani, *Academic Freedom* 203–36.

Pavela, Gary. "Academic Freedom for Students Has Ancient Roots." *Chronicle of Higher Education* 27 May 2005: B8. Print.

People for the American Way. *Buying a Movement: Right Wing Foundations and American Politics.* PFAW, 1996. Web. 1 Oct. 2006.

———. "Pat Robertson Calls Liberal Professors 'Racists, Murderers, Sexual Deviants and Supporters of Al-Qaeda.'" PFAW, 21 Mar. 2006. Web. 4 Oct. 2006.

———. "700 Club's Pat Robertson Comments on Liberal Professors." PFAW, 21 Mar. 2006. Web. 4 Oct. 2006.

Pérez, Emma. "Ward Churchill Is Neocon Test Case for Academic Purges." *WBAI.* WBAI, 15 Feb. 2005. Web. 1 Oct. 2006.

Post, Robert. "The Structure of Academic Freedom." Doumani, *Academic Freedom* 61–106.

Rabban, David. Foreword. Gerstmann and Streb ix–xiv.

"Report of the ADE Ad Hoc Committee on Changes in the Structure and Financing of Higher Education." *ADE Bulletin* 137 (2005): 89–102. Print.

"Report of the Investigative Committee of the Standing Committee on Research Misconduct at the University of Colorado at Boulder concerning Allegations of Academic Misconduct against Professor Ward Churchill." U of Colorado, 16 May 2006. Web. 9 Oct. 2006.

Scott, Joan. "Academic Freedom as an Ethical Practice." Menand, *Future* 163–80.

Spacks, Patricia Meyer, ed. *Advocacy in the Classroom: Problems and Possibilities.* New York: St. Martin's, 1996. Print.

Stanton, Domna. "The Paradox of Academic Freedom." *MLA Newsletter* 37.3 (2005): 3–5. Print.

Survey Report Table 4. *American Association of University Professors.* AAUP, n.d. Web. 30 Nov. 2006.

"Sweezy v. New Hampshire." Metzger, *Constitutional Status* 234–70.

Talbot, Margaret. "Subversive Reading." *New York Times* 28 Sept. 2003: n. pag. Web. 23 Aug. 2006.

"Time Is of the Essence." *Chronicle of Higher Education* 6 Oct. 2006: A25. Print.

Van Alstyne, William W. "Academic Freedom and the First Amendment in the Supreme Court of the United States: An Unhurried Historical Review." *Law and Contemporary Problems* 53.3 (1990): 79–154. Print.

Walfield, Mike. "The ALA Library: Terrorist Sanctuary." *Front Page Magazine* 8 May 2003: n. pag. Web. 30 Nov. 2006.

Wilson, Robin. "A Not-So-Professorial Watchdog: Anne Neal Has Never Worked at a College, but She Has Become a Leading Critic of Left-Wing Faculty Members." *Chronicle of Higher Education* 10 Nov. 2006: A10. Print.

It's Not about the Book

MICHAEL BERNARD-DONALS

During the 2006 MLA convention in Philadelphia, I wandered into a session sponsored by the association at which David Laurence and one or two members of the Task Force on Evaluating Scholarship for Tenure and Promotion were presenting some of the task force's preliminary findings. Okay, I didn't exactly wander in: I'd heard John Guillory talk about expanding the idea of scholarship—unlinking it from publication and thinking instead (along the lines of the Boyer Commission, but with more nuance) of the different ways in which our academic work, what we tend to think of as research but which gets "cashed" almost exclusively as publication—at an ADE seminar in the summer of 2004 and knew instantly that his ideas could help loosen some orthodoxies with which we've been living in our profession. Because Guillory's call had very much to do with unseating the scholarly monograph from its supreme position in the academic order, I should say that, having made the connection, I anticipated what the task force had to say. I also vaguely remembered filling out a survey like the one described by members of the task force (but then, as a department chair, I fill out a lot of surveys). Finally, I'd been talking with some of my colleagues in the field of rhetoric and writing studies, with whom I shared the concern that the task force hadn't paid enough attention to the differences between the traditional fields in English and other language departments and other fields, often housed in these departments, whose work wasn't principally hermeneutic and thus not scholarly monograph material. (I'm

The author is Nancy Hoefs Professor of English and an affiliate member of the Mosse/ Weinstein Center for Jewish Studies at the University of Wisconsin, Madison.

thinking here not just about rhetoric and composition but also about applied linguistics, creative writing, folklore, and ESL.) How, I wondered, would the task force account for these faces of our field?

Of course, not having read the task force's report, I listened intently and jumped to all sorts of conclusions about what the report would leave out. Having jumped to these conclusions, I complained to Laurence about these (supposed) omissions. Gracious and patient as ever, he simply said, "Read the report." So when Rosemary Feal invited me to do just that in the spring of 2007, in preparation for some remarks I'd make at the Midwest Modern Language Association's convention in November of that year, I agreed. And as nearly everyone who wrote in *Profession 2007* has noted, it is an elegantly written and marvelously comprehensive report. What started out as an investigation into a nagging concern that the constriction in scholarly publication venues would make it harder for probationary faculty members to get their first books published (first books being the gold standard for tenure) ended up as a thoughtful diagnosis of the changing economics of postsecondary faculty work, in which fewer faculty members are working harder in an ever-broadening field with less support and with greater demands in all three areas of academic labor (teaching, research, and service). The report also makes excellent recommendations about how to ameliorate the situation. Some of the most sensible are rethinking whether the monograph should really be the sole criterion for tenure, reconsidering whether the dissertation really does what it's supposed to do, and being honest with probationary faculty members about what it takes—and should take—to get tenure and be promoted to associate professor. That the task force recognized the extraordinarily complex terrain on which the "book crisis" was (or, as it turned out, wasn't) playing out just makes me all the more embarrassed about the conclusions I jumped to in the early winter of 2006–07.

Now that I've read the report, I realize that it isn't really about the book. Instead, it's a broad assessment of the nature of faculty scholarly work and the obstacles to evaluating that work fairly. But because of this change of focus, the report raises questions for me, some of which remain from the first time I heard the preliminary results of the task force's work and some of which have arisen in my subsequent readings of the report. As one who has chaired a large English department at a Research I institution for four years, who has been a writing program administrator (WPA) for seven years (while also chairing the department), and whose work at public research universities over a seventeen-year career has always crossed the disciplinary boundaries between literary study and rhetoric and composition, I've been a probationary faculty member, and I have mentored probationary faculty members in a wide array of subspecialties in the field of English studies, and in both ways I have crashed into obstacles to a sensible and fair evaluation of scholarly work any number of times. Thus I'd like to discuss four issues that the report raises but does not adequately address, to my mind anyway, and to urge the MLA to take these up in as systematic a way as possible. These issues have to do with the array of subdisciplines in the modern languages, fields that aren't necessarily literary or literary-critical; with the race and ethnicity of probationary faculty members and what obstacles in evaluating scholarly work are tied to the question of race and ethnicity; with the intransigence of the status quo in university and college committees (particularly promotion and tenure committees) beyond the departmental level; and with what we mean by service and who should do it.

The first concern, about the nature of scholarship in fields that aren't principally literary-critical in their methodologies, was one I had harbored early on, and it was not allayed when I read the full task force report. The report's executive summary notes that even at its inception the task force was charged to examine "current standards and emerging trends in *publication requirements* for tenure and promotion" (9; emphasis added), as if forms of research that remain unpublished are beyond the scope of evaluation for tenure and promotion, let alone the task force's purview. But as Guillory has been telling us for some years now, partly in response to a similar conclusion reached by Ernest Boyer in 1990, there's a great deal of research done by scholars at the university that either never sees print (it doesn't get into peer-reviewed journals or books) or does see print but has a profound public reach that, ironically, doesn't receive the imprimatur of the scholarly journal industry. I know that this neglect occurs in subfields covered by the ADE and ADFL whose methods are principally literary-critical: just think of members of our faculties whose research on the reception histories of texts like *Candide* or *Huckleberry Finn* has led them to become engaged with public humanities programs that involve outreach to nontraditional students or members of the community but whose annual report form has no place to put such activities except under the category of "service."

But this neglect is especially prevalent in fields like applied linguistics, ESL, and rhetoric and composition, in which a great deal of research—on second-language learning, on dialect shifts, on the assessment of first-year students' writing, on the effectiveness of new media in student information-seeking practices—has its greatest impact on the effective administration of programs or on the learning of large numbers of students through the creation of educational policy. Let me give a couple of examples. I worked for many years at a public university with a nationally respected writing program, a program that had taken a number of years (and a number of directors) to get off the ground, that, once it was established, instantly became a model for other collegewide writing or writing-across-the-curriculum programs. The director of the program was an untenured assistant professor in the English department who, by arrangement with the university's provost, had a great deal of latitude about when to turn on the tenure clock for promotion to associate professor. The director—widely respected because of the research she had done on best practices in writing across the curriculum, on student outcomes, and on one-on-one tutoring to support writing-intensive courses, most of which was used internally by the university administration or circulated as conference presentations or as PDF documents on the writing program's Web site—had a very difficult time convincing her English department colleagues that the work she had done as a WPA (research-intensive work) should count as scholarship in the traditional triad of faculty work. Teaching? Maybe. Service? Probably. But certainly not scholarship. And because the director was seen principally as an administrator—by agreement with the provost and with the Department of English, to which her tenure line was assigned—with released time from teaching to run this widely respected writing program, she also had a very difficult time making the case that her work as a WPA should count as scholarship. Senior faculty members in rhetoric and composition programs strongly counsel their graduate students not to take jobs as WPAs until they have already earned tenure. Administrators will tell you that your work administering a writing program won't count against you at tenure time, but since such work takes away from time otherwise needed to conduct research and since even the research you do in the context of the program won't be seen as real research, you're very likely to get dinged because you haven't published enough.

The report does make the case that evaluators of faculty work should be more generous in understanding that

> service, traditionally viewed in research institutions as the least significant of the scholarship, teaching, and service triad, should be seen as a crucial part of faculty work that overlaps with—and involves—both other elements. (25)

It goes on to describe the sorts of public scholarship such generosity of definition might entail, citing the report of the MLA's Commission on Professional Service—making "knowledge available to government, industry, the law, the arts, and nongovernmental organizations" and "serving on a state or local humanities council, helping a school system revamp its curriculum, working on a community literacy project, writing a script for public television, and consulting on expert testimony for Congress" (25). But it leaves out of the mix the possibility of writing (or ESL) program administration and the scholarship such work involves. (I wonder if anyone would tell Guillory that his work on reconsidering the nature of scholarship was "service" because it was done, at least in part, in the context of his work as chair of the English department at NYU.)

Part of the problem may be that the task force's assessment of what counts as faculty work relies on the report of the Commission on Professional Service (see esp. 4, 17–18, and 24–26). That report—entitled "Making Faculty Work Visible: Reinterpreting Professional Service, Teaching, and Research in the Fields of Language and Literature"—makes a distinction between "intellectual work" and "academic and professional citizenship" (2). It's a distinction that the commission itself suggests may not hold up under scrutiny, but it is telling nonetheless. Intellectual work, which comprises teaching, research, and service, involves the various ways faculty members "can contribute individually and jointly to the collective projects and enterprises of knowledge and learning undertaken to implement broad academic missions" (15). Academic and professional citizenship in the area of service includes working on committees and task forces and participating in the development of policy that sustains the institution in which one works (18–19). The first category, intellectual work, "should point beyond itself and its immediate context" (16) and is thus expected to be visible—that is, presented publicly in person or in print—as intellectual work, while the second category of work is limited to the institution itself. The problem is that much of the work in the second category also involves significant investment of time and intellectual labor, not to mention academically sound and discipline-specific methodologies to carry that work out, work that could be peer-reviewed in other circumstances but is not here because of its use in institutional contexts. Much of this work is disseminated to other institutions and put to use (and thus reviewed) in other programs, making what is at first the work of institutional citizenship a far broader contribution—and one that is, as a result, measured by far more rigorous standards of review—than the commission (and the task force) may realize. All this suggests that the MLA, in its subsequent work on the nature of scholarship—or on any subject—would do well to consider facets of English and foreign language study (that sometimes still look a little odd to literature professors) like composition and rhetoric, applied linguistics, and creative writing, whose scholarly work doesn't take on the forms that work in literary-critical fields takes on and has effects in contexts, sometimes very public contexts, beyond the classroom or the readership of scholarly journals and books.

Another issue that gave me pause as I read the report was the question of diversity—not just racial, ethnic, or cultural diversity, recognized in the report as something to consider when examining the data on the rates of successful tenure and promotion cases in the MLA's fields, but also disciplinary diversity, which is to some extent inextricably linked to racial, ethnic, and cultural diversity. Part of what gave me pause was simply the brevity with which the issue of race and ethnicity was addressed in the report: the issue of "hiring, exiting, promoting, and tenuring" faculty members of color was mentioned only late in the report and then only as an issue, among others, that requires "further study and more precise documentation" (59). Indeed. Another question I had as I read the report—particularly those sections that deal with the emerging areas of study in language and literature, the methodologies that attend those areas, and the extent to which those areas challenge the ways in which scholarship can and should be evaluated—was why the task force hadn't made the connection between the obstacles faced by faculty members of color and the obstacles faced by faculty members whose areas of study and whose methodological approaches differ from the more or less orthodox areas of literary-critical study. (This connection is made in "Making Faculty Work Visible" but only in a single paragraph on page 27, on the special burden in the area of service placed on minority faculty members.) In my experience, faculty members whose work focuses on traditionally underrepresented minority literature and language—or whose approaches weave together ethnic-studies methodologies and literary-theoretical ones or whose research involves outreach to and face-to-face work with members of marginalized communities—are often people of color or members of traditionally underrepresented groups themselves. As Juana María Rodríguez writes in an essay responding to the report of the ADE Ad Hoc Committee on the Status of African American Faculty Members in English, also published in *Profession 2007*, the increasing demands placed on probationary faculty members for tenure and promotion and the difficulties encountered by faculty (particularly junior faculty) members of color as they navigate the currents of academic work are not unrelated. I'd even say they're very clearly related.

I know this because I waded through reams of studies and materials on just these issues as a member of my college's Equity and Diversity Committee during the 2006–07 and 2007–08 academic years. The committee was formed during the summer of 2006 by the dean of the College of Letters and Science as part of his work to improve the climate in the college and—through the college, the largest unit by far on this very large public campus—the university. The first stage of the committee's work involved reviewing studies on the status of faculty members of color at peer institutions and on our own campus. One incredibly valuable source of information about our campus came from our Women in Science and Engineering Leadership Institute (WISELI), which was established through an NSF grant a decade ago and has quickly developed into a powerful research center that addresses impediments to women's advancement in academia, principally in the STEM (science, technology, engineering, and mathematics) disciplines but in others as well. Among the many initiatives supported through WISELI is a regular series of Climate Workshops for Chairs, which—along with other resources—provides a wealth of data, collected for department chairs to understand the health (or lack of it) of their departments' climate, on the degree to which members of the faculty, doing very different kinds of work, feel as though they are being supported academically and personally by the academic institution. Taken together with data from other publicly funded research universities, the results from the Climate Workshops surveys suggest that faculty members of color find higher hurdles to tenure than their white counterparts when their work is being evaluated. The results also provide some of the reasons why.

Two reports—one by WISELI, the *Study of Faculty Worklife*, and the other by the Equity and Diversity Committee at the University of Wisconsin, Madison, particularly its reading dossiers—suggest many things, but for the MLA's task force, two stand out. First, there is a significant gap between the tenure and promotion rates for faculty members of color and for white faculty members. In the College of Letters and Science, for example, the overall tenure rate between 1987 and 1999 for all junior faculty members was about sixty-five percent over a nine-year period. (This means that they were all hired during this time and that sixty-five percent received tenure within nine years of their initial hire.) This rate of tenure is consistent with the findings in the task force's report (27–28) that of the sixty (of one hundred) doctoral students in English and foreign languages who find tenure-track employment, about thirty-four receive tenure at the institution where they were hired. There are very small differences when the data are disaggregated by gender. But when they are disaggregated for gender and race, one discovers much larger differences, particularly for junior women faculty members of color. While minority male faculty members are tenured less frequently than majority male faculty members over the course of nine years, by a rate of about five percent, minority women faculty members are tenured at a rate about twenty percent lower. (The data from other large public research universities suggest that what we discovered on our Equity and Diversity Committee and what is reported in the results of WISELI surveys is true across the country.)

Second, as shown by the WISELI climate survey results, there is a correlation between the levels of support reported by minority faculty members and the levels of support reported by faculty members whose work is considered nonmainstream in their discipline. In general, most faculty members who responded to the WISELI survey reported that they were "very satisfied" or "satisfied" with the level of support they received both from their departments and from the university community. Faculty members were also able to report whether their work fell into the mainstream of their discipline and whether they were members of a traditionally underrepresented minority group. When the results of this survey were disaggregated, there were again significant differences. Of the groups that reported a higher rate of dissatisfaction with the support their work received from their departments and the university, three stand out. The first group—no surprise—was composed of faculty members working in the humanities. The other two groups were minority faculty members and those faculty members who reported that their work was considered to be less in the mainstream of their fields than that of their colleagues. While the WISELI data suggested rates of satisfaction on only one campus (ours), I imagine that they are not dissimilar to rates of satisfaction reported by faculty members at other institutions like ours.

Taken together, these results suggest that there is further work to be done by the MLA to see whether some of the obstacles to the tenure and promotion of faculty members of color are structurally related to those faced by faculty members working in areas of scholarship that involve noninterpretive research, research that involves working outside the traditional university space or that involves the writing and other cultural production of marginalized communities. I know from the experience of moving tenure and promotion cases through my department and from there to divisional committees that junior faculty members whose work is in ethnic studies or whose research involves outreach or whose essays appear in journals that are not considered mainstream literary-critical ones receive a great deal more scrutiny and far more questions—about their work's "fit" in a department or college or about its intellectual heft—than do literary scholars whose work employs methods more familiar to those charged with vetting it. The studies with which I'm familiar and my experience as a department administrator suggest that there is a clear relation between faculty diversity and methodological diversity, and, unless it is explored, members of the profession and of the MLA will never fully understand the obstacles to assessing scholarship produced by faculty members of color and in areas of English and foreign language study that aren't principally literary-critical.

One reason for these obstacles is what the task force's report calls the "status quo" on department faculties (23). The report notes, for instance, that an astoundingly high number of department chairs report not having any familiarity with peer-reviewed scholarship in electronic journals and other formats, when a growing proportion of work in the modern languages is finding a readership—and a pretty wide one at that—in these newer formats. This part of the report suggests that we're either just not paying attention to the way the field is being transformed by electronic media or we just don't care. But I'd like to stick up for my colleagues who serve as chairs—and who are, often enough, paying close attention to how our disciplines are being transformed—and note instead that some of the obstacles to assessing new developments in faculty work might originate outside our departments. Specifically—and this is something toward which the report points but does not give serious consideration—one of the obstacles to promotion and tenure and the fair evaluation of cases may be divisional or external committees beyond the department.

The report, for instance, points to the "startling" conclusion that at institutions where there has been no explicit decision to reform the criteria by which tenure and promotion decisions are to be made, expectations for junior faculty members nonetheless rose in all areas of scholarly work (23). The report goes on to explain how departments can do better to acclimate new faculty members to the changing roles and raised expectations (23–24). But this solution puts the onus on department chairs and the faculty members themselves, when in fact the rise in expectations is often driven from the top down, as the report also makes clear (23): with the prevalence of rankings like the ones published in *U.S. News and World Report* and with cries for accountability by taxpayers and legislators, administrators sometimes see an increase in the number of c.v. lines among their faculty members as a way to quantify the rising standards. Such pressure becomes especially burdensome not in the department's assessment of a junior faculty member but between the department and the provost. Members of divisional committees may or may not be members of the MLA, the ADE, or the ADFL, and they may or may not be interested in truly interdisciplinary work or research that involves community outreach or diversities of different kinds. I was told by a colleague and fellow department chair that one of the assistant professors in his department, after an overwhelmingly positive vote in the department, was denied tenure at the divisional committee level at least in part because there was no one qualified to present his case. The scholar had a cultural studies approach to his period and had published his work at presses that took a similar approach, but once his work hit the divisional committee—made up of scholars in the humanities with very different approaches to the work (the case was presented by a linguist)—all bets were off. I've run into similar situations at my institution, and I hear story after story of junior colleagues whose (especially) interdisciplinary work is encouraged by the department but is put seriously into question—if not used as a justification to deny tenure—by committees further up the line that are more traditional in their approach to scholarly work. It's understandable that divisional committees are more conservative than departments: after all, they're composed of faculty members from across the spectrum of the humanities who—as a collective—cannot be expected to understand the trends in disciplines far afield from their own. But incidents like the ones I've just described suggest that the insights of the MLA task force's report need to be shared with members of other professional societies—the AHA, the APA, the NCA— so that we're all on the same page and the faculty members in other areas of the humanities, those who sit on divisional committees with us and who evaluate our colleagues' work, can discuss and debate what does and doesn't, what should and shouldn't, count in evaluations of scholarship for promotion and tenure.

Finally, let me turn to the question of the expanding workload that all members of the profession have experienced over the last decade or two, a phenomenon to which the report rightly points. The second section, "The Shifting Composition of the Faculty and the Shifting Nature of Academic Work" (17–19), most clearly describes the problem: while the number of students entering higher education over the last thirty years has grown significantly and while the number of faculty members hired at colleges and universities has also grown, the growth in tenure-track positions has not grown nearly as quickly as full-time or part-time positions off the tenure track (18). As the report also makes clear, these trends have a direct impact on the workloads of tenure-track faculty members:

> The dramatic increase in the number of part-time NTT [non-tenure-track] faculty members and in the number of term-limited full-time NTT faculty members puts increased demands and pressure on all full-time tenure-track and tenured faculty members.

OK, so far, so good. But the passage concludes:

> "[T]he casualized work force is not—and should not be—responsible [for work reserved for tenured and tenure-track faculty members]: service on

> department committees and in departmental governance; student advis-
> ing; teaching upper-level undergraduate and graduate courses; directing
> dissertations; and, less concretely but no less importantly, contributing to
> intellectual community building in the department and outside it, in the
> college and in the university. (19)

I find in this statement a remarkably condescending attitude.

Now, it may be that "NTT faculty members appear satisfied with some aspects of their jobs, especially their workload and the level of control over their professional time" (19). But these same faculty members are dissatisfied with "their organizational status, perquisites, and future prospects" (19). I would be dissatisfied too if I worked a full-time job but had no say in the governance of the organization in which I worked, no say in the direction of that organization, and no say about its future hires or its strategic planning. A colleague of mine, who is a full-time non-tenure-track faculty member charged with program administration, told me that she'd tried for years to "get noticed" and garner a role in the governance of the department (the program not only serves an important group of undergraduate students but also pulls in a significant amount of privately generated money to the department). After trying for a while, she just gave up, contenting herself with the fact that, left alone, she could pretty much do what she wanted. This colleague is incredibly smart, has a significant research agenda, runs a program that draws students to the major, and should have a governance role in the department. Thus with the restructuring of the university, which involves a growing number of non-tenure-track faculty members teaching our courses, running our programs, and involving themselves in the lives of our departments, we should also rethink how we distribute the labor that it takes to run these departments. There are very capable people off the tenure track—people with research agendas and smart ideas about governance who are marvelous and thoughtful teachers—whose energy and intellectual capital we could use to reinvigorate some of our departments and who could change for the better how we think about faculty work. True, some of them don't want to be as involved in the department as their colleagues on the tenure track are obliged to be. But some of them do, and we should give them the support they need so that they can. Their participation would alleviate some of the pressure on tenure-track and tenured faculty members. In this brave new world of academia, we should empower all our faculty members—on or off the tenure track—to have a hand in reshaping it, so that the reshaping is not done for us (or maybe to us) by someone else.

As I said at the outset of this essay, I'm deeply grateful to the MLA Executive Council and to the members of the task force for directly and forcefully examining the obstacles to the fair and equitable assessment of faculty work, particularly the work of assistant professors as they make their way toward tenure and promotion. And I'm grateful to David Laurence, whose gentle prodding got me to consider more thoughtfully the implications of the task force's work. The report makes clear that while the crisis in scholarly publishing is not yet having deleterious systematic effects on the assessment of faculty scholarship for tenure and promotion, it is likely to in the future; the report also makes clear that, in the meantime, there are changes that we as a profession can put into practice to ameliorate those effects. They include making the assessment of scholarly work more transparent, rethinking the monograph as the gold standard for tenure, considering alternatives to the dissertation as a monograph's first draft, and broadening our conception of scholarship so that it's not equated so unequivocally with publication.

Because it's not just about the book but also about the rapidly changing nature of academic work, including scholarship and what it means to be a teacher-scholar in colleges and universities, and about how—at our most realistic and at our best—we assess that work, I'd urge the MLA to continue its study of the relation between the rates of tenure for people of color, particularly women of color, and the evaluation of nontraditional or multidisciplinary work—in ethnic studies, rhetoric and composition, language and linguistics—in more or less traditional English and foreign language departments. Let the MLA examine how scholarship involving outreach, work in nonuniversity communities, and work associated with program administration can be fairly evaluated so that it counts as research. When we consider the nature of scholarly work, we should more energetically involve fields (including creative writing, rhetoric and composition, applied linguistics, and folklore) that sometimes feel marginalized by the more traditional, literary-interpretive fields under the purview of the MLA. And let the MLA also pursue ways to draw on the talents and insights of those in the profession who aren't on the tenure track, for whatever reason, and thereby change the future of the profession. As a member of the MLA, I look forward to doing this work.

WORKS CITED

ADE Ad Hoc Committee on the Status of African American Faculty Members in English. "Affirmative Activism." *Profession* (2007): 150–55. Print.

Boyer, Ernest L. *Scholarship Reconsidered: Priorities of the Professoriate*. Princeton: Carnegie Foundation for the Advancement of Teaching, 1990. Print.

Equity and Diversity Committee of the College of Letters and Science. "Faculty

Diversity and Excellence: A Report and a Practical Vision for the Future." U of Wisconsin, Madison, Sept. 2007. Web. 22 Sept. 2008.

MLA Commission on Professional Service. "Making Faculty Work Visible: Reinterpreting Professional Service, Teaching, and Research in the Fields of Language and Literature." *Modern Language Association.* MLA, 1996. Web. 12 June 2008.

"Report of the MLA Task Force on Evaluating Scholarship for Tenure and Promotion." *Profession* (2007): 9–71. Print.

Rodríguez, Juana María. "The Affirmative Activism Project." *Profession* (2007): 156–67. Print.

Study of Faculty Worklife at the University of Wisconsin-Madison. WISELI. U of Wisconsin, Madison. 2003. Web. 12 June 2008.

We Need to Talk: Scholarship, Tenure, and Promotion in the Balance

DANA RINGUETTE

There are twenty summary recommendations made in the *Report of the MLA Task Force on Evaluating Scholarship for Tenure and Promotion;* my department is already (and has been for some time) doing eighteen of them. I point this out not to sing our praises but to suggest that the "complex situation," as the report calls it, of trends that must be addressed before they become a crisis is already being addressed (5). It is not going to be resolved once and for all, mind you, because these are issues that must be continually engaged. Nonetheless, there are many examples, I suspect, of departments already addressing and employing the practices, calibrations, conceptions, and facilitations recommended by the task force. It's just that such examples or models are not, as far as I can tell, emanating from doctoral programs or traveling in a trickle-down fashion. The discussion we should have on these recommendations must stop being "vertical"—as if the PhDs sent to master's and baccalaureate institutions go brain-dead or incommunicado when (and if) they find a position—and must become dispersed horizontally across the spectrum of departments, colleges, and universities.

While the report focuses on specific issues, as it must, the ramifications of what it reports and recommends should engage us in much more fundamental and sweeping—not to say abstract—issues. Consider, for example, recommendation 7, which states, "Departments and institutions should

The author is professor of English and chair of the English department at Eastern Illinois University. A version of this article appeared in the Winter 2008 issue of the ADE Bulletin.

establish mentoring structures that provide guidance to new faculty members on scholarship and on the optimal balance of publication, teaching, and service" (5–6).

The value of setting up "mentoring structures" seems to me beyond question, but what draws my attention here are the issues embedded in what mentors or mentoring structures will do: "provide guidance . . . on scholarship and on the optimal balance of publication, teaching, and service." The first, providing guidance on scholarship, is indeed the focus of the task force's emphases on "revising the meaning of scholarship" (27) and on "rethinking the preeminence of the monograph" and "revaluing the essay" (38). But the second, "providing guidance . . . on the optimal balance of publication, teaching, and service," strikes me as much more difficult, and there's little in the report that provides direction on this because, of course, it was beyond the charge assigned to the task force.[1] Yet because the issue is raised and in effect if not intention emphasized in the report, I think we have a responsibility to address it once again—and again and again, if necessary. If nothing else, the relative silence in the report on the "optimal balance" may reflect a whole profession's ambivalence and uncertainty about the relations among the academic triad. Determining what the optimal balance of publication, teaching, and service is will require a far-reaching reevaluation of what we do. But the good news is that this reevaluation, as I say, has long since started. Many just have not noticed.

Consider what the possible effects would be should we (and I mean all of us) act on the conviction that the relation of publication to teaching—not to mention to service—is currently out of balance, that the emphasis given to publication is excessive—is out of whack and unsupportable (intellectually, educationally, and economically)—and that, as a result, the emphasis given to teaching is insufficient. The probable effects would resonate throughout the entire institutional structure (in my situation that would mean department, college, and university), but certainly one effect would be giving preeminence to our teaching, conceiving of it as the vehicle, the enabling condition, that gives meaning and significance to research and service. We might teach more, or of course we might teach less, depending on the institution, because a greater emphasis on teaching should not mean simply additional classes, especially for those who somehow manage to teach four, five, even six classes every semester. Such effects, in other words, would make it necessary for us not only to talk about what we do or should teach but also, for example, to ask, What is the optimal teaching load? What should be our expectations for publication—or for other scholarship that reaches beyond the boundaries of one's department and campus—given that optimization? Where does service fit in?

Another consequence would be a plausible end to the modeling of our professional lives and aspirations on the example set by the natural and physical sciences, an example that was shaped into its present form by the extensive federal investment in research and development during the 1950s. This model, as the report indicates clearly, is still with us, even though the developing and developed exigencies and circumstances of our discipline and responsibilities would seem to run counter to it. Over the past decade or so, many writers, not to mention the report itself, have shown how universities and liberal arts colleges have continued to mimic the Research I model despite the deleterious effects it has had on faculty members across the spectrum of institutions.[2] We all say we teach, but professional prestige depends on publication and, more important, on recognition for publication.

Not surprisingly, as the report notes briefly, we are also confronting the same shortcomings that have been bedeviling our colleagues in the sciences for some time. James Jasper has briefly summarized the institutional and individual consequences of those problems or limitations:

> [The model of the natural sciences] means a division of labor into departments and disciplines that only make sense if they correspond to objective aspects of the world out there that can be divided into tiny fragments. It means evaluation criteria that turn to the disciplines. Only other experts in your sub-subfield can judge your work, so peer review is used not only for publications but also promotions. It means a lopsided emphasis on research more than teaching, despite occasional lip service to the contrary (those outside experts who review you for promotion cannot evaluate your teaching). And finally, it means the ability to attract outside grants.

As it turns out, according to an ongoing series of articles in the *Chronicle of Higher Education* focusing on teaching, a pressing concern over the past decade in the sciences is faculty resistance to finding and using different, more effective methods of teaching undergraduate science classes. The irony should not be lost on us that we in the humanities might have a great deal to teach scientists about how to put into practice in the classroom the recommendations of the National Science Foundation in this respect. But they aren't listening to us, just as we aren't listening to one another and persist in following a model of the relation of teaching and scholarship that even they have difficulty sustaining (Brainard). I'm just as alarmed as the task force is by what appear to be (according to their surveys) the current demands on faculty members, and, frankly, I'm depressed by what appears to be department chairs' "predominant satisfaction with the status quo," despite what the report observes as "an increased emphasis on teaching since the mid-1990s" (21). If these circumstances indeed exist, then it seems clear that in our discipline we are desperately intent on believing what we are already inclined to believe, intent on being satisfied with what we are already inclined to think. In other words, to borrow from Charles Sanders Peirce, we have blocked the way of inquiry, which pretty much obviates from the start the "new conjuncture" noted in the report that "demands new thinking, new flexibility and openness, and new solutions" (27). Not to consider at least rethinking the status quo is an untenable position because it risks our own intellectual and educational integrity. As Peirce also observed, "to avoid looking into the support of any belief from a fear that it may turn out rotten is quite as immoral as it is disadvantageous" (123).

Faculty members at regional and comprehensive colleges and universities must believe otherwise. We have been more or less compelled (to good effect, I think) to believe that our work in the classroom, in our reading and writing, and in committee must be associated. When we do good research, we are refining and redefining what it is we do in the humanities, both for ourselves and for our professional audiences. This kind of work makes one a better teacher, not only for the practice of intellect it demands but also for the understanding of the profession one then takes back to the classroom and, for that matter, to every department or university committee. Any research worth doing involves, even necessitates, thinking about what we're doing and why, if only because it involves such a dynamic commitment of energy, time, and scheduling. Publication of research, which is in practice outwardly directed beyond the confines of the department and university, must move also inward. The research a colleague does, for example, into the aesthetic values underlying an obscure novel may lead her to think about high and low art in ways that change her syllabi, to shape the way she presents material in the classroom, and to think about the curriculum when she serves on committees. It also sends her to conferences where she talks to people from other universities about their teaching, service, and research.

Such work, I would contend, is no less viable, valuable, or worthwhile than that conducted in literature and language departments at large, research-oriented institutions; and doing such work does not mean having to fashion concessions, dispensations, or "accommodations" (a term often seen in discussions of differences in expectations for scholarship among Research I universities, comprehensive institutions, and liberal arts colleges, but that I'm happy to see avoided in the task force report). Accommodation should not carry with it the assumption of second-rate recognition or, worse, second-tier work. Rather, such accommodation should become a measured, purposeful fine-tuning or adjustment. And the consequence, consistent with the recommendations in the report, is that quantifying scholarship in terms of how many articles and books one has published becomes less important than the sustained, worthwhile engagement that demonstrably and meaningfully contributes to the work of one's department and, by extension, the profession. Such a model of research and scholarship encourages and assists in the time it takes to do careful, consuming, rigorous, integrated study. Perhaps more important, this model contributes less to the building up of a single ego (whether individual or institutional) and more to the advancement of a community's knowledge and conditions. It is a model that creates an environment in which such study is encouraged but not regarded as binding entitlement to the isolated professor or the institution. In other words, our research either moves into the classroom, into curricula, and ultimately into the lifeblood of the department, or it goes nowhere at all.

The isolation of program from program, of school from school, of doctorate-granting university from MA I university or college, of such master's-granting institutions from baccalaureate ones, of colleague from colleague, and so on, is so ingrained, is so much the status quo ante, that we regard this state as an objective, nearly immutable truth, when on reflection we recognize that it is a conventional form we may have inherited but continue to propagate at nearly every level. Take conventional teaching practices—and the evaluation of those practices—as a case in point. In preparing to teach or to write, college and university professors read one another's books, articles, and reviews in print or online as a matter of course, even though we (writer and reader) are displaced individually in terms of distance, time, association, and medium. But we rarely witness—or read—one another's teaching, even though one's colleagues are just across the hall or in the same building and classrooms are within walking distance. Our writing involves a collaboration to which we adapt, but our teaching in practice occurs in isolation: once we close our classroom doors, we leave our closest peers behind. So it's no surprise that such a structure is reproduced in the rigid hierarchies that arise among graduate students, adjuncts, and junior and senior faculty members and in the separations among our specialties. One of our basic functions as teachers—to risk a broad generalization—is to help students learn and become accustomed to the fact, as we learned in our own educations, that they have not read enough or read as widely as they can or might. And yet, as teachers early in our careers, assured that we are competent because we have excelled in advanced studies in particular fields, we have generally missed the opportunity to see one another's classes as a resource. We have, as William Carlos Williams might put it, instantiated "the virtual impossibility of lifting to the imagination those things which lie under the direct scrutiny of the senses, close to the nose" (14).[3] To make this example reach further, I think that enacting the recommendations of the report is going to require a concerted effort to listen to and learn from one another.

Let me then add another way of thinking about this issue, which might also, I hope, double as an additional path of inquiry into our mutual concerns. The ongoing "general anxiety" that the report cautions the discipline of literature and language to avoid before it is too late is already a crisis that doctoral students have absorbed in PhD programs (7). But it is not a crisis in my program—it is not a crisis in a literature and language program in a comprehensive, MA I, regional, state-assisted (alas, like so many others, no longer really state-supported) university. And those students, when they come to us as applicants and candidates for positions and even when they find themselves transformed as newly arrived faculty members, are always—and I don't think I'm exaggerating—surprised yet relieved to find this out. Instead they confront another issue, which in many cases may be initially just as unsettling but soon becomes much less an obstacle than an opportunity: how to value, give emphasis to, and articulate their teaching in ways they have never before been prepared to anticipate, except often in some incredibly condescending way ("comprehensive universities are less interested in your scholarship than in your teaching—don't make the mistake of giving a scholarly presentation during your on-campus interview"). It's as simple as that. They may have thought about how to present (or preserve) themselves as researchers, and they may even have had the odd, isolated teaching experience that somehow dovetailed into their research areas. But they have not thought about—indeed, what chances have they had to do so unless they have had to endure years on the job market in temporary positions?—what it means to be primarily a teacher in a community of research, writing, and scholarly exchange.

It is in this light that I read further manifestations of anxiety documented in the report:

> The task force believes that the declining number of tenure-track positions in relation to the total number of positions accounts in large measure for the widespread anxiety in the profession about standards for tenure and promotion. This anxiety may also be understood as unease about the continued escalation of quantitative demands for scholarly production, the extension of such demands to a widening circle of institutions of higher learning, and the harm being done to scholars and scholarship as demands increase. As a result of our survey of 1,339 department chairs, we clearly see increasing pressure on the system of scholarly production and the mechanics of its evaluation. Scholars and institutions

> have adapted to changing circumstances over the years as requirements for tenure have expanded and demands have been increased throughout the profession. But the results have taken their toll on individual scholars and institutions—and on the academy's infrastructure as a whole—and strained the profession in ways that are intensely serious but not yet well understood or articulated. (26)

I would ask that we also consider the converse situation: the possibility that an equally important factor in the declining number of tenure-track positions is the overemphasis on publication and recognition as the defining mark of an educator in language and literature. While this reading is another way of describing what doctoral candidates may absorb and inhabit as yet another form of the "general anxiety" the report draws attention to, I simply want to suggest that we continue to put our profession at risk by not foregrounding more fully—for ourselves first and foremost, but subsequently for others—our job as primarily teachers and educators. Despite the report's welcome endorsement, following John Guillory's work, of a "more complex and expanded view of the sites of scholarship," wherein teaching and service are regarded as "forms of scholarship," I fear that such approval does not go far enough, especially when current administrative, legislative, and public support for the investment in a literature and language program clearly favors temporary, part- and full-time faculty members at the expense of tenure-line faculty members (22–23). This is precisely where programs in "flagship" institutions disregard the work of programs in "comprehensive" institutions at their peril, because, first, this *is* where a disastrous "trickle-down" effect occurs as programs in comprehensive institutions are unable to hire new PhDs, and, second, comprehensives have much to offer that will help doctorate-granting programs describe and present themselves more effectively. There is a third effect that requires mention. As much as I appreciate the report's call for "expanding the definition of scholarship and the body of work to be evaluated for tenure," when the time rolls around for tenure and promotion, the process returns almost inevitably, it seems, to the types, qualities, and quantities of publication (40). This circularity may be in one sense inevitable given the charge assigned to the task force, but I think it also underwrites implicitly the status quo that is difficult for us to rethink.

To return to an earlier assertion, teaching is not, I would contend, a form of scholarship; rather, it is, for so many of us already, the enabling condition for what we do in the classroom, our offices, and our studies. This statement does not make simply a semantic or rhetorical distinction, as important as such distinctions may be. Acting on such a conviction allows us to reconsider what we do and how we do it, allows us to generate different grounds on which to make effective common cause, and allows more and fuller collaboration across institutional missions and boundaries. Perhaps now it is even more urgent for us to act as teachers to change how we (and our work) are regarded by those legislators, administrators, parents, and interested parties who, I believe, really want to support us but haven't yet the means to do so productively. They want students to become the kind of readers we are and can teach them to be: willing to read, to engage the complex and imaginative uses of language manifest in what we read, to work toward understanding, to think hard and then to rethink, and to try to articulate that thinking. After all, perhaps the most pressing and prevalent issue, common to us all in this discussion of standards and evaluation, pertains to the growing number of non-tenure-track positions in our institutions gained at the expense of tenure-line positions. It's then not really an issue of tenure lines alone, or the tenure and promotion process that follows, but of whether we can make it clear why permanent teaching positions are so important for the intellectual and educational well-being of programs, teachers, and students (see also Steen; Steward, in this issue).

The report makes clear to me that its recommendations must be taken on by all of us, in all departments and institutions. One answer does not fit all. But I would also suggest that it is not—and should not be—simply a matter of each department, categorized and distinguished by the type of institution, developing different answers according to differing institutional missions. Separation by institutional missions (Carnegie doctorate, master's, and baccalaureate) should not be an obstacle, should not prevent us (and again, I mean all of us, no matter what institution) from learning from one another, from paying more attention to one another.

NOTES

The author would like to thank Randall Beebe, Linda Coleman, Ruth Hoberman, David Laurence, Leroy Searle, Richard Sylvia, and Robyn Warhol for their counsel and responses regarding this commentary.

1. "To address this set of issues, the Executive Council charged the Task Force on Evaluating Scholarship for Tenure and Promotion first and foremost 'with examining the procedures used to evaluate scholarly publications for tenure and promotion'" (8).

2. The reader will no doubt be able to supply a long list of references here and should also consult the extensive list of works cited in the report itself. In addition to that list I would add Kolodny; Searle; Sosnoski; and Watkins.

3. In fairness to Williams, I should supply his entire sentence (even as it, for me, suggests a valuable correlation between writing and teaching): "But the thing that stands eternally in the way of really good writing is always one: the virtual impossibility of lifting to the imagination those things which lie under the direct scrutiny of the senses, close to the nose" (14).

WORKS CITED

Brainard, Jeffrey. "The Tough Road to Better Science Teaching." *Chronicle of Higher Education* 3 Aug. 2007: A15–18. Print.

Jasper, James. "How the Research-University Model Has Killed the Creativity of Humanists and Social Scientists." *Chronicle of Higher Education* 7 Feb. 2002: n. pag. Web. 1 Nov. 2007.

Kolodny, Annette. *Failing the Future: A Dean Looks at Higher Education in the Twenty-First Century.* Durham: Duke UP, 1998. Print.

Peirce, Charles Sanders. "The Fixation of Belief." *The Essential Peirce: Selected Philosophical Writings.* Ed. Nathan Houser and Christian Kloesel. Vol. 1. Bloomington: Indiana UP, 1992. 108–23. Print.

Report of the MLA Task Force on Evaluating Scholarship for Tenure and Promotion. Modern Language Association. MLA, Dec. 2006. Web. 23 Sept. 2008.

Searle, Leroy F. "Institutions and Intellectuals: A Modest Proposal." *Profession* (1996): 15–25. Print.

Sosnoski, James J. *Token Professionals and Master Critics: A Critique of Orthodoxy in Literary Studies.* Albany: State U of New York P, 1994. Print.

Steen, Sara Jayne. "Living with Our Words: What English Department Administrators Should Know about the Language of Higher Education Policy." *ADE Bulletin* 141-142 (2007): 49–54. Print.

Watkins, Evan. *Work Time: English Departments and the Circulation of Cultural Value.* Stanford: Stanford UP, 1989. Print.

Williams, William Carlos. "Kora in Hell: Improvisations." *Imaginations.* Ed. Webster Schott. New York: New Directions, 1970. 6–82. Print.

On the Tyranny of Good Intentions: Some Notes on the MLA Task Force Report

W. B. CARNOCHAN

The academy enjoys a good crisis. The clash described by Hannah Arendt, between the values of authority and tradition, on the one hand, and the centrifugal forces of the modern, on the other, probably qualifies as an educational crisis—though I think not a corrigible one (Steiner 145). More often the crisis is fathered as much by self-importance as by facts (we have unhappily learned to say) on the ground. In the 1980s and early 1990s, crisis mongering, led by conservatives like Allan Bloom, was everywhere. The canon was dying. The end of Western Civilization, if not of Western civilization, was at hand, apocalypse a day or two away. At the time, I wrote a book that took a less gloomy and, I thought, more historical view (*Battleground*). Much as I would enjoy attributing the subsequent diminution of crisis mongering to that book, realism suggests that events merely ran their course as things dwindled into normality.

Now we have another crisis or the supposition of one, the "tyranny of the monograph," first named by Lindsay Waters. Notwithstanding some economic realities, I think this crisis, too, is in good part factitious. That does not mean, however, that I suppose all is perfectly well. Rather, I think that forces set in motion long before 1970, the date offered by the MLA Task Force on Evaluating Scholarship for Tenure and Promotion as the moment when the tyranny of the monograph took hold, have produced a moment of self-recognition. At heart, any tyranny has been that of good intentions paving the way to a traffic jam with its attendant anxiety—and

The author is Richard W. Lyman Professor of Humanities emeritus at Stanford University.

an MLA task force. These concerns originate not in some recent fetishizing of the monograph, whenever it might be dated, but in the institution, tenure itself, that has been to the advantage of many of us and one that we would be unhappy to do without.

A quick tutorial in historical views of tenure can be had at the Web site of the American Association of University Professors (AAUP). Most striking is the evolution of tenure from a guarantor of academic freedom to a means of quality control. I leave the job of charting that shift in meaning to others, but the notion of a probationary period, articulated in the AAUP's "1940 Statement of Principles," has been crucial to the transition from things as they once were to what they are now: "After the expiration of a probationary period, teachers or investigators should have permanent or continuous tenure." Then in 1969 the association stated in principle what was already the case in practice: "Beginning with the appointment to the rank of full-time instructor or a higher rank, the probationary period should not exceed seven years." Having myself been appointed an instructor in 1960, then advanced to assistant professor when the rank of instructor was effectively abolished, I recall that the change provided me an extra year of probation, eight rather than seven, for which, not being a fast worker, I was duly grateful. The serious question, however, is not seven years or eight but the temporal imperative itself and the implications that go with it.

If there is to be a probationary period, there needs to be a limit of time, and seven years—with its sabbatical associations—comes more or less naturally to mind. Yet any deadline will be in a measure arbitrary and entail assumptions about what the probationary period is supposed to prove and how it needs to be proven. A period of two or three years would be reasonable on some sets of assumptions: teaching ability or collegial reliability can be demonstrated in less than seven years. So the seven-year rule carries the presumption that something needs doing that may take that long to do. And seven years is long enough—isn't it?—to write a book. What lies behind the rule and its implicit valuation of the book is the valuation of qualities like patience and the ability to pursue a line of thought in an extended argument. These are not the same qualities as sheer brainpower, notwithstanding any illusion that departments and university administrations may harbor to the contrary, and many a monograph is a lot of plodding along and only a little actual invention—in the words of Waters, "narrow and passionless" ("Rescue" B8). Surely that is the main reason the market for the product has slumped; no one would argue that Harvard could not afford the luxury of publishing monographs in the humanities whenever it chose, even if the potential audience numbered in less than three figures. And why suppose that someone who writes a dull mono-graph would be more likely to write an inspiriting essay?

When Waters looks at the shape of humanistic careers, he is also right that a first book is unlikely to be the best or most important thing one ever manages to write (unless it is the only thing), but it may serve as an earnest of what will come. Waters points to the case of Edward Said: first a "rather conventional" monograph on Conrad in 1966 ("Tenure" 97) and, I would add, an article about Swift in 1969 that still has resonance, followed by *Beginnings* in 1975 and *Orientalism* in 1978. Would Said have written *Beginnings* or *Orientalism* had he not begun with Conrad and Swift? Could he have? The article that he called "Swift's Tory Anarchy" has foreshadow-ings of his own later career as both a rebel and a responsible member of the intellectual and academic establishment. Some contrarians might add, Shouldn't Said's early experience in academic scholarship have guided him better in *Orientalism*, notable for its abundance of error as well as for its large cultural impact? The discipline of the monograph imparts to the struggling acolyte a sense of the stakes in getting things as nearly right as possible. It can also be formative, as with Said—a testing of the grounds of one's identity, scholarly and otherwise.

Benign intentions lie behind the institution of tenure and the proba-tionary time limit, no doubt about that. When I was working on the book that became my first—it was about *Gulliver's Travels*—I recall Norman O. Brown, then famous for his *Life against Death*, in which he wrote about Swift's "excremental vision," putting a question to me: "Are you trying to do justice to Swift?" I hesitated and said yes. He said, "Well, I wasn't trying to do justice to Swift. When you get tenure, then you can do something really subversive." Not that I ever did, but the feeling that I could if I figured out what it should be was itself enhancing. As for the probation-ary time limit, it began life as a well-intended guarantee against perma-nently subordinate roles for teachers who were permitted to stay on and on. (That subordinate roles have now multiplied in the form of part-time positions is a separate story.) But when you combine tenure, the seven-year probationary period, and the natural desire of universities to improve themselves, what you get is a "tyranny of the monograph" that, on a less heated account, is the predictable consequence (hindsight makes predict-ability easy) of a systemic arrangement that has grown ever more pervasive over time.

And, for all the mechanization of the tenure process, there remains an underlying subjective truth: to this day, and I would forecast for some time to come, the book retains its allure. Call it a monograph if you will, but anyone who has written one, then seen and held it in hand, knows that the object in question is a book, whether or not it is also that more abstract, far less thrilling thing called a monograph. As "social constructionists," writes Donald E. Hall, "we should be able and willing to admit readily that there is nothing sacred about the monograph as such. A book as a thing carries with it no transcendental value" (84). Of course. But as social constructionists (how could we not be?) we assign the book, a solid thing that incorporates and seems to endow our poor forked words with permanence, something approaching transcendental value. The idea of demoting the book to the ordinary status of ordinary things feels like a shaking of foundations. Don't aspirants to tenure, probably almost all of them, want to write a book if they can, no matter how much they may feel oppressed by the tyranny of a system that forces them to do it? Writing a first book may not be great fun, but it feels good to have done it. Unless up-and-coming workers of the academic world themselves unite in some unimaginable way to throw off their chains, it will be difficult to effect large-scale change: in their secret hearts, I think those who are up-and-coming—like those of us who have preceded them—are largely accepting of things as they are. Who would not prefer to have a book in hand rather than some scattered essays, even in gilt-edged journals? The MLA task force reports that most department chairs "seem to approve of the status quo" (35), which might not be the case if junior faculty members were in revolt or even greatly disquieted.

If I read things right, then, it follows that even if the monograph were quickly dislodged from its role as the main or only criterion for awarding tenure, the result would be to exacerbate, at least in large research universities and at least for a period of time, a sense of class in which those who write books are perceived, and self-perceived, to occupy a higher station than those who write "only" essays. This might be countered by a system of other rewards that acknowledged equal value to different varieties of work, but I frankly doubt that administrators, whether at the departmental or decanal level, would be immune to the inherited pressures of caste and of the marketplace.

Lacking in the report of the MLA task force is any numerical accounting: How many monographs on literature and language are published in a given year? Has that number actually fallen? How far? We hear of "the reduced output from or, in some cases, the phasing out of the humanities lists of academic presses" (13). But Waters reports that academic presses published increasing numbers of titles throughout the 1990s ("Rescue"), and at the Stanford University Press, singled out in the report as "reducing" its humanities list (20), the number of titles in the humanities overall has in fact continued to climb or at least remained stable. I doubt that the "diminishing availability of publishing outlets in the fields represented by the MLA" (13) is the substantial problem it is represented to be. Leafing through the advertisements in *PMLA*, one does not get a feeling of decline and fall. Surfeit is more like it. But if the number of titles has not diminished, or not diminished much overall, then the question becomes, Which presses are publishing what titles and how many? The answer seems to be that, as some large research universities cut back in certain areas, other institutions continue to shoulder the load, not only supporting individual authors but also enhancing their own public visibility. The University of Delaware and, among smaller institutions, Bucknell, Fairleigh Dickinson, and Susquehanna publish over one hundred fifty books a year combined, many of them in the humanities and often valuable. That is not a small number. But although the responsibility has fallen more on these institutions, the awkward, usually unacknowledged but universally understood truth is that they have less standing than (the obvious elephant in this room) Harvard (or other favorites of *U.S. News*) and that administrators at Harvard or its competitors in the prestige wars will in general be less welcoming to monographs, whatever their merits, from less visible institutions than to monographs (should there be any) that find their way past Harvard's own formidable portcullis. Were it not for the usual habits of discretion, a task force recommendation addressed to universities at the top of the food chain might have been, Get over the prestige hang-up, tell your young faculty members that their monographs will be judged solely on their merits, and mean it.

Of course the monograph as a book may die a slow natural death if the Internet takes over in the humanities as it has in the sciences. It is not hard to imagine such a scenario. And, while the MLA task force frets about the "inexperience" of doctoral institutions in evaluating electronic publications (42), that is not the heart of the matter: you can evaluate an electronic publication in the same way you evaluate anything else, except that (being of the old school) you may want to read it in printed form. Doctoral institutions have little experience evaluating electronic publications not because they pose a unique challenge but because they are not, or not yet, accepted currency. As the task force says, "probationary faculty members will be reluctant to risk publishing in electronic formats unless they see clear evidence that such work can count positively" (43). Once again, if departments and universities commit themselves out loud to the proposition that work will be judged only on its merits, not on its site of publication, there could be a sea change. If electronic publications become accepted currency, no special difficulty will arise in judging them. The long-term value of the MLA report may lie less in its devaluation of the monograph than in its endorsement of "new sources and instruments for knowing" (44).

Some apprehension probably remains about the democratic untidiness of the Internet, stuffed as it is with every kind of commentary. Though evaluating electronic publications should be like evaluating anything in print, there may be the risk of too much evaluation in the relentless give-and-take of Web-based discourse. But, with care, the evaluation could be handled more evenhandedly than in the current system, which, for all its emphasis on peer review, operates in ways that admit covert influence. I think the skeptic who told Waters that the system is a "joke" greatly exaggerates, but not without some cause ("Rescue" B8). An author submits a manuscript to a press. The editor asks who would be a good reader. The author comes up with an acquaintance (but not too close an acquaintance) or a teacher (but not the supervisor of the author's dissertation) or anyone thought to be favorably disposed. The editor nods ambiguously but acts on the suggestion while also turning to someone thought to be authoritative and impartial. Then those on the receiving end of the request (usually) put their best foot forward; not many readers want to sink a career before it has begun, and criticism is typically cast as constructive. Subsequently, the book goes out for review—and, *mirabile,* some reviewers think less well of it than readers for the press. The conventions that govern reviewing material in print differ from those that govern reviewing manuscripts for publication. And the same considerations hold true, I think, in tenure reviews. Sometimes the candidate is asked to suggest referees—and the bias of referees in general is more often than not in the candidate's favor even though candor is expected as well. The high proportion of candidates who receive tenure when they come up for consideration implies the normal leanings that operate within the system—though that implication is not to denigrate the accomplishments of those who work their way through.

What might happen if electronic publication became the norm? First, reviews of a monograph would be reviews of something already in print, and the conventions governing that exercise, as they are now, could be maintained if the right procedures were established. Caroline Levine proposes "a centralized process of peer review" for electronic publications: "[i]n every field, each year, a panel of scholars would be appointed or elected to act as peer readers of manuscripts" who would issue, or not, an imprimatur (102). But, as Levine recognizes, all would be free to bypass the system if they chose, and Levine's proposal as it stands strikes me as unworkable. Who would appoint or elect the panels? Could the distinction between publications with an imprimatur and those without ultimately stand up? Within the context of the Web, the panels, however chosen, would resemble a politburo without real authority. I think the free-for-all of the Web would quickly engulf the system. But if we change the ground rules, letting individual institutions devise their own procedures, conventions governing evaluation could become more like reviews of work in print as they exist now and less like the sometimes slanted judgments about particular manuscripts and tenure cases. In a mythically objective world, a coherent system could be devised for reviews and reviewing on the Internet to replace the process that now takes up so much time and energy on the part of administrators, readers, and referees alike.

For candidates coming up for tenure, unable to have much or any part in the assignment of referees, such a system might not count as a reassuring prospect. Nor do I think it would necessarily be good from an institutional standpoint: however mechanized the tenure process has become, this new procedure would be even more so. Still, mediated by common sense, it could relieve pressures in a system that, if not in crisis, is straining at the seams. How long the old hankering for a book in hand will remain to console or haunt us cannot be known—but probably not forever.

If electronic publications become acceptable currency, that will take care of the current traffic jam. What it will not take care of are any systemic problems associated with the particulars of tenure as an institution or the criteria for achieving it. Whatever one thinks of the monographic requirement, the drift toward demanding a second book "in progress" is pushing things to or beyond their natural limits. And on the Internet, after all, publication is instantaneous. In that new world, why not ask for two books or three? It is time to look beyond the dominance of the monograph as standard currency to the whole system within which its exchange value has been established. Few would choose to surrender the freedom from constraint that comes with tenure, but neither the good intentions that brought the system into being nor its undeniable benefits should shield its network of conventions from some renewed, deliberate, and thoughtful scrutiny. Some recommendations of the MLA task force address questions that touch on these big issues. "Departments and institutions," reads recommendation 2, "should calibrate expectations for achieving tenure and promotion with institutional values, mission, and practice" (11). Here lies a hint, couched in committee prose, of something that would take us a few steps beyond the status quo; but without a less oblique, more frank, and more direct examination of the issues at hand, it is hard to imagine how fundamental change will come about.

WORKS CITED

American Association of University Professors. "1940 Statement of Principles on Academic Freedom and Tenure with 1970 Interpretive Comments." *American Association of University Professors.* AAUP, 1940. Web. 3 June 2008.

Bloom, Allan. *The Closing of the American Mind.* New York: Simon, 1987. Print.

Brown, Norman O. *Life against Death: The Psychoanalytical Meaning of History.* New York: Vintage, 1959. Print.

Carnochan, W. B. *The Battleground of the Curriculum: Liberal Education and the American Experience.* Stanford: Stanford UP, 1993. Print.

———. *Lemuel Gulliver's Mirror for Man.* Berkeley: U of California P, 1968. Print.

Hall, Donald E. "A More Capacious View of Scholarship." *Profession* (2007): 83–88. Print.

Levine, Caroline. "Rethinking Peer Review and the Fate of the Monograph." *Profession* (2007): 100–06. Print.

Report of the MLA Task Force on Evaluating Scholarship for Tenure and Promotion. Modern Language Association. MLA, Dec. 2006. Web. 20 Oct. 2008.

Said, Edward W. *Beginnings: Intention and Method.* New York: Columbia UP, 1985. Print.

———. *Joseph Conrad and the Fiction of Autobiography.* Cambridge: Harvard UP, 1966. Print.

———. *Orientalism.* New York: Vintage, 1978. Print.

———. "Swift's Tory Anarchy." *Eighteenth-Century Studies* 3.1 (1969): 48–66. Print.

Steiner, David. "K–16: Our Dogmatic Slumbers." *Profession* (2007): 141–49. Print.

Waters, Lindsay. "Rescue Tenure from the Tyranny of the Monograph." *Chronicle of Higher Education* 20 Apr. 2001: B7–9. Print.

———. "Tenure, Publication, and the Shape of the Careers of Humanists." *Profession* (2007): 93–99. Print.

Coauthoring: What Every Department Should Know

LARA LOMICKA ANDERSON AND GILLIAN LORD

Introduction: Defining Coauthorship

In recent years, several articles have contributed to a wider understanding of the role of linguists and applied linguists[1] in language departments (e.g., Katz and Watzinger-Tharp; Kramsch; VanPatten). One issue for the applied linguist that surfaces consistently in language departments, primarily in discussions held during tenure and promotion reviews, is that of co- or multiauthorship[2] of publications, which may be a somewhat foreign concept to many of the applied linguist's literary colleagues.

Coauthorship is difficult to define, not just in academia but beyond it as well. Many dictionaries offer a simplistic definition of the term: *coauthor* refers to a joint author or collaborator; coauthoring is a process by which more than one author takes on the task of creating a written work. While a collaborating author does contribute to a publication, it may not be clear to an applied linguist's department chair what that contribution entails. This article examines the notion of collaboration in academia, to identify both its benefits and challenges; to investigate the number of coauthored articles in journals familiar to applied linguists; and to offer suggestions for departments, chairs, and faculty members to address this issue more effectively in their institutions.

Lara Lomicka Anderson is associate professor of French and linguistics at the University of South Carolina, Columbia. Gillian Lord is assistant professor of Spanish and applied linguistics at the University of Florida. A version of this article appeared in the Winter-Spring 2008 issue of the ADFL Bulletin.

Who Collaborates?

Collaboration in literature, creative works, and even philosophy is not un-heard of. Considerable attention has been paid by literary analysts to the concept of author and whether an author is a solitary genius or not. Jack Stillinger makes the case that a great number of literary works we know as single-authored are actually the product of more than one contribu-tor, although society in general and scholars in particular are reluctant to recognize this fact. He goes on to claim that acceptance of joint author-ship will not happen as long as "critical appreciation of a masterwork re-quires it to be the product of a single organizing mind" (138). M. Thomas Inge and Holly Laird both examine coauthoring and collaboration from a philosophical and literary perspective, noting that authors have always, in one way or another, benefited from the mediation of another contribu-tor to their works, be it the monks who made transcripts, the typesetter at the printing press, or the editor of a book. Inge encourages academia to recognize this ongoing process of collaboration:

> On a practical level, recognizing that the concept of the solitary genius, or of the divinely inspired author, is a myth calls for no drastic change in the ways we teach and write. . . . But there should be a change in attitude about how we discuss our literature and culture so that we do not constantly downgrade authors according to the extent to which they compromise with the pragmatic and economic forces of time and place.
> (630)

Others have commented on the role of multiple contributors in the concept of author. Lisa Ede and Andrea Lunsford present three differ-ent ideas of coauthorship ("Why Write"). The first involves cocreating a work at every stage of the process, from drafting the outline to the actual writing; they describe the result as true collaboration. The second idea involves authors' contributing separate sections and then putting the work together. In this type of authoring, each person works on a particular con-tribution and then collaborates in the assembling at the end. The third type of coauthorship is group writing, in which many people contribute sections but only a few meet to assemble the work. All these models are present in work done outside academia, but the degree to which they are manifested in academia is uncertain and undefined.

Collaboration in Academia

Regardless of how we define *collaboration*, in academia it supports a double standard: it is the norm in some disciplines; in others it is shunned. Ede and Lunsford note, "As a rule, writers in the humanities have tended to ignore co-authorship, both in writing and in teaching, while colleagues in the sciences and the professions have long used it as a major mode" ("Why Write" 157). It would seem, then, of benefit to both authors and readers to examine further the role of collaboration in academic scholarship. For the sake of simplicity and brevity, we limit the following discussion to the issue of collaboration in humanities-related fields, although coauthoring in the sciences and social sciences has been the norm for some time: style manuals in the sciences specifically treat the issue of coauthoring (e.g., *ACS Style Guide* 14; *Scientific Style* 17).

In the humanities, coauthoring has not yet achieved such acceptance. The past MLA president Linda Hutcheon, who herself worked collaboratively on a variety of projects, has become well known for her promotion of collaborative work in academia. She notes:

> Outside the rhetoric and composition world—where collaborative *pedagogy*, at least, has become a norm—we have lacked such a model. As a profession, we have developed instead a model of the humanities researcher as, to cite Jonathan Arac, "the figure of the creator, treated as a distinctive, single, isolated individual," not unlike the Romantic genius.
>
> ("Presidential Address" 524)

Hutcheon argues that we should not try to be Romantic geniuses in our scholarship; rather, we should collaborate, drawing on one another's strengths. The standard academic model of the single author is adversarial by nature, because we are conditioned to attack one another rather than help one another, even as we recognize the potential benefits of working together. "Arguing is easy," she claims; "constructive engagement is harder" ("Creative Collaboration" 5). Hutcheon's works challenge scholars in academia to "explore—and enact—the possibility of positive alternatives to this adversarial vision of the academy" (4–5), but only a few scholars have accepted or acted on this challenge.

Ede and Lunsford, who in a variety of books and papers on the subject are among those few, note the double standard in academia today: we encourage collaboration in teaching and even through collaborative writing projects, yet we fail to recognize the value of collaborative scholarship. They emphasize:

> Whether one is an undergraduate hoping to do well in a class, an assistant professor working to meet explicit and implicit criteria for tenure and promotion, or a senior faculty member striving to gain national recognition for his or her scholarly work, everyday practices in the humanities continue to ignore, or even to punish, collaboration while authorizing work attributed to ... individuals.

They go on to claim that regardless of what we do, it is more how we do it that matters: "success in the academy depends largely on having one's work recognized as an individual accomplishment" ("Collaboration" 357).

Although some academics have promoted and encouraged collaboration, it remains relatively disregarded in scholarly publications in our departments. A recent MLA report highlights the disconnect between the growing practice of coauthoring and its lack of scholarly recognition. The report calls for "a broad, intellectually driven approach to teaching language and culture in higher education" (MLA 1), requiring "sustained collaboration among all members of the teaching corps" (6).

To Collaborate or Not to Collaborate: Challenges

Responsibility and Credit in Collaborative Works

In the field of applied linguistics, there is no established convention for working together or for listing coauthors, nor is there an established way to determine who receives the credit for a coauthored piece (Long). From this uncertainty, problems arise: for example, one author may not do his or her share of the work, or the issue of proprietorship may surface—one author may feel that because she or he came up with the idea, she or he deserves more credit than her or his coauthors.

How authorship is listed in a publication is not consistent. Some authors prefer to rotate the order of their names; others prefer an alphabetical listing; others use notes to indicate roles. Some publications put the person who initiated the paper in the first position, but in some social science labs the main author is listed at the end. The preposition *with* may indicate a lesser contribution. Finally, when coauthoring involves differences in rank or power (senior vs. junior faculty members, faculty members vs. students), it is often difficult to determine the extent of contribution to the work by different parties. There have been cases where the person of lesser rank or power does a significant part of the work without receiving due credit.

These issues become of paramount importance when it is time to evaluate faculty members for promotion, tenure, or merit pay. Because there is no established convention for the listing of authors and because coauthoring is still not accepted by many in the humanities, departments tend not to have any policy for evaluating a collaboration. This lack of formalized or consistent practices in departments can discourage collaborative work; it can also lead to conflicts or problems when colleagues are reviewed, especially junior colleagues.

Additional Considerations for Junior Faculty Members

Junior faculty members may benefit the most from coauthoring. They can build on collaborations and connections made during graduate school to form a new network of peers in their field. Coauthoring may increase the strength of their work, teach them valuable lessons through the writing process, and build their reputations as scholars. Further, they can benefit from working with more experienced colleagues, who serve as mentors. Janet Pérez mentions coauthoring as one of the key practices in which department chairs can engage to help their faculty members. She encourages chairs to coauthor articles with colleagues and points out that doctoral students in the sciences coauthor an average of six articles during their graduate careers. J. Chris Leach, Michael Loroz, Ronald W. Melicher, and Russel Wermers indicate that in finance "early-career coauthoring with a mentor can provide significantly increased later-career research output for a faculty member" (2). Whether working with peers or with senior colleagues, junior faculty members could use such collaboration to build on and expand their current research agendas, to network in their field, or to engage in a mutually beneficial mentoring relationship.

Coauthoring: The Norm or the Exception?

Clearly, coauthoring is not the norm in many fields of the humanities and is the norm in the sciences and social sciences. In many ways, the field of applied linguistics falls between the humanities, as it is often housed in language departments, and the social sciences, whose work it closely resembles in terms of data collection and analysis. The field continues to grow: language acquisition courses are gaining in popularity at the graduate and undergraduate levels, and more scholars are investigating issues related to language learning. The issue of how to approach, categorize, and credit coauthored work needs to be addressed in departmental policies sooner rather than later. A first necessary step in helping departments establish such policies is to examine the facts.

That coauthoring in applied linguistics studies is increasingly prevalent in practice and publications is confirmed by an examination of the primary journals and organizations in the field.

We chose ten top journals in applied linguistics for analysis to determine precisely what role collaboration plays in their publications. Our choice was based primarily on Udo Jung's analysis of the top language learning and teaching journals, using such criteria as whether a work breaks new

TABLE 1
PERCENTAGE OF COAUTHORED ARTICLES, BY YEAR

Journal	2000	2001	2002	2003	2004	2005	2006	Average
Applied Linguistics	21	33	41	41	47	25	38	35
CALICO Journal	50	33	43	38	55	32	52	42
Canadian Modern Language Review	41	40	36	18	55	52	33	40
Foreign Language Annals	33	35	28	22	54	25	31	33
International Review of Applied Linguistics	26	42	6	35	48	29	25	31
Language Learning	57	48	67	55	47	64	32	51
Language Learning and Technology	23	30	42	36	46	40	25	35
Modern Language Journal	38	40	50	36	37	29	37	38
Studies in Second Language Acquisition	24	50	19	29	40	37	72	37
System	46	34	26	36	56	47	41	41
Average percentage	36	39	36	35	49	38	39	38

ground, reports important research findings, and presents new methods and materials. But our survey added journals for English as a second language (ESL), foreign languages, and technology in language learning (a growing field that should also be recognized). On our final list, these ten journals were consulted: *Applied Linguistics, CALICO Journal, Canadian Modern Language Review, Foreign Language Annals, International Review of Applied Linguistics, Language Learning, Language Learning and Technology, Modern Language Journal, Studies in Second Language Acquisition,* and *System.*

In each of these journals, we counted the number of articles published each year from 2000 to 2006 (articles included responses but not book reviews or editorial introductions to specialissues), then calculated what percentage of them were written by two or more authors. Table 1 displays these percentages by year for each of the journals investigated; figure 1 presents the data visually.

A number of interesting observations emerge from this exercise. Over the seven-year period the lowest rate of coauthored publications was still about one-third of the total number of publications (*International Review of Applied Linguistics*), while many journals ranged considerably higher,

FIGURE 1
AVERAGE PERCENTAGE OF COAUTHORED ARTICLES, 2000–06,
BY JOURNAL

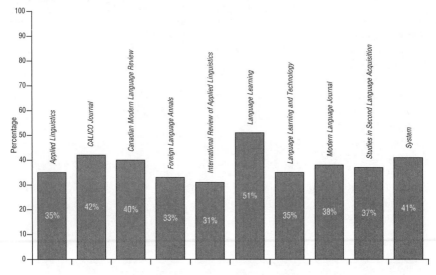

topping out at over 50% (*Language Learning*). These averages indicate that coauthoring is fairly common in applied linguistics scholarly outlets.

To see if there was any trend in coauthoring over those years, we also looked at the averages for each year (fig. 2). There is no clear pattern of increase or decrease in coauthorship. The overall average remains consistent: between 35% and 40% of all articles published in these journals come from collaborative authors. (It would be interesting to compare these averages with those from the 1980s and 1990s, as we suspect there was a steady increase in collaboration then.) Many factors can contribute to variation— for example, the spike in 2004, when 49% of all articles were coauthored, might have resulted from the topics covered in special issues. Or it might have been pure coincidence. It is perhaps not valuable, therefore, to examine a particular year. Overall, there is a strong presence in these top-rated applied linguistics journals of collaborative work. As Sally Magnan, past editor of the *Modern Language Journal* notes:

> In SLA research, we have relied on coauthorship for some time now. For example, in the *Modern Language Journal*, which I edited for fourteen years, it is now more common to find coauthors or multiple-author teams than it is to find articles by single authors. This trend developed steadily over my editorship, in line with the growing interdisciplinary nature of research. (152)

FIGURE 2
AVERAGE PERCENTAGE OF COAUTHORED ARTICLES, BY YEAR

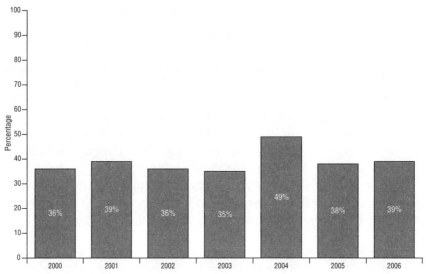

CONCLUSIONS AND RECOMMENDATIONS

Although applied linguistics scholars recognize the benefits of collaborative endeavor, there continues to be a lack of official policy regarding coauthored work, not only in departments and universities but also in the very organizations that promote applied linguistic research. Clearly, this is an issue that must be addressed, but the question is where to begin.

Considerations for Faculty Members Interested in Coauthoring

Collaboration with one or more authors certainly has its advantages. First, it may be necessary to team up with someone who has expertise that you do not. This type of collaboration is slowly gaining popularity in the humanities:

> [T]oday many important and exciting research projects in the humanities . . . simply cannot be carried out by a solitary . . . scholar. What has become a commonplace for many in the natural and social sciences— scholars in physics and political science, for instance, carry out almost all their research as part of groups or teams—is now a feature of work across the humanities. (Ede and Lunsford, "Collaboration" 361)

Collaboration can also provide scholars with a larger pool for data (from different languages, levels, types of institutions) and easier entry into a particular field for data collection. An applied linguist conducting research on an aspect of language variation may want to look at this construct across several languages, levels, and institutions. Having one or more collaborators could not only reduce the length of time for data collection and analysis but also make the project more interesting because it is broader.

Collaboration demonstrates one's ability to work with others, as it involves both cooperation and compromise. Two scholars coming together to share knowledge keep each other accountable for errors, provide an additional lens through which to examine data, and together accomplish the task more efficiently. There is less ego involvement, since the work and ideas are shared. Finally, coauthoring can be personally satisfying: one learns more, one grows more as a scholar.

Coauthorship does present challenges. If the authors do not have complementary skills, their collaboration and the finished product may be weak. They may have very different working styles or habits:

> The dynamics of any collaborative research will be affected by a number of differences. . . . [P]ersonal preferences shaped by ideologies of the autonomous author will continue to make solitary scholarship and single-author publication seem the natural choice to many. . . . [L]ogistics are far from inconsequential: the seemingly simple paperwork requirements for a large collaborative project can daunt the most enthusiastic group member. (Ede and Lunsford, "Collaboration" 363)

While one author may thrive on down-to-the-wire creativity and writing, the other may prefer consistent writing over a longer period of time. Also, writing with others may be difficult when one has a particular writing style: "Of the many other challenges to collaboration and concepts of multiple authorship, questions of methodology and style stand out as particularly problematic as well as potentially productive" (364). There are also issues of responsibility: how to determine who will be accountable for which task in a project.

Coauthoring is not suitable for every person or every project. Often, contrary to popular assumption, it results in more rather than less work for each author. The choice of collaborator is of foremost importance. Fruitful coauthoring requires complementary skills (Stafford-Yilmaz and Zwier) rather than skills that will conflict or compete. It is also imperative that coauthors be able to work together in terms of personality. Once the project and coauthors are established, it should be determined early on who will do what and when and how the revision process will proceed. Constant contact, by e-mail, telephone, and meetings, is necessary. The last key to collaboration is the willingness to collaborate, because coauthoring often requires more revision, more rethinking, more critical examination of one's work than sole authoring does. The product may be stronger in the end, but the process may be more difficult.

Faculty members who consider engaging in collaborative work should also have published some single-authored works, to show their ability. And they should be prepared to educate colleagues and supervisors as to the complexities and issues involved in coauthorship.

Considerations for Departments

Department chairs and promotion committees can be daunted by the prospect of evaluating a colleague's collaborative work. It is especially difficult to judge a coauthored work when the coauthor works in a field with which the chair or committee members are unfamiliar. Coauthoring, at least for now, remains highly reflective of field—as evidenced, for example, by the difference in rates of coauthorship between literature and applied linguistics. Even subfields vary in the degree to which coauthoring is accepted. Technology-related language acquisition studies, for example, lend themselves more naturally to collaborative endeavor.

There are ways to evaluate a faculty member's coauthored work. One can examine the journals in which such works appear, to see if the coauthorship is typical or not of the field. It can be helpful to ask the faculty member to explain or describe the role that she or he played in the collaboration process. (A word of warning, though: in many cases of collaboration, it may be hard to tease apart different roles and tasks, as the whole project is generated from brainstorming and evolves in true partnership at every step of the way.) It may be useful to see how the authors are listed on the publication. Sometimes there are notes explaining why authors are listed in a particular order. One should consider with whom the faculty member does most of his or her collaboration. Coauthoring with peers often is a sign of equal contribution; coauthoring with a senior faculty member or graduate student can be a sign of lesser or greater contribution and responsibility for the work.

The discussion and data presented here apply to a small proportion of work in applied linguistics, which is a small proportion of work in linguistics in general. As a starting point, however, they point strongly to the popularity and effectiveness of collaborative efforts among colleagues. As departments and organizations begin to recognize the value of coauthorship and establish policies for evaluating such work, more faculty members can begin to engage in these fruitful collaborations.

NOTES

1. The term *applied linguistics* does not enjoy an easy or accepted definition among those in this and related fields. It is well beyond our scope or intention to attempt a definition of what applied linguistics is and encompasses. For the purposes of this paper, we mean the primary current interpretation of the term: a focus on the investigation of language acquisition, in both learning and teaching. Our intention is not to ignore or slight fields such as sociolinguistics, language variation, translation and interpretation, lexicography (in which coauthoring is indeed quite common as well) but rather to delimit our investigation so that it is a manageable and logical one. We encourage researchers in related fields to carry out their own investigations of coauthoring, in order to supplement the information provided here.

2. From this point forward, for the sake of simplicity, we use the term *coauthor* to refer to authoring by two or more authors.

WORKS CITED

The ACS Style Guide: Effective Communication of Scientific Information. 3rd ed. Ed. Anne M. Coghill and Lorrin R. Garson. New York: Oxford UP, 2006. Print.

Ede, Lisa, and Andrea Lunsford. "Collaboration and Concepts of Authorship." *PMLA* 116.2 (2001): 354–69. Print.

———. "Why Write Together?" *Rhetoric Review* 1.2 (1983): 150–57. Print.

Hutcheon, Linda. "Creative Collaboration: Alternatives to the Adversarial Academy." *Profession* (2001): 4–6. Print.

———. "Presidential Address 2000: She Do the President in Different Voices." *PMLA* 116.3 (2001): 518–30. Print.

Inge, M. Thomas. "Collaboration and Concepts of Authorship." *PMLA* 116.3 (2001): 523–630. Print.

Jung, Udo O. H. "Paris in London Revisited or the Foreign Language Teacher's Topmost Journals." *System* 32.3 (2004): 357–61. Print.

Katz, Stacey, and Johanna Watzinger-Tharp. "Toward an Understanding of the Role of Applied Linguists in Foreign Language Departments." *Modern Language Journal* 89.4 (2005): 490–502. Print.

Kramsch, Claire. "Second Language Acquisition, Applied Linguistics, and the Teaching of Foreign Languages." *Modern Language Journal* 84.3 (2000): 311–26. Print.

Laird, Holly. "A Hand Spills from the Book's Threshold: Coauthorship's Readers." *PMLA* 116.2 (2001): 344–53. Print.

Leach, J. Chris, Michael Loroz, Ronald W. Melicher, and Russel Wermers. *Research Productivity in Finance Academia: Mentoring versus Peer Coauthorship.* U of Colorado, 2007. Web. 14 Mar. 2008.

Long, Sheri Spaine. "Editor's Message: Do We Value Collaborative Scholarship?" *Foreign Language Annals* 40.4 (2007): 567. Print.

Magnan, Sally. "The Promise of Digital Scholarship in SLA Research and Language Pedagogy." *Language Learning and Technology* 11.3 (2007): 152–55. Print.

MLA Ad Hoc Committee on Foreign Languages. *Foreign Languages and Higher Education: New Structures for a Changed World. Modern Language Association.* MLA, May 2007. Web. 14 Mar. 2008.

Pérez, Janet. "The Proactive Mentor: Suggested Strategies." *ADFL Bulletin* 24.2 (1993): 39–44. Print.

Scientific Style and Format: The CSE Manual for Authors, Editors, and Publishers. 7th ed. New York: Rockefeller UP, 2006. Print.

Stafford-Yilmaz, Lynn, and Larry Zwier. "Coauthoring from the Horses' Mouths." *TESOL Matters* 13.4 (2003): n. pag. Web. 14 Mar. 2008.

Stillinger, Jack. *Multiple Authorship and the Myth of Solitary Genius*. New York: Oxford UP, 1991. Print.

VanPatten, Bill. "What Is Second Language Acquisition and What Is It Doing in This Department?" *ADFL Bulletin* 30.3 (1999): 49–53. Print.

New Alignments, New Discourses

KARIN C. RYDING

The report of the MLA Ad Hoc Committee on Foreign Languages touches on a number of issues in foreign language teaching today from several perspectives: logistical, paradigmatic, curricular, and administrative. In that report, committee members were at pains not to single out any language in particular, even though the situations for Spanish and for less commonly taught languages (LCTLs) differ greatly. Evidently, the report has resonated with language professionals across the country, because it touches on knotty, core issues that every foreign language department faces but that are rarely discussed outside departmental boundaries.

By convening this committee, the Modern Language Association took a key step in approaching three substantive ideological divides: between language and literature, between traditional academic curricula and government programs, and between the worlds of teaching and research. Each of these divides has its own history, its own advocates, its own critics, and its own inertia, heavily weighted down by the legacy of past practice and discipline-fed mythology.

The ad hoc committee's report and its recommendations show a shift of attention and intent on the part of the MLA leadership to reexamine goals and curricula, to assess the impact and implications of global security issues on language and culture teaching, and to realign itself with other professional and advocacy groups for an agenda that is both short-term and long-term, academic and public. The report aims to stimulate experimentation with new curricular models that go beyond national security

The author is Sultan Qaboos bin Said Professor of Arabic at Georgetown University.

priorities; that build on a broad, intellectually driven base; that are highly visible; and that fortify our fields across the board.

I would like to address some issues faced by Arabic in particular and other LCTLs in general, both from the point of view of rising demand for these languages and from the point of view of how they and their cultural traditions fit (or don't fit) into traditional language and literature departments. Has the impact of expanded hiring in critical languages such as Chinese, Persian, Urdu, Korean, and Arabic had a jarring or constructive effect on these departments? Has it had any effect on them? Except for profound and extensive diglossia, the problems that confront Arabic aren't unique, but these and other problems have risen to salience because of the urgency with which they need to be addressed and resolved.

Journalists, lobbyists, military officers, and government officials all want to know what the short-term solution is to ramping-up problems, not the long-term solution, and the answer I have to give is that there is no short-term solution; there are only short-term measures, which are partial at best and ineffective at worst. The short-term measures are even misleading in some respects because although they provide a quick fix (a teacher in a classroom, for example), they disguise a lack of quality, of well-designed curricula, of materials, and of professional experience or expertise.

For long-term purposes and to ensure high-quality academic programs, federal and other funding is needed to address crucial shortcomings in research and publication on issues directly related to individual LCTLs, especially those outside the Indo-European language family. In high-context cultures such as Arabic, there is a need not only for sustained, in-depth, professional discourse research and analysis but also for the translation of that analysis into effective and multifaceted classroom learning resources.

To illustrate this need, it is recognized that Arabic speakers function in a continuum of linguistic competence that encompasses an extensive range of performance. They calibrate their linguistic interactions according to a number of sociolinguistic factors, including the formality of a situation, the location of a situation, and the people involved in it. This range of competence is of course acquired over a long period of time that includes both formal and informal learning experiences. To aim for communicative competence close to that of an educated native speaker in Arabic means that the goals are complex in ways unparalleled in most other languages. This complexity is one reason that Arabic is classified by the Department of State as being in category 3 of languages, "superhard," languages "that are exceptionally difficult for native English speakers" ("Language Learning Difficulty").[1] Arabic is the only Semitic language in this category; the other members of the small superhard category are Cantonese, Mandarin Chinese, Japanese, and Korean. Arabic is superhard essentially because of diglossia, the existence of two (at least) distinct varieties of a language, one specialized for everyday interaction and the other for more formal purposes, including writing.[2]

Everyday Arabic vernaculars are a form of primary discourse; they are acquired as mother tongues and used in all informal settings and situations. The more formal level is a form of secondary discourse, reserved in the Arab world for reading and writing, for scripted discourse, and for professional and academic functions.[3] It is this formal level of language that is taught as Modern Standard Arabic to learners of Arabic in virtually every case. Therefore, whereas Heidi Byrnes has noted a particular privileging of primary discourses in the teaching of European languages (49), I have identified what I call "reverse privileging" of traditional Arabic in foreign language classrooms: the narrow focus on written and formal Arabic at the expense of communicative skills in Arabic vernacular discourse ("Teaching" 16). This exclusive focus on secondary discourse has left the field with many discouraged, disabled, and disappointed students who never feel at home in ordinary spoken Arabic situations even though they can read at advanced levels. There is therefore a great deal to be done in terms of legitimizing the teaching of spoken Arabic vernaculars, as well as in funding and guiding the linguistic research that must underpin the development of effective classroom materials and approaches.

In terms of faculty and departmental organization, despite the pressing need for qualified and highly trained LCTL faculty members, I have seen little change in the structure, values, or goals of academic departments. Frankly, the two-tier system of foreign language instructors on one level and literary specialists, linguistics specialists, or area specialists on another is well and thriving. I think change in Middle Eastern language departments may come even more slowly than change in departments focused on Western languages—for many reasons, not the least of which is the covert but widely shared orientalist suspicion that too extensive or too profound an understanding of the other culture will cause learners to go native, an academic and also diplomatic taboo that one transgresses at the price of social and professional exclusion or even ostracism.

Inasmuch as there is now extraordinary demand for professional Arabic specialists, our lives and fields have changed dramatically. These days, everyone who gets a master's or PhD in Arabic literature or linguistics has many job offers. Academic, government, consulting, intelligence, and military positions abound. In a way, we could keep on doing the same old thing and still have plenty of demand for our expertise and services.

Yet we have an opportunity here to expand and improve the universe of discourse between East and West, to examine carefully and objectively the deep tensions between the Arab world and the West by acknowledging the richly textual culture of the Arab world; its imperial legacies; its literary heritage; its sacred texts; its pioneering efforts in medicine, science, linguistic analysis, and mathematics; and the way that these key medieval narratives have constructed a vast cultural terrain that underlies the reference knowledge of every native speaker. A shift to the examination of non-canonical texts, even in the medieval period, would enrich and enlarge our understanding of the Arab world. We can also imagine other types of shift that would radically alter our way of looking at contemporary Arabic by revaluing and including elements of popular culture, which would mean that academic programs would have to deal seriously and thoroughly with the world of colloquial Arabic, still a strong taboo. As a high-context culture, the world of everyday embedded Arab cultural practices, knowledges, norms, institutions, ethics, and values is truly teachable only if we include a network of quotidian signifying practices: written, drawn, built, chanted, broadcast, spoken, woven, carved, designed, sung.

Perhaps the time has come for us to interrogate our choices and experiment with our definitions of objects of cultural and linguistic study. Approaches to understanding the Arab world and foregrounding a new critical practice would benefit from re-visioning and redefining the textual cultures of different periods, the multiple paths of symbolic production, and the role of neglected discourses in what Michael Holquist calls "the dense particularity of our everyday lives" (xix).

NOTES

1. Until recently there were four categories, and Arabic was classified as a category 4 language. This system has been revised into the three-tier system.

2. Hebrew, which shares many features with Arabic, is a category 2 language, classified as "hard"—"with significant linguistic and/or cultural differences from English," but not superhard ("Language Learning Difficulty"). For further discussion of diglossia and the teaching of Arabic, see Alosh; Al-Batal; and Ryding, "Proficiency," "Discourse," and "Teaching."

3. Many intermediate levels exist between the acrolect, or most formal language, and the basilects, the most informal spoken forms of Arabic. See my "Educated Arabic" for bibliography and discussion.

WORKS CITED

Alosh, Mahdi. "Arabic Diglossia and Its Impact on Teaching Arabic as a Foreign Language." *International Perspectives on Foreign Language Teaching*. Ed. G. L. Ervin. Lincoln: Natl. Textbook, 1991. 121–37. Print.

Batal, Mahmoud al-. "Diglossia Proficiency: The Need for an Alternative Approach to Teaching." *The Arabic Language in America*. Ed. Aleya Rouchdy. Detroit: Wayne State UP, 1992. 284–304. Print.

Byrnes, Heidi. "Toward Academic-Level Foreign Language Abilities: Reconsidering Foundational Assumptions, Expanding Pedagogical Options." *Developing Professional-Level Language Proficiency*. Ed. Betty Lou Leaver and Boris Shekhtman. Cambridge: Cambridge UP, 2002. 34–58. Print.

Holquist, Michael. Introduction. *The Dialogic Imagination: Four Essays*. By M. M. Bakhtin. Ed. Holquist. Trans. Caryl Emerson and Holquist. Austin: U of Texas P, 1981. xv–xxxiv. Print.

"Language Learning Difficulty for English Speakers." *Languages of the World*. Natl. Virtual Translation Center. 2007. Web. 24 June 2008.

Ryding, Karin. "Discourse Competence in TAFL: Skill Levels and Choice of Language Variety in the Arabic Classroom." *The Teaching of Arabic as a Foreign Language*. Ed. Mahmoud al-Batal. Provo: Amer. Assn. of Teachers of Arabic, 1995. 223–31. Print.

———. "Educated Arabic." *Encyclopedia of Arabic Language and Linguistics*. Vol. 1. Leiden: Brill, 2005. Print.

———. "Proficiency despite Diglossia: A New Approach for Arabic." *Modern Language Journal* 75.2 (1991): 212–18. Print.

———. "Teaching Arabic in the United States." *Handbook for Arabic Language Teaching Professionals in the Twenty-First Century*. Ed. Kassem Wahba, Zeinab Taha, and Liz England. Mahwah: Erlbaum, 2006. 13–20. Print.

Literature? C'est un monde: The Foreign Language Curriculum in the Wake of the MLA Report

NICOLETTA PIREDDU

Since its publication, the report of the MLA Ad Hoc Committee on Foreign Languages, "Foreign Languages and Higher Education: New Structures for a Changed World," has made me meditate on various academic issues, but my real-life epiphany occurred a few months ago, when I attended a pre-K–8 school open house. The principal, who was illustrating the school's radical curricular revisions, shared with his audience the dilemma that plagued him during the restructuring of his program: Would it be moral to fragment the students' daily schedule even more by adding a foreign language requirement? Despite its avowed dedication to outstanding literacy and, needless to say, to diversity of all sorts, not to mention the need to prepare new generations for a multicultural, global world, the school ultimately chose to remain faithful to a monolingualist ideology. Ironically, two days later, while waiting at the doctor's office, I found in a 2007 issue of *U.S. News and World Report* an article that discussed the Pentagon's deployment of civilian anthropologists "to help understand Iraq's 'human terrain'" (Mulrine). Recruited by the military as cultural analysts, these social scientists provide troops with observations about the complex local dynamics of Iraqi society, its symbols, and its relation with power players, which are then translated "into action for soldiers" (36).

There I was, confronted with two extreme manifestations of what the MLA report defines as the "instrumentalist" view of language and culture

The author is associate professor of Italian and comparative literature and director of the Comparative Literature Program at Georgetown University.

(235). On the one hand, a narrow conception of foreign idioms as mere communicative tools, so limited in scope that they can be easily sacrificed in favor of other activities and expressive means allegedly endowed with higher educational value—practicing hand bells, for instance. On the other hand, a clear understanding of the usefulness of translingual and transcultural competencies, co-opted, however, for strategic intelligence purposes.

In the face of such examples, which are anything but isolated cases, it is unquestionable that we, as academic educators in foreignness, can and have to play a pivotal role in supporting what, at the opposite end of the spectrum, the MLA report presents as the "constitutive aspect of language" (236). By combining advanced expressive competencies and profound cultural awareness, language as a "complex multifunctional phenomenon" (235) can foster understanding of self and other and offer tools to resist reductive or aberrant instrumentalizations. But how do we persuade students to come to us in order to acquire that expertise? With its suggestions for curricular and institutional change, the report promises to keep the academic debate on the mission of language departments in higher education alive and kicking for quite a while.

The report's reflections and recommendations regarding the present and future of foreign language teaching are in line with a wider pedagogical and scholarly reconceptualization of the humanities, from the proposal to rename the field of comparative literature as comparative cultural studies to the self-examination of English departments about the role of linguistic competencies—written and oral, literary and more broadly cultural—in the undergraduate curriculum of the third millennium. We have long accepted that an approach to literature as the quintessence of Arnoldian sweetness and light is history. The curricula of many foreign language departments and the scholarship of numerous faculty members already reflect the radical changes brought about by the advent of cultural studies, as the report also observes (237). Therefore a systematic commitment to a broader notion of cultural literacy in the entire foreign language sector is sensible, provided that individual academic institutions do not implement the report's call for transformation only as a pragmatic response to short-term needs (like the government's fixation on certain foreign languages as weapons to get to know the enemy) or as expressions of ephemeral fashions.

At the same time, the flaws that have been ascribed to the cultural studies approach can work as caveats for a scenario that looms in the report— namely, the risk of building a pop foreign language undergraduate major that teaches everything and nothing, devoid of a precise focus and of methodological rigor. I endorse the idea that literature should constitute not a single but one of the discourses in the undergraduate foreign language curriculum (a comparatist myself, I have happily occupied the translingual and transcultural territory since my undergraduate days). Yet I believe we should prevent literature from becoming the Cinderella in the cluster of disciplines that are summoned to contribute to the new integrative approach to the major. I am not saying this to reinstate the rigid two-tier language-versus-literature system we inherited.

In an ideal academic world, blessed by the perfect synergy of administrative support, interdisciplinary collaboration, departmental restructuring, and individual faculty members' innovative pedagogical and scholarly practices, the programs envisioned by the MLA report could successfully develop a variety of cultural contents and approaches while preserving each professor's areas of specialization and following precise goals set by the faculty as a whole. In more realistic frameworks, however, the foreign language major might turn into a bad copy of an area studies program, in which jack-of-all-trades educators offer a bit of everything, sacrificing coherence and depth in the name of an illusory extensiveness: a touch of history here, a pinch of geography there, a bit of politics, some literature—possibly contemporary and noncanonical texts so as to appear more progressive—a fleeting look at cinema, art, religion, society, and a taste of food. In other words, a program that, precisely for its lack of a well-defined identity or intellectual rationale, could be housed in any academic unit, offering administrators a tempting pretext to dismember us. The danger haunting this allegedly wide-ranging and flexible model of education in institutions with limited resources or different priorities is hence a certain banalization of the curriculum, which may backfire precisely against the expectation that foreign language departments will lead the way in this transformation.

As we redesign our course contents in the wider cultural and cross-cultural context suggested by the report, let us keep in mind that we can gain even more in this new configuration by preserving the centrality of the literary text and highlighting its specific dynamics, capitalizing on the skills that we can export from literary analysis to other disciplinary areas. Instead of apologizing for the nature of our knowhow, trying to ascribe value to a supposedly ineffectual literature through other disciplines that we often perceive as stronger and more respectable, we (just as our colleagues in English departments) should present our discipline as able to throw light on other cultural phenomena, as the forge of messages and interpretive strategies that modify or even create those adopted in other areas.

Like all that belongs to the aesthetic rather than to the practical realm, literature too often seems a curricular luxury, a surplus with maintenance costs that, especially in periods of shrinking budgets, are considered less and less justifiable. Yet we should defend this apparently superfluous educational wealth without either enclosing it in a vacuum or excessively diluting it in a disciplinary melting pot. I would apply to literature the observations that a character in Henry James's *The Ambassadors*, Chad, makes about the great force of the new art of advertising: It is "infinite like all the arts. . . . In the hands, naturally, of a master. . . . With the right man to work it *c'est un monde*" (359). A literary text itself is a world. Students should rediscover it not as a self-contained enclave but as the center of an interdisciplinary network connecting individual feelings, collective drives, historical reasons, geographic contexts, social issues, ideologies, all of them transfigured through a sophisticated and imaginative use of language. And we—to evoke James once again—are the right men (and women), the masters, to make it work as such and to help students draw from it fundamental competencies that are crucial to a wide spectrum of academic units and professions.

If the language specialists envisioned by the MLA's report are expected to make an active, receptive, and creative use of language (see Saussy), it is literature more than any other sectorial discipline that, as it conveys content, calls attention to language and fosters critical thinking and inventiveness. The training in discourse analysis, writing, and expository skills and the art of effective and creative argumentation that we can offer students are at least as exportable and useful as any other, more applied expertise. We can enrich our students' reading and interpretive adventure if we teach students not simply to treat the literary text as a cultural phenomenon but also to analyze cultural phenomena as texts, reading their lines but also between the lines, with rigorous and well-defined tools.

Professional retooling in any job is at once a challenge and an opportunity. I think we have to be open to this translingual and transcultural turn but not attempt to transform ourselves into eclectic Renaissance men and women under the illusion of our limitless capacity for development and credibility. We should resist the pressure to tailor curricula to the alleged tastes and expectations of undergraduates at large in the hope of stealing a few students from other departments or of retaining a couple of not-too-committed majors. The danger of this strategy is the creation of a simplistic, although apparently more appealing, course of study that is in fact quite distant from the "deep cultural knowledge" that the MLA report recommends (236). With that kind of outcome we will fail to gain the respect of other academic units and above all of our own pool of customers who are interested in acquiring valuable and measurable expertise of some sort.

Perhaps—why not—we should also try to reeducate students (who sometimes choose a foreign-language major with the idea that it will be less demanding than other sectors of the humanities) and require some retooling of them so that, with careful mentoring, they can strike a balance in their academic experience between practical training and intellectual investigation for its own sake. Experience has taught me that students' preferences are not so homogeneous and predictable as we might think; students do not always lean toward more applied material. In several of my interdisciplinary courses, they have sometimes explicitly asked for more literary content, precisely because they wish to be exposed to materials and approaches that they would not get in other academic units. I have students who, from other undergraduate majors and even from the law school, come back to my classes to read, write, and talk about literature, to compensate for the too matter-of-fact and unimaginative nature of their specialization and to keep alive a certain analytic frame of mind and humanistic background that they consider fundamental for a well-rounded education but also for their more practical career goals. There must be some truth in what we hear is the increasing demand for philosophy and humanities graduates for jobs in business and management.

Although I am not implying that these represent the priorities of most students, I feel we should not neglect interests and choices of that kind by throwing the (literary) baby out of the (cultural) bathwater. In this respect, it is ironic to find, in the same issue of *Profession* where the MLA report was published, an article by Jane Gallop and one by James F. Slevin, both addressing the losses that literary studies have undergone by making too many concessions to nonliterary fields. While the MLA report is asking the foreign language major to dethrone literature in some way, Gallop highlights the paradox, in English studies, of the shift from the New Critical heritage to new historicism and cultural studies. "While the move to understand literature within culture is theoretically good," she writes, "the problem is that we generally don't do cultural history nearly as well as our colleagues in history departments, who have professional training in historical methods. We have become amateur, or rather wannabe, cultural historians." At the same time, she adds, English has given up "the most valuable thing," which transformed scholars "from cultured gentlemen into a profession: close reading." Her point is that, without trying to resurrect the New Critical ideology from which close reading emerged, the practice this reading technique allows us to gain with literary texts in literature classes is a powerful and "widely applicable skill, of value not just to scholars in other disciplines but to a wide range of students with many different futures" (183). We may add that precisely because it forces us to pay attention to details and to substantiate our observations with specific evidence, close reading helps us avoid generalizations and reflect on those "differences in meaning, mentality, and worldview" that the MLA report underscores as the objective of a reconceptualized foreign language education (238).

Likewise, in his defense of academic literacy as "the most crucial work" of the discipline of English, which is also a call for "a greater public understanding . . . of what humanistic inquiry is" (200, 203), Slevin reminds us that, despite "our radically expanded conception of studiable cultural texts," English "is fundamentally an interpretive discipline grounded in close reading of how language works in art, in discourse more generally, and in the world understood as knowable in part through the mediating force of cultural objects" (206).

I think that departments of foreign languages and literatures can play a complementary role to the English departments' "complex work of inquiry and critical exchange" (Slevin 203) by not disavowing the value of how the foreign language discipline teaches in order to unrealistically overstretch its contents and competencies. The alliances that the MLA report suggests be forged with other departments have already led, in many universities, to solid collaboration for general education humanities and writing courses. This kind of synergy is convenient to English, because it helps English professors manage their usually massive enrollments; it is equally beneficial to foreign language units, allowing them to escape their isolation and to introduce elements of their cultures well beyond the major. As we know, however, reaching out with courses in English is a blessing and a curse for a foreign language major program. The price to pay for more visibility is a weakening of the language component. To strike a balance between these two poles, a transformed foreign language academic program might offer—and encourage majors to take—comparative and interdisciplinary collaborative courses as electives[1] and add to their elective basket courses offered in English by other departments (history, economics, art history, government) on topics that are related to the foreign country whose language they are learning and that reflect students' specific interests.

By relying on external specialists, we would jettison the hubristic assumption of an exhaustive and solid cultural and transcultural formation within our departmental walls and at the same time preserve the foreign language through the entire four-year major. I fully endorse the MLA report's insistence on the need to strengthen foreign language competence at the undergraduate and graduate levels as well as throughout the spectrum of academic disciplines in the humanities and social sciences (242). We need to offer intensive undergraduate language courses, teach upper-division courses in the target language, and integrate classroom study with a meaningful study-abroad experience. Furthermore, we are asked to equip students with both sophisticated training and tangible skills; we should give them clear signals regarding the demands at stake in the language learning process. Often their language performance (especially written) is paradoxically better in grammar classes than in upper-division courses that emphasize literature or culture, not simply because of the increasing complexity of the material but also because of the tacit supposition that students' ideas matter to teachers more than their expressive skills and that the grade will reflect this hierarchy, overlooking grammatical, syntactic, and stylistic flaws. If we really wish to ensure "language to the end"—as Haun Saussy, a member of the ad hoc committee, synthesizes one of the objectives of the restructured undergraduate language major, namely, the central and active presence of the foreign language throughout the curriculum, up to fourth-year courses—it is worthwhile clarifying standards and enforcing rules more rigorously instead of favoring, perhaps unwittingly, a dangerous downward leveling for fear of losing majors.[2]

While of course we must do our best to respect our students' thoughts, we would do students a disservice by not encouraging them to obtain the accuracy and maturity expected of educated near-native language users. To foster "deep translingual and transcultural competence" by bolstering "the ability to operate between languages," as the MLA report recommends, does not mean diminishing the value of advanced language training; rather, it makes that training an integral component of this new, expanded target—the creation of "informed and capable interlocutors" (237) who, in addition to interacting proficiently in the target language with educated native speakers, can relate to the foreign culture and simultaneously meditate on their own national tradition. Therefore, a fortiori, precisely because so much is now involved in language learning, it becomes of paramount importance to pursue the goal of advanced competence with renewed pedagogical tools, even if—as the MLA report observes—it is rarely attainable (237). To borrow a Machiavellian simile, the foreign language educator who aspires to produce graduates with near-native proficiency but must accept the lesser goal of teaching students to speak a foreign language well enough to get by should act like the clever archers mentioned in *The Prince*. Determined to hit a target that appears too distant and aware of the limited strength of their bows, they "pongono la mira assai più alta che il loco destinato, non per aggiugnere con la loro freccia a tanta altezza, ma per potere, con lo aiuto di sì alta mira, pervenire al disegno loro" 'aim much higher than the destined place, not to reach such height with that arrow, but in order to be able to attain their design with the aid of such high aim' (51; 20).

Translation occupies a leading position among the pedagogical tools that can enhance linguistic rigor and creativity while foregrounding cultural awareness. The MLA report clearly urges the development of translation and interpretation programs. But, on a smaller scale, in my ideal foreign language transcultural curriculum I would insert a mandatory course on practices and theories of translation, revolving around texts taken from a variety of contexts (literary and nonliterary) yet also able to foster student reflection on the phenomenon of "carrying across"—across languages, cultures, identities, historical and geographic milieux, value systems, and ideologies.

Needless to say, the successful implementation of innovative educational strategies depends on an institutional commitment to recruiting language teaching personnel trained in and for the profession and not simply native speakers of the target language.[3] Making this commitment means putting an end to the paradoxical and rather perverse dynamics of an academic system that, after releasing a bountiful supply of graduate degrees in the discipline, too often responds to the demands of that discipline by not hiring its own products and preferring cheaper substitutes.

Only in this way can we really build solid and lasting joint ventures between language and literature faculty members. Because of the variety of language department configurations, I would leave to each department the choice of how to devise and implement this "shared educational mission" (MLA 241). However, be it a collaboration between expertises in the two fields or an intervention that is more directly pedagogical and mutual, constant dialogue and exchange on curricular matters, transcending monopolies and power struggles, are essential to the joint creation of a cogent four-year program that can ensure a verticality in linguistic, literary, and cultural competencies.

I happen to think that, far from increasing the popularity and the enrollment figures of a foreign language major, the weakening of the language component leads to the death of the culture altogether. This observation applies as much to the survival of BA programs as to the future of PhD graduates and faculty members. It is unfortunate that both at the MLA convention and at several other scholarly conferences in foreign literatures and languages most papers are delivered in English. Likewise, it would be refreshing and certainly beneficial to our profession to see more nonnative speakers (graduate students and professors alike) publish their research in the target language.

I hope that the MLA report will revamp the concept of defamiliarization, increasing the incentive to tackle a different language and culture as complex living entities that force us to open up to otherness, crossing borders to foreignize ourselves.[4] On that note, I conclude with a quotation from a very translingual and transcultural Italian writer, Claudio Magris, which, in this context, I hope will sound not like an elegy to a defunct discipline but rather like an ode to its unlimited transformative power:

> La frontiera è duplice, ambigua; talora è un ponte per incontrare l'altro, talora una barriera per respingerlo. . . . [L]a letteratura, fra le altre cose, è pure un viaggio alla ricerca di sfatare questo mito dell'altra parte, per comprendere che ognuno si trova ora di qua ora di là—che ognuno, come in un mistero medievale, è l'Altro. (52)

> The border is twofold, ambiguous; sometimes it is a bridge to meet the other, sometimes a barrier to reject the other. . . . [L]iterature, among other things, is also a journey to try to debunk this myth of the other side, to understand that each of us is sometimes on this side and sometimes on the other—that each of us, as in a medieval mystery, is the Other.
>
> (my trans.)

NOTES

A shorter version of this essay was presented at the conference Fostering Translingual and Transcultural Competencies at Georgetown University, 24 April 2008. I am grateful to Serafina Hager, convenor of the Faculty of Languages and Linguistics at Georgetown University and chair of the Italian department, for offering me the opportunity to contribute to this event. I wish to thank Rosemary Feal and all my colleagues who attended the conference for their generous encouragement and insightful comments.

1. Resources permitting, the "credit-bearing discussion module in the target language" suggested in the report for interdisciplinary courses taught in English (239) is, ideally, an effective compromise between language skill enhancement and cross-cultural enrichment outside the foreign language major. I emphasize the resource constraints, however, because, in the real-life scenarios in which most of us operate, I am afraid not too many foreign language departments can afford to ask their staff systematically to maintain regular course offerings and simultaneously contribute to extradepartmental pedagogical venues. Few foreign language faculty members would be happy if, despite the best administrative intentions, supplementary discussion modules became for them a teaching overload without compensation of some sort.

2. Far from endorsing elitism per se, my observations on academic performance expectations in foreign languages and cultures take into account the current debates in United States secondary education about the need for more demanding high school curricula and in particular the recent popularity of International Baccalaureate (IB) programs not only in wealthy areas of the country but also in less affluent districts. See, for instance, Mathews and Hill. Significantly, besides the promise of rigorous college-level skills and the IB's successful integration of different subject areas, the appeal of the IB according to its supporters lies precisely in its transcultural approach to education, thanks to its international focus and its strong emphasis on the foreign

language component as a prerequisite for global citizenship. The hostility vented at the anti-Americanism of the IB indirectly brings back to the foreground an essentially monolingual and monocultural perspective, a perspective that, just as it overlooks the plurality of languages and cultures rooted in United States soil, can also be considered responsible for the endangered status of foreign language, literature, and culture studies at the university level.

3. For instance, an applied-linguistics specialist is a much-needed and valuable presence in any language department, providing the liaison between language and literature in a contextualized, culturally rich, unified language-and-content curriculum.

4. I have in mind foreignization as the translation strategy that, in contrast with domestication, disrupts the codes of the target language by calling attention to linguistic and cultural differences instead of aiming at an unproblematic intelligibility. See Venuti.

WORKS CITED

Gallop, Jane. "The Historicization of Literary Studies and the Fate of Close Reading." *Profession* (2007): 181–86. Print.

James, Henry. *The Ambassadors*. Ed. Leon Edel. Boston: Houghton, 1960. Print.

Machiavelli, Niccolò. *The Prince*. Trans. and ed. Angelo M. Codevilla. New Haven: Yale UP, 1997. Print.

———. *Il principe e altri scritti*. Ed. Gennaro Sasso. Firenze: Nuova Italia, 1963. Print.

Magris, Claudio. *Utopia e disincanto: Storie, speranze, illusioni del moderno*. Milan: Garzanti, 2001. Print.

Mathews, Jay, and Ian Hill. *Supertest: How the International Baccalaureate Can Strengthen Our Schools*. Chicago: Open Court, 2005. Print.

MLA Ad Hoc Committee on Foreign Languages. "Foreign Languages and Higher Education: New Structures for a Changed World." *Profession* (2007): 234–45. Print.

Mulrine, Anna. "The Culture Warriors: The Pentagon Deploys Social Scientists to Help Understand Iraq's 'Human Terrain.'" *U.S. News and World Report* 10 Dec. 2007: 34+. Print.

Saussy, Haun. *Enlarging Language Study*. 28 Jan. 2007. Web. 24 June 2008.

Slevin, James F. "Academic Literacy and the Discipline of English." *Profession* (2007): 200–09. Print.

Venuti, Lawrence. *The Translator's Invisibility: A History of Translation*. London: Routledge, 1995. Print.

The MLA Report on
Foreign Languages:
One Year into the Future

MICHAEL E. GEISLER

Over the past year, I have had the privilege of discussing the MLA report "Foreign Languages and Higher Education: New Structures for a Changed World" (MLA Ad Hoc Comm. on Foreign Langs.) with colleagues at the University of Minnesota, Twin Cities (at a workshop organized by the Center for Advanced Research on Language Acquisition), as well as at Wesleyan University, at Brown University, and at the AATG-sponsored session of the 2007 MLA convention in Chicago.

All these events were very well attended, and all sparked wonderful discussions. Interestingly, the meetings drew more colleagues primarily involved with language education than those on the literature-culture side of the two-tier system we described: clearly, those of us who work in teaching language, which is tantamount to saying those of us who engage our students at the critical juncture when they are trying to decide whether or not to pursue the study of a foreign language and culture, rightly felt that the report acknowledged the critical role we play in the future of our profession.

A pleasant surprise was that the relatively fewer colleagues from the literature-culture side did not quibble much with the substance of the report. Almost everybody I talked to agreed that we cannot keep doing business as usual, that we have to find a way of integrating beginning and

The author is professor of German and vice president for the Language Schools, study-abroad, and graduate programs at Middlebury College.

intermediate language with whatever cultural content students study after that—and that, indeed, some of that cultural content needs to be integrated into every step of a typical four-year undergraduate cycle.

Several people from the audience came up to me after each presentation and said the same thing others had written in response to the first article in *Inside Higher Ed*, after the first MLA presentations of more than a year ago, before the report was officially released. They professed a passionate interest in language and culture but were turned off from pursuing an advanced degree in foreign languages by the prospect of having to spend the remainder of their career studying literature—and only literature—when they were interested primarily in language and culture. Several said they would still be in the profession today, teaching foreign languages, if they had been given the option the MLA report recommends, that is, to focus on language and linguistics and cultural area studies.

On the other hand, there were colleagues who responded by saying, This is not new, we all do cultural studies in one way or another, at least as one option in our curriculum; do any undergraduate institutions still offer exclusively literature-oriented foreign language curricula?

The short answer is yes, but the committee reached this conclusion in two ways, both of which merit an explanation.

Many undergraduate curricula in foreign languages now include offerings that are often somewhat loosely subsumed under the common rubric of cultural studies (e.g., courses on film, media, or popular culture or broad thematic courses designed to attract a large cross-disciplinary audience). But these courses typically do not provide students with much geopolitical or regional background information specific to the countries associated with the foreign languages we teach—no more than is provided by traditional literature courses. The MLA report uses the term *cultural area studies* instead of *cultural studies* to draw attention to the need for specific historical, political, and institutional reference knowledge, without which cultural discourses (including literary discourse) cannot be fully understood. This sort of reference information was provided in the past by area studies programs, but with the decline of area studies expertise in the social sciences,[1] this crucially important synthetic approach to cultural "thick description" (in Clifford Geertz's classic term) was lost in increasing disciplinary specialization, as Daniel Yankelovich rightly laments:

> During the cold war, the disciplines cooperated with each other in the interest of understanding the varied aspects of particular regions, nations, and clusters of nations. Programs of area studies gained a certain

momentum. Knowledge, teaching, and research about a region like Latin America was integrated, not compartmentalized. . . .

But when the cold war ended, the specialized disciplines regained the upper hand, and area studies lost out. Ironically, today, at the moment when area studies are most badly needed, the internal pull within higher education toward specialization and separatism exercises the most influence. . . . The world remains fractionalized, even polarized. Ethnic, racial, national, and religious divisions may be growing even more important, not less.

Given their expertise in analyzing cultural narrative, I believe foreign language departments are best equipped to meet this national need for both linguistic and cultural area studies expertise.

The second approach to the question about the existence of true literature-only departments led the committee to recognize that, from one language to another, for both historical and economic reasons, departments differ in what they offer. The pressure to change has been greatest in languages that had to struggle for enrollments, such as French and German; the pressure was less strong in Spanish. Arabic and Chinese traditionally enrolled students with a much more utilitarian outlook on language study; thus many Arabic and Chinese departments or sections have been more responsive to the marketplace than the Western languages and have not focused on canonical literature as their raison d'être.

However, despite the occasional offering in French cinema or business German, the literary canon remains the coin of the realm in most foreign language departments.

I take my own discipline, German, as an example. German departments actually have been under sufficient pressure in recent years to have to figure out where the students are and what their needs are. Following the example of Georgetown, where Heidi Byrnes and her colleagues implemented the "Developing Multiple Literacies" curriculum in 2000 (*Summary*), German departments around the country have transformed themselves from departments of German literature to departments of German studies, featuring courses on such topics as business German, Berlin in the twenties, German identity, and contemporary German culture and media. Yet if one looks more closely, especially at the upper levels, one often finds the usual suspects:

Sturm und Drang (Storm and Stress)
German Classicism
German Romanticism
German Bourgeois Realism (Stifter, Grillparzer, Heine, Grabbe, Storm, Fontane)

German Expressionism (Wedekind, Werfel, Trakl, Kaiser, Toller, Lasker-Schüler)
German Literature since 1945

In suggesting that a curriculum focused exclusively (or almost exclusively) on literature is too narrow for preparing students to work in a global environment, I am not suggesting that we stop teaching literature altogether. I cannot think of many major discussions of German culture for which some work (or works) by German writers would not provide an excellent framework as a catalyst for focusing students' minds.

That said, the price our students pay for being left in the dark about major cultural discourses beyond the scope of literature (and there are many cultural issues in which writers, for various reasons, do not get involved) is too high. If we have not noticed this price, our students certainly have, and, just as important, so have employers and other graduate disciplines. That is one of the reasons why traditional foreign literature departments have become marginalized in much of academe.

To illustrate further, I digress and hark back to my days as a student of English and American literature, since I studied English as a foreign language during both my undergraduate and beginning graduate years.

In order to understand American culture, I read James Fenimore Cooper and Edgar Allan Poe, Mark Twain and F. Scott Fitzgerald, William Faulkner and Ernest Hemingway, Sylvia Plath and Theodore Roethke. I studied the interventionist drama of Arthur Miller but not the stirring cascades of John F. Kennedy's political rallying cries or the transformational energy of Martin Luther King's rhetoric of the inspirational; I plowed through Upton Sinclair's muckraking masterpiece *The Jungle*, but nobody introduced me to the eloquence of Edward R. Murrow's challenge to McCarthyism during the historic *See It Now* broadcast of 9 March 1954:

> This is no time for men who oppose Senator McCarthy's methods to keep silent, or for those who approve. We can deny our heritage and our history, but we cannot escape responsibility for the result. There is no way for a citizen of a republic to abdicate his responsibilities. As a nation we have come into our full inheritance at a tender age. We proclaim ourselves—as indeed we are—the defenders of freedom, what's left of it, but we cannot defend freedom abroad by deserting it at home. The actions of the junior senator from Wisconsin have caused alarm and dismay amongst our allies and have given considerable comfort to our enemies, and whose fault is that? Not really his. He didn't create this situation of fear; he merely exploited it, and rather successfully. Cassius was right: "The fault, dear Brutus, is not in our stars, but in ourselves." Good night, and good luck.   (qtd. in Friendly 40–41)

This was a pivotal moment for the United States, a moment in which the future of the republic depended on the eloquence and personal courage of one individual.

Yet by the standards of the curricular vision dominating modern foreign language departments today, Murrow's broadcast would not make its way into a classroom or a textbook, since it is not literature in the narrow definition of the term. Together with Murrow's opening salvo against McCarthyism, "The Case of Lt. Milo Radulovich," the *See It Now* broadcast on McCarthy was a defining moment for an age.

Another attempt to save a republic, two thousand years earlier, has become part of the canon over time: Cicero's philippic against Catilina is now standard reading in Latin courses. Murrow's statement has not yet reached that status. Yet I would argue that, to understand the forces that have shaped contemporary United States identity and public discourse, the Murrow broadcasts are as essential as the poems of Theodore Roethke or the novels of John Updike. The point is not which of these important texts (important for different reasons) a particular instructor should or would choose but that there should be such a choice, for both instructors and students.

I believe that a student of American culture who knows Cooper and Fitzgerald, Faulkner and Hemingway but is not familiar with the major speeches of Lincoln, Kennedy, or Martin Luther King; Frederick Jackson Turner's classic "The Significance of the Frontier in American History"; the films of Frank Capra; Marshall McLuhan's medium theory; Robert Bellah's paradigm-setting essay "Civil Religion in America"; Watergate and the public discourse about it, including Carl Bernstein and Bob Woodward's 1974 book *All the President's Men*; an influential television series like *The Mary Tyler Moore Show*, which had a significant impact on the women's movement in the United States; or the rituals and major metaphors of American football and baseball will never fully understand American culture.

Casting such works in the binary of high versus popular culture, as some critics of the MLA report have done, is missing the point: high-culture and low-culture texts, political oratory and major social commentary—they are all part of a larger cultural narrative, key elements that our students need to know, no matter which register the elements belong to. What the elements are will differ from department to department and from one instructor to the next. In this rich collection, many choices are possible and defensible, including the choice to privilege canonical literature. Yet canonical literature should not be the only way students have to study a foreign language and culture beyond the intermediate sequence.

But what is the core of our enterprise, if it is not traditional literature? I submit that it is the study of cultural narrative and linguistic discourse (in any one of its manifestations), with historical and cultural relevance the criterion for inclusion or exclusion.

Things will not change until curricula change in graduate departments of foreign languages. Many colleagues who teach so-called content courses[2] in foreign language departments have raised the issues of how to teach the new curriculum, who is qualified to teach it, and how those qualifications can be passed on to new instructors coming up through the pipeline. How are we going to teach students about the political system, the media, the social structure, the major issues of public discourse, traditions and identity formation, history, and patterns of leisure? Do we now all have to become experts in all those areas?

The obvious answer is an emphatic no. We cannot, and will not need to, turn ourselves into historians, economists, political scientists, and cultural anthropologists. Our students do not need to understand regression analysis to become familiar with the political system and traditions of the German-speaking countries. Most Germans are familiar with the German political system, and most Germans do not understand regression analysis. To understand the historical factors that have shaped contemporary Germany, our students need to be somewhat familiar with the results of the Thirty Years War, which created the Westphalian system of nation-states. They also need to know what happened in Germany and Europe around 1815, 1848, and 1871 and the major data points from 1914 to the present. They don't need to know the theory of historiography, the years of the Black Plague in Europe, or even the Treaty of Rapallo. They do need to know something about the historically constructed mentality that turned perfectly ordinary citizens (before 1933 and in many cases after 1945) into mass murderers; they need to know why the Bonn and then the Berlin Republic succeeded where the Weimar Republic had failed; they need to know what the *Bundesliga* is (German premier soccer league), what the "Wunder von Bern" means, what the underpinnings of the German welfare state are, and why, given the constitutionally mandated role played by political parties in Germany, the kind of mess that the Democratic Party finds itself in these days would be almost impossible in Germany (although other kinds of messes happen).

Students need to know the central cultural metaphors or "key words" (in Raymond Williams's apt phrase) that are generated by various historical traditions and discourses. When the German news magazine *Der Spiegel* publishes an investigative report about top-level German business executives committing massive tax fraud (see "Steuerflucht"), our students, at the end of four years, should have the conceptual parameters in hand to understand why German politicians and intellectuals are much more concerned about the impact this will have on German society than their American counterparts would be in a parallel situation over here, and why they are right in worrying about that impact.

Traditional disciplinary specialists, whether they are historians or political scientists or sociologists, cannot cover such a wide spectrum of different registers of cultural knowledge.[3] Needless to say, neither can literary specialists.

So what we need, and whom we need to train, are cultural area specialists, teacher-scholars who combine native or near-native proficiency in a second language with a solid grounding in language teaching methodology and a good grasp of the essentials of the cultural narrative, broadly defined, that a competent journalist has after a couple of years of being "embedded" in the target culture.

How do we get there?

1. Let's reevaluate the primacy of the native speaker ideal and its pedagogical implications: to clone, in the language classroom, fully inculturated speakers of French or Italian or Japanese.[4] Without an Archimedean point, anchored in the learner's identity, coupled with the awareness of the liminality involved in every cultural crossover phenomenon, all we get are very articulate parrots. (We have all encountered the occasional very gifted near-native speaker of a foreign language who has nothing to say but says it beautifully.) That is why the MLA ad hoc committee's report calls for "translingual and transcultural competence" (237): translingual and transcultural competence implies liminality (see also Bhabha), not a complete exchange of identities.
2. Let's say good-bye to the grand narratives. The curriculum I listed above, covering German literature from the eighteenth to the twenty-first century, is such a grand narrative. The idea of cultural area experts could easily lead to the misunderstanding that we are now asking our students to cover an even grander narrative, since the arc of cultural expertise we built has a span that reaches from literature to politics, sports, and the basics of the economic system. Let us instead consider contributing to, or adapting, Scott McNealy's concept of "currikis"—an online dynamic archive of seminal cultural texts, an archive permanently under interactive construction, but let's make sure that there is some professional quality control involved in such an endeavor.
3. For those of our students who spend a semester or year abroad in one of the countries whose language they are studying, we should shape their study abroad to round out a fully articulated cultural area studies curriculum. Senior work, whether or not it involves a thesis, should be mapped out by students and academic advisers before departure, with the overarching goal of maximizing the opportunity for cultural field research through a mainstreamed academic experience (where possible, based on linguistic proficiency) combined with guided independent study (e.g., portfolio work) or internships.

4. Let foreign language courses focus less on content and more on process. Let us teach students how to access, evaluate, critique, and utilize existing repositories of information instead of trying to squeeze a hopelessly inadequate mini-archive of French life or French literature between the covers of traditional textbooks.

5. Parenthetically, for promotion and tenure we must seriously question the usefulness of the monograph as the gold standard of research accomplishment and tenurability. For tenure decisions in foreign languages, we need to know whether our younger colleagues are sufficiently conversant with the cultural narrative of the country or countries whose language they teach to engage our students about these discourses in a way that earns them the students' respect. In the age of the Internet, it is unrealistic to expect faculty members to keep up with cultural and political developments in such a way as to be a step ahead of their Internet-surfing and text-messaging students and, at the same time, to expect them to publish two books about very specialized topics before they come up for tenure. In this context, I applaud the MLA Task Force on Evaluating Scholarship for Tenure and Promotion for recommending in its report that "[d]epartments and institutions should recognize the legitimacy of scholarship produced in new media, whether by individuals or in collaboration, and create procedures for evaluating these forms of scholarship" ("Report" 11). It is nothing short of ludicrous that these days "40.8% of departments in doctorate-granting institutions report no experience evaluating refereed articles in electronic format, and 65.7% report no experience evaluating monographs in electronic format" (11).[5]

6. We need more multidisciplinary, multimedia, peer-reviewed online journals (like *Southern Spaces*) as well as dynamic, endowed, and managed Web archives, and we need to find a way of financing such endeavors, of encouraging and professionally rewarding both junior and senior colleagues' contribution to such projects, and of evaluating the results.

7. This focus on process would bring us back to the one skill that no other discipline has developed to the same level of sophistication as have departments and scholars of foreign languages, cultures, and literatures: the critique and analysis of narrative across a wide variety of texts, including (but not limited to) literary texts. If you are concerned about the balance of breadth and depth in the training of future foreign language teachers, this is where their depth will be: the ability to read and deconstruct cultural narratives on the basis of the particularities of the target language. To the extent that we are trained in foreign languages and literature, we are also trained in the analysis of narrative. We understand how cultural identity and specificity are created and re-created, written and rewritten, through narrative. The tools of our trade are the analysis of narrative, whether it be through Foucauldian or Derridean deconstruction; narrative theory; discourse analysis; and the examination of major cultural metaphors in the tradition of George Lakoff and Mark Johnson's work.

8. To translate into reality the recommendations of the MLA Ad Hoc Committee on Foreign Languages, we need regular summer offerings for foreign language instructors on both the high school and college-university levels, such as the

NEH seminar Citizenship and Culture: French Identity in Crisis, offered this summer by Michael Kline and Nancy Mellerski at Dickinson College.

I conclude by citing a play I recently saw at the Public Theater in New York City, Richard Nelson's *Conversations in Tusculum.* As Cicero discusses with Brutus and Cassius the decline of Rome's republican traditions under Caesar, he reads to Brutus a list of words—neologisms—he has created in Latin "so we could understand the great Greeks," since, as he reminds Brutus, "all civilization comes from them." Among these words are "Element. Quality. Vacuum. Moral. Individual. Definition. Property. Infinity. Comprehension. Appetite. Instance. Image. Difference. Notion. Science. Species." Then he says, "I was amazed. I hadn't realized. . . . You don't realize all we didn't know. All we didn't have words for. How many more words will we need? How much more is there to know, to try and say?" (78). It is fascinating that Nelson has Cicero reflect on the influence of another culture on Rome, at the very instant when the nation they both love and cherish is most threatened from within, when Roman political traditions and cultural identity are in jeopardy. By acknowledging the influence of the foreign on one's own identity, Nelson appears to be saying here, through Cicero, that we have no identity of our own. This influence depends on words. The new words Cicero created in Latin for concepts that had become crucial elements of Roman identity and culture were necessary because there were no Latin words for them before. He was able to perform this work as cultural mediator because he was able to read and understand a foreign language, Greek—but also because he inhabited the liminal position that allowed him to selectively appropriate those (linguistic) aspects of Greek culture that seemed most relevant and productive to him in the context in which he lived: Rome in the twilight of the republic.

NOTES

An earlier version of this paper was given at the annual meeting of the Northeast Conference on the Teaching of Foreign Languages (NECTFL), New York, March 2008.

1. For an interesting introduction to the area studies debate in the field of political science, see Bates.

2. I believe that, by using the term *content courses,* foreign language departments are buying into a dichotomy that is not their own; it was developed by university administrators to separate upper-division content from lower-division language study for the sole purpose of being able to justify distinctions in faculty salary and status between the two. The old adage "Content from the beginning, language to the end!," as appealing as it sounds, is pleonastic and predicated on the very binary it purports to

deconstruct. Nobody can learn a language—any language—in a contentless classroom environment. The only reasonable question is which content is appropriate for discussion at which level.

3. Which is not to say they won't try. In the field of history, Pierre Nora and his collaborators have actually attempted to define the core elements of French identity, through their monumental *Lieux de mémoire*. This work is a magnificent achievement and might make a good general model for a similar project in foreign languages that would give students access to building blocks of French (or German or Arabic) identity. However, in its present form it is clearly—and legitimately—intended as a resource for French historians, not for instructors of French language and culture. As such, it presents us with certain pedagogical problems that have to do as much with the selection of identity modules (not all of which are of the same relevance to foreign language teachers as they are to historians) as with the fact that this is a work designed by the French for a French discourse. At the most, it encompasses a community of advanced French specialists from other cultures. It is clearly not a work designed for students who do not yet have basic reference or background knowledge. As Ed Knox put it in an eloquent critique of unrealistic expectations created by some overenthusiastic advocates of traditional cultural studies, ". . . it is difficult enough to unpack a Barthes with students who have never seen a Tour de France, or a *lieu de mémoire* with young people who understandably can't 'remember' a referent they have yet to learn about. How . . . are we to facilitate for the foreign language student access to the transcultural or postcultural, without passing first through the cultural?" (672).

4. This reevaluation is all the more appropriate since there is an ongoing discussion among applied linguists about the native speaker ideal as a pedagogical concept. See, for instance, Cook.

5. The other distressing practice unearthed by the MLA task force is that "translations were rated 'not important' by 30.4% of departments (including 31.3% of foreign language departments), as were textbooks by 28.9% of departments" (11). In plain English, this means that one-third of American educational institutions believe it is of "no importance" that we have access to the ideas created by the rest of the world through translations of their research results.

WORKS CITED

Bates, Robert H. "Area Studies and the Discipline: A Useful Controversy?" *PS: Political Science and Politics* 30.2 (1997): 166–69. Print.

Bellah, Robert N. "Civil Religion in America." *Daedalus* 96.1 (1967): 1–21. Print.

Bernstein, Carl, and Bob Woodward. *All the President's Men.* New York: Simon, 1974. Print.

Bhabha, Homi K. "How Newness Enters the World." *The Location of Culture.* London: Routledge, 1994. 212–35. Print.

Cook, Vivian. "Going beyond the Native Speaker in Language Teaching." *TESOL Quarterly* 33.2 (1999): 185–209. Print.

Friendly, Fred W. *Due to Circumstances beyond Our Control. . . .* New York: Vintage, 1967. Print.

Geertz, Clifford. *The Interpretation of Cultures.* New York: Basic, 1973. Print.

Knox, Edward C. "Between Cultural Studies and Cultural Competence." *French Review* 72.4 (1999): 669–75. Print.

Lakoff, George, and Mark Johnson. *Metaphors We Live By*. Chicago: U of Chicago P, 1980. Print.

McLuhan, Marshall. *Understanding Media: The Extensions of Man*. New York: Mentor, 1964. Print.

McNealy, Scott. "Education in the Participation Age." ConnectEd: Conf. on Global Educ. Monterey Conf. Center, Monterey, CA. 22 Jan. 2008. Opening plenary address.

Murrow, Edward R., narr. "The Case of Lt. Milo Radulovich." *See It Now*. CBS. 20 Oct. 1953. Television.

MLA Ad Hoc Committee on Foreign Languages. "Foreign Languages and Higher Education: New Structures for a Changed World." *Profession* (2007): 234–45. Print.

Nelson, Richard. *Conversations in Tusculum*. New York: Faber, 2008. Print.

Nora, Pierre, et al., eds. *Realms of Memory: The Construction of the French Past*. Ed. Lawrence D. Kritzman. Trans. Arthur Goldhammer. New York: Columbia UP, 1998. Print.

"Report of the MLA Task Force on Evaluating Scholarship for Tenure and Promotion." *Profession* (2007): 9–71. Print.

"Die Steuerflucht der Reichen." *Der Spiegel* 18 Feb. 2008: 20+. Print.

Summary: Developing Multiple Literacies. Dept. of German, Georgetown U. 4 Sept. 2004. Web. 11 May 2008.

Turner, Frederick Jackson. "The Significance of the Frontier in American History." Amer. Historical Assn. Convention. Chicago. 12 July 1893. Address.

Williams, Raymond. *Key Words: A Vocabulary of Culture and Society*. Rev. ed. New York: Oxford UP, 1983. Print.

Yankelovich. Daniel. "Ferment and Change: Higher Education in 2015." *Chronicle of Higher Education* 25 Nov. 2005: 14. Print.

The Language Program
Director in Curricular and
Departmental Reform

GLENN S. LEVINE, CHARLOTTE MELIN, CORINNE CRANE,
MONIKA CHAVEZ, AND THOMAS A. LOVIK

Since its release in 2007, the MLA report "Foreign Languages and Higher Education: New Structures for a Changed World" has stimulated lively debate about the teaching of foreign languages in the United States. In the report, the MLA Ad Hoc Committee on Foreign Languages recommends that curricular and governance structures of foreign language programs be transformed to create an educational environment in which students will attain "deep translingual and transcultural competence" (237). The salutary effects of this discussion cannot be underestimated. The release of the report was followed by dialogue sessions at numerous conferences and focus sections in professional journals including the *ADFL Bulletin*, the *German Quarterly, Die Unterrichtspraxis / Teaching of German*, and the *Journal of Language and Literacy Education*. The summer 2008 "Perspectives" column of the *Modern Language Journal* (*MLJ*) continued that conversation by publishing the reactions of diverse stakeholders to the committee's recommendations. The arguments for a national foreign language policy will be aired in forthcoming *MLJ* issues. Indeed, a year after the report's

Glenn S. Levine is associate professor of German at the University of California, Irvine. Charlotte Melin is associate professor of German at the University of Minnesota, Twin Cities. Corinne Crane is director of the Basic Language Program in the Department of Germanic Languages and Literatures at the University of Illinois, Urbana. Monika Chavez is professor of German and second language acquisition at the University of Wisconsin, Madison. Thomas A. Lovik is professor of German at Michigan State University.

release, dire news about program closures, severe cutbacks, and financial strains (for example, at the University of Florida, the University of Southern California, and the University of California, Berkeley) has renewed concern about the learning of languages beyond the "critical" group that currently receives government funding (Brockman). The crisis in foreign language education is palpable and can no longer be considered in abstract terms.

At the same time, the paradigm shift in language education depicted by the MLA report is not without controversy. In particular, its accounts of the two-tiered system, communicative language teaching, and articulation rely on tenacious, but in our view not entirely accurate, narratives about language education. It is our conclusion that discussion of these narratives requires the participation of language program directors. Despite the report's observation that "[t]he presence of linguists and second language acquisition specialists on language department faculties is also an essential part of this vision" (240), it does not describe their contributions.[1]

Our collaborative response to the MLA report is undertaken in an effort to insert that voice into the debate and to urge careful reexamination of its narrative strands from the perspective of language program directors. While we hold differing views on a number of issues and do not wish to imply unified opinion among our colleagues, we have found much ground for consensus concerning the vision that language program directors can bring to foreign language education at the departmental, institutional, and national level. They have long grappled with the structural problems identified in the MLA report, and we are gratified to see this metadiscussion move from the periphery to the center of dialogue about the crisis in language teaching. In this essay, we analyze three facets of the bifurcation model that are the backbone of the MLA report and propose that to reform the system effectively more nuanced conclusions should be drawn regarding the situation of foreign language education in the United States. Our aim is to suggest ways departments can move beyond outdated paradigms (including those implied by the report itself) and identify the types of contributions that are critically needed from language program directors to set in motion the kind of educational transformation that is the ultimate goal of the MLA report.

THE TWO-TIERED SYSTEM

The MLA report aspires to a profound transformation of language education across all levels, proceeding from the central concern about "[t]he standard configuration of university foreign language curricula, in which a two- or three-year language sequence feeds into a set of core courses primarily focused on canonical literature" (236). This structure, it finds, produces "a division between the language curriculum and the literature curriculum and between tenure-track literature professors and language instructors in non-tenure-track positions" (236). That critique should sound familiar, since in 1997 Dorothy James incisively diagnosed the structural division in language departments. A decade later, much has occurred to dismantle the two-tiered language-literature divide. To be sure, the lion's share of lower-division language courses is taught by graduate student teaching assistants and adjunct lecturers (MLA 236). Yet in the day-to-day and semester-to-semester work of helping students learn a new language and culture, language teachers and faculty members, even when they occupy discrete positions, share many common intellectual investments that bridge the divide. At large universities, the work of the language program director is positioned where these networks intersect.

But how real is the two-tiered divide in terms of curricular offerings? Data collected by the MLA invite a more nuanced understanding of the two-tiered system problem. The 2001 MLA study "Successful College and University Foreign Language Programs, 1995–99: Part 1" reports that for introductory language courses at United States institutions, 68.5% place more emphasis on culture than literature, while 30.2% indicate equal or more emphasis on literature (Goldberg and Welles 185). For advanced courses, the corresponding data show that 53.4% place more emphasis on literary texts and 43.9% place equal or more emphasis on nonliterary texts. The data are further sorted to indicate types of literature and approaches used and show that 49.6% of departments use a combination of canonical and noncanonical literature (186). Taken in aggregate, the data indicate that nearly a third of introductory courses emphasize some literature, although admittedly the nature of its inclusion is unknown, and that nearly half of all advanced courses (43.9%) emplasize some nonliterary texts. To sum up, the survey information available does not clearly indicate a rigid division of language versus literature, although some obvious differences exist between lower- and upper-division courses.

These general data about postsecondary curricula suggest that in terms of course content the two-tiered system began to dissolve at least a decade ago. There is also ample evidence about an evolution of learners and course content that makes the two-tiered model outdated. Numerous *ADFL Bulletin* reports on successful programs confirm the creativity of departments in analyzing and reforming the structure of foreign language education during the period of the MLA departmental study (see issues 35.1, 35.2-3, and 36.3 in particular). In addition, an abundance of qualitative and quantitative research on program articulation, the use of literary and nonliterary texts in the foreign language classroom, and approaches to building an intellectually challenging undergraduate curriculum is available (see Bernhardt and Berman; Byrnes and Sprang; Eigler; Maxim, "Expanding" and "Integrating"; Mittman; Rankin).

On an institutional level, faculty teaching assignments and the growth in double majors (Goldberg and Welles 177) also argue for the conclusion that foreign language education in the United States has moved or is moving beyond the two-tiered structure. Faculty members in small departments and liberal arts colleges have long been expected to teach the full spectrum of learners. University faculty members at research institutions also regularly teach at the undergraduate and graduate levels— including film, culture, or other nonliterary courses. Some departments experience the greatest enrollment pressure at the third-year course level as increasingly well-qualified freshmen with the equivalent of beginning and intermediate language courses move directly into upper-division content courses. Enrollment options that allow high school students to elect college courses, immersion programs, and study abroad render the two-tiered system obsolete. Thus some students never experience the lower tier in college—and most college students taking language courses to satisfy a basic requirement never move into the upper tier.

While the two-tiered system may characterize some institutions and live on as a concept in the minds of some faculty members who influence the training of graduate students for academic careers, it is in many respects not the dominant model. We contend that it is vital to the transformation of foreign language education that the bifurcation model not become an enabling narrative that distracts from the urgent need for reform. The problems of continuity are real and ongoing in areas related to curricular articulation and departmental power sharing, but when the problem is described as bifurcation, many complexities in the current situation are obscured. Our claim is simply that on the ground in language departments, faculty members, lecturers, and graduate students have already responded in multiple and sophisticated ways to the so-called cultural turn in language departments. The narrow-minded literature faculty members sharply criticized in the report are a vanishing species.

Faculty research and teaching do not display a one-dimensional insistence on the primacy of literary texts, as is evident from the heated discussion of German studies that played out in the pages of the *German Quarterly* in 2007 (see Trommler and the responses in issues 80.1 and 80.2). Rather, faculty members openly acknowledge that they grapple with a shifting, interdisciplinary educational landscape where the linguistic, historical, literary, and rhetorical dimensions of all text forms are read through the lens of cultural theory, aesthetic history, identity politics, and other approaches. Indeed, the same graduate students and adjunct instructors who in the bifurcated model sit on the opposite bank of this divide have been trained in these modes of analysis, and they have also received extensive professional development from language program directors and others regarding pedagogy. While it is true that departmental faculties hold much decision-making power (MLA 236–37), they by no means have sole control of curricula. Academic freedom notwithstanding, factors such as administrative directives, textbook marketing, and financial constraints influence how programs operate. Today, the two-tiered divide of yore is a multidimensional puzzle made up of the diverse identities of faculty members and language teachers rather than a dichotomy held in place by curriculum. The divides we grapple with are less a product of a language-literature hierarchy than divisions according to agency, class, resources, or mere longevity in a department.

Though the MLA report praises the transformation of scholarship and pedagogy that has taken place at many institutions, its assertion that "[t]he two-tiered configuration has outlived its usefulness and needs to evolve" casts doubt on the commitment of foreign language departments to embrace change (237). Yet in our experience, language departments have long demonstrated flexibility and a willingness to change their curricula, technologies, and teaching approaches, even though some of this change is more reactive than proactive. True, few departments have chosen to undertake a curricular overhaul of the type hinted at by the MLA report.[2] However, in privileging the two-tiered system as an antagonist and proposing the articulated four-year curriculum model as its remedy, the MLA report does not go far enough in its recommendations. Hierarchies of power and knowledge are not sufficiently questioned, and the investments of various stakeholders are not considered. One area in which this becomes evident is the discussion of communicative language teaching.

Reconsidering Assumptions of Communicative Language Teaching

The underlying critique of communicative language teaching advanced by the MLA report is that it constrains student achievement. To simplify this point for the sake of argument, when instruction focuses primarily on oral self-expression rather than on the full complexity of language and culture, intellectual scope is lost. Moreover, communicative language teaching is often equated with proficiency-oriented teaching, and by implication it is assumed that current teaching—particularly in lower-division language classes—is not sufficiently invested in issues of literacy. At stake, however, is not merely a dichotomy of written versus oral modes of communication but also what those modalities represent both in the classroom and in the target culture. In other words, communicative language teaching is often disparaged for focusing too heavily, and too uncritically, on everyday communication at the expense of a sophisticated exploration of the range of authentic second-language registers and discourses.

Intellectually challenging content is, we agree, needed at the postsecondary level, and foreign language departments are well advised to maintain a broad educational vision for their programs, but it should be remembered that proficiency-oriented teaching and communicative language teaching developed as a response to teaching methods that were ineffective and mismatched with students' interest in learning language for instrumental purposes, such as travel, study or work. Little hard evidence exists that postsecondary educators have uncritically construed proficiency-oriented or communicative language teaching as simply oral expression (see Liskin-Gasparro). MLA data, in fact, show that few programs (23.1%) report more emphasis on oral communication than on reading and writing (Goldberg and Welles 185). Where instrumental language learning does occur, it is most visible in language courses for special purposes (such as Business German or Medical Spanish) that attract highly motivated students with advanced-level fluency and specific professional goals.

A reconsideration of communicative language teaching is, indeed, advisable in the light of current second language acquisition research. The ACTFL Proficiency Guidelines, like the subsequent National Standards, were initially developed based on the professional experience of teachers rather than through data-collection procedures that could provide empirical evidence of proficiency levels. Later, the speaking guidelines were used to conceptualize writing, reading, and listening norms. As second language acquisition researchers have widely acknowledged, there are many open questions about teaching methodology that deserve validation studies for writing and listening not acting as predictors for language proficiency (Liskin-Gasparro). Although qualitative analysis techniques are now evolving that could eventually lead to a better appreciation of the type of intuitive-experiential knowledge that produced the guidelines, legitimate questions can be asked about their validity. The same point can made for the National Standards or other frameworks for curricular reform that derive from a knowledge base of professional experience rather than empirical evidence. The epistemological status of that knowledge base should not be reason enough to reject them, but it should prompt serious reflection about the claims that can be made for any teaching approach.

To their credit, the ACTFL Proficiency Guidelines became a tool for dissemination of professional standards, and this effort yielded, among other things, outcomes assessment instruments suited to measuring student achievement in a variety of language skill areas, in a variety of ways, and in a variety of forms (see Zimmer-Loew), to the betterment of second language education in the United States. Calls for accountability in postsecondary education will likely increase the use of assessments, data-collection methodologies, and quantitative as well as qualitative research that contributes to an understanding of educational outcomes. There is considerable momentum at the national level to move language programs in the direction of skill development and proficiency as a measure of competence. To some extent this trend is dictated by the decision by the National Council for Accreditation of Teacher Education to adopt Advanced Low as the required proficiency for teachers of French, German, and Spanish. It is also influenced by the federal government's infusion of new money into the study of languages for strategic purposes. This development is putting increasing pressure on programs to ensure that their graduates are indeed able to achieve the proposed thresholds. While the research shows that undergraduate programs do not typically achieve this threshold easily, it is essential that departments have serious discussions about the goals of their curriculum and how they intend to bring students in all courses toward a common competency goal that is understood, shared, and supported by all faculty members and reflected in every course.

In this environment, discussion of communicative language teaching, proficiency, and national standards must now become more nuanced. Communicative language teaching has provided a vital starting point for departments to reflect on the relation of form and meaning in second language instruction, but we now need an expansion of these constructs to advanced levels of language learning. Literacy, genre, and discourse—constructs that address the relation of language, content, and context and place texts in a central position—will be useful for considering how to stage language learning across broader curricula.

There also is a pressing need to connect curricular goals with theories of learning and research into pathways to learning and learning outcomes. Second language acquisition has enjoyed—some may argue, endured—spirited debates about the relation of language use and language acquisition (see Kasper) as well as about the cognitive and social dimensions of language learning (see Lafford). Regardless of one's position in these professional debates or toward communicative language teaching, this method and its fundamental tenets have been subjected to rigorous scientific investigations and linked to cognitively and socially oriented theories of learning. Similarly, as constructs of literacy and text become increasingly focal in the reconceptualization of foreign language curricula, it will become important for the field to examine and assess their associated learning theories through research that is grounded in scientific theory and inquiry.

The challenge, then, is how to envision radically diverse curricula that are theoretically and empirically sound and that help learners achieve advanced competencies, curricula that work in every institutional context and at the same time articulate with other educational systems. Frequently in a university department the language program director has the most experience with articulation and the broadest knowledge of relevant research and thus has or should have a strong voice in this transformation.

Articulation of Curriculum

The irregular enrollment patterns described above mean that the solution of creating an internally articulated departmental curriculum taught primarily in the target language will not remove the problems created by an absence of foreign language policy at the national level. At the department level, the success of the internally articulated curriculum depends on the ecology of the department. If learners were to progress through a carefully staged sequence of courses, departments could feel confident about bringing students to the advanced proficiency levels recommended in the MLA report. That achievement is a worthy goal. However, in departments where students enter at levels beyond beginning-intermediate courses or move in and out of the language sequence as they juggle requirements for multiple majors, the path to advanced translingual and transcultural competence will be quite different. Complicating the situation are administrators who strenuously remind departments to manage the curriculum effectively, make sure that classes are well enrolled, avoid "boutique seminars" of limited appeal, remove outcomes assessments if they prove to be impediments to degree progress, and promote study-abroad opportunities only as long as they do not interfere with graduation rates and tuition revenue. Thus a curriculum aiming for advanced transcultural and translingual competence cannot come about by simple resolution; complex issues of internal articulation and administrative demands and restrictions must be brought to bear.

If enrollments are of pressing concern, it is troubling that the learners' desires so far have gone largely ignored. While communicative language teaching developed in response to perceived student needs to communicate in authentic, functional contexts, little attention has been paid to student expectations regarding new approaches to multiple second-language literacies. Rigorous survey research on learners' curricular goals and expectations is sparse, and the little that exists appears to have minimal influence on departmental discussions about curriculum. Yet solid empirical investigation of learner goals and expectations could contribute greatly to the complex sort of internal articulation described above.

Similarly, it is uncertain whether and how curricula that target translingual and transcultural competence and multiple literacies would be able to articulate with K–12 language teaching and learning. A disconnect between secondary and postsecondary curricula could raise concerns about content articulation as well as potentially jarring student expectations and motivation. Coming from a communicative language teaching approach at the secondary level, students might find the new literacies at the college level exciting, but for some students the experience could be alienating.

Based on this potential disconnect and contrasted with internal articulation, systemwide articulation (K–16) depends not on internal curricular integration but on external standards that introduce yet another type of bifurcation. Perhaps paradoxically, it appears that institutions that are more likely to have a four-year integrated curriculum (liberal arts colleges and private institutions) are less likely to be engaged in K–12 outreach or to have a language program director. Public universities, though, are more likely to have language program directors and on the departmental level may find it more difficult to develop an articulated four-year curriculum because of the enrollment issues cited above. In primary and secondary education in recent years, K–12 articulation has raised significantly the quality of teaching of foreign languages in high schools and has been facilitated by the ACTFL Proficiency Guidelines, as well as the National Standards, which have made expectations more transparent and more translatable to diverse educational settings (see Lally). This experience should encourage colleagues in postsecondary departments to foster reciprocal connections with K–12 and community college and other university-level educators while still valuing the distinctness of education at different levels and in different educational contexts. Successful articulation requires more than the search for a common denominator—it is a division of labor that is based on the mutual respect of all stakeholders.

An additional issue related to articulation is instruction in the target language. The push for more courses in the target language, which the MLA report supports, cannot be taken as given and should be approached in a nuanced way. Articulation is not vertical but lateral and multidirectional. Department size and ecology determine course offerings. In a small department whose primary function is language instruction, all courses may be taught in the target language. Larger departments, by contrast, offer a mixture of gateway courses, lecture courses in English for students from all fields (with or without a trailer section in the target language), language courses at a variety of levels, and content, theory, or linguistics courses in the target language or in English. Graduate seminars in many cases combine readings in the target language with discussions in the language of choice because of the intellectual complexity of the material. This mixed language model has spread as departments have sought to attract students from across their home institutions and is the vehicle for interdisciplinary collaboration. Therefore, it does not suffice to advocate only for target-language instruction; the ecology of both the department and the institution must be considered, along with the specific goals and priorities of its students and faculty members.

Language Program Directors and Second Language Acquisition Scholars

Language program directors, we suspect, read the MLA report with mixed emotions, wondering whether it is a genuine reform initiative or an effort to reposition literature while still retaining in some ways its position at the top of the academic hierarchy. The MLA report's observation that "[t]he presence of linguists and second language acquisition specialists on language department faculties is also an essential part of this vision" is a welcome endorsement of the language program director, but it does not foreground sufficiently what this presence has already accomplished and why it is so urgently needed in the near future (240).

Language program directors throughout the United States have backgrounds in applied linguistics, second language acquisition, literature, and other fields (Katz and Watzinger-Tharp 494), with qualifications and expertise matched to the profile of their departments. Departmental ecology is an important determinant of who serves as language program director and whether an institution has one. Liberal arts colleges may have little direct knowledge of language program directors because these professionals work primarily at large research universities and medium-size institutions. Moreover, the structure of appointments is very different. Some language program directors oversee the educational vision of their departments—supervising upper-division courses, curriculum development and articulation across all levels, and initiatives in the use of instructional technology. Others concentrate effort in the beginning-intermediate language program or function more as a course coordinator. Some are tenured or tenure-track, others are not. Regardless of these differences, every foreign language department in the United States has a vested interest in understanding the level of professionalization expected of language program directors because they are the faculty members who mentor graduate students as they teach, usually by teaching the methodology course for these future professionals.

Although every language program director brings different qualifications to the table, most are well positioned to make deliberate, data-based decisions, and that decision process is very different from informal planning based on untested beliefs or generalized recommendations. Absent from the MLA report, and indeed from the position paper by the same committee (Pratt et al.), is an acknowledgment of the role this type of informed decision making needs to play in the transformation of foreign language education. Our discussion as collaborators for this essay has led us to reflect on several issues regarding language program directors and second language acquisition research that are particularly pertinent in that transformation process:

1. Having a language program director in a department signals a division of labor; departments are well advised to avoid the trap of turning this work distribution into conceptual bifurcation. Departments can benefit greatly from this specialization.
2. Given the regular interactions with teaching assistants, faculty colleagues, and administrators in their departments, language program directors are able to form insights about learning and teaching from a larger, programmatic perspective, insights that are motivated by a desire to enhance teaching and deepen learning. Yet language program directors can also become professionally overburdened in the process. The alignment of preparation, administrative duties, teaching, and research is not neat, and ideally it should be for tenure and promotion purposes.
3. The dramatic cycles in the teaching of foreign languages are driven by forces that lie beyond the control of individual faculty members. International politics, economics, immigration, national education policy, reductions in public funding for higher education, and changing student demographics powerfully impact which languages are taught, as well as where and how they are delivered. Programs that are weakened by low enrollments, inefficient management of course offerings or stagnant curricula, or isolation are more vulnerable to these pressures. The language program director is frequently the one faculty member in the department who is professionally engaged on a daily basis in teaching, research, and service related to these external issues.
4. It is unrealistic to assume that every faculty member will obtain knowledge about second language acquisition research; in fact, it is difficult even for specialists to keep up with the many branches of research. As the field of second language acquisition grows, with an attendant increase in subspecializations,

the gap between research and practice or awareness among language teachers of what the field is about will also grow. A striking bifurcation is already developing between second language acquisition research and pedagogical practice; thus departments should not automatically assume that hiring a second language acquisition expert will solve the problem of finding a language program director or that the presence of a specialist will shore up the curriculum or resolve divides. In some departments, linguistics may need to be afforded a greater role. Departments should identify where the expertise of these specialists (and what kind of expertise) is critically needed and how all faculty members can best be informed about new research on second language acquisition, curriculum, and teaching.

5. Collaboration across departments and interdisciplinarity are potential outcomes for institutions that have or plan to hire language program directors. As a faculty group whose research can include second language acquisition, sociolinguistics, applied linguistics, literature, pedagogy and curriculum, intercultural competence, and reading and writing studies, language program directors have scholarly expertise that is brought to bear in differing ways on questions of second language education. What knowledge is important for our students and how that knowledge is constructed is part and parcel of the type of research in which language program directors engage. What students read, why digital culture transforms the way we think, and how we define culture in the twenty-first century are all open to question. Many of our past assumptions are no longer viable. Undergraduate liberal arts education is being thoroughly redefined as we seek to teach students to be global citizens in an increasingly complex world.[3]

The MLA report's discussion of continuing priorities contains many commendable recommendations (243–44), and yet here, too, we urge further reflection. Many of the priorities carry with them a tacit assumption that language learners are primarily affluent students. In particular, enrichment courses, intensive courses, and study-abroad options may be out of reach for students from less affluent backgrounds who work summers and many hours during the academic year to make ends meet. More attention needs to be given to providing incentives to study foreign languages and supporting and encouraging nontraditional groups of language learners. More emphasis is needed as well on the role of student agency in the study of foreign languages.

For those departments that have not yet moved beyond the two-tiered model, the MLA report is likely to come as a welcome incentive to reenvision foreign language education. For the rest of us, the time has come to leave the narrative of the language-literature divide. Our situation has grown far more complex than the solutions that can be derived by conceptualizing the problems facing foreign language education through such binary categories.

In a recent editorial in the *Chronicle of Higher Education*, Will H. Corrall and Daphne Patai argue, "[i]f foreign languages, whether underenrolled or not, are to survive today, they need to stake a claim for their intrinsic value and their relationship to the study of foreign cultures." Much of the discussion of the MLA report has been devoted to exploring the bond between language and culture, especially literature. We need, however, a yet more radical exploration of their intrinsic value than has occurred to date. If we truly believe that language, literature, and culture are essential to humanity, we must be able to articulate that visionary argument and ground it in research. It is hard to imagine the success of such a project without the voice of language program directors.

RECOMMENDATIONS FOR LANGUAGE DEPARTMENTS

The MLA report, the position paper by that same committee (Pratt et al.), several of the response papers (Bousquet; Pfeiffer; Wellmon), and many other contributions to the current debate over curricular and structural reform of postsecondary language education advocate the active participation of linguists and language experts in curricular and structural change in language departments. We strongly support their admonitions that departments hire linguists and language acquisition specialists and integrate them into the departmental program, and we recommend that they recognize that language program directors with backgrounds in literature and other areas can make valuable contributions to our profession. New language program directors should be engaged not only in creating and coordinating curriculum and training graduate students and adjunct faculty members but also in teaching courses in their field as an integrated component of their department's undergraduate and graduate curricula. In addition, they should be able to contribute to the professional development of faculty members not explicitly trained in language teaching and learning issues, so that all department members rethink advanced courses as forums for both literature-culture learning and ongoing language training (Pratt et al. 290). To be sure, these recommendations are fruitful only in a departmental culture where pedagogical contributions are supported and rewarded—including for tenure—and where participation in discussions concerning teaching and learning is the norm for all department members.

In the face of administrative actions at many colleges and universities that compromise the existence of advanced language study, even in the so-called critical languages, there is indeed an urgent need for foreign language departments to engage in proactive curricular and structural reforms. To take up this important work without the contributions of a scholar trained to deal with the complexities of language learning and curriculum would be akin to building a bridge without the services of an engineer.

NOTES

The idea for this essay originated in conference discussion at the 2007 meeting at the University of Iowa of the American Association of University Supervisors, Coordinators, and Directors (AAUSC) German Section that was held in conjunction with a meeting of German chairs representing departments of the Committee on Institutional Cooperation, a consortium of twelve research universities. The essay represents the views of the authors, however, with no claim to represent the views of the AAUSC or other entities.

1. Pfeiffer, for example, concludes that a stronger voice for colleagues currently engaged as language program directors would have been beneficial (296).

2. For example, the German departments at Georgetown University and the University of Texas, Austin, have undertaken large-scale curricular and programmatic changes. Georgetown in particular led the way in the first years of the decade in integrating cultural content from the beginning of introductory German and focused language instruction through the most advanced literature courses.

3. For poignant discussions of the large-scale educational reform in higher education, see Jones, McCarney, and Skolnik; Suárez-Orozco and Qin-Hilliard. For discussions of and calls for reform in language education, see Byram; Phipps and Gonzales.

WORKS CITED

Bernhardt, Elizabeth B., and Russell A. Berman. "From German 1 to German Studies 001: A Chronicle of Curricular Reform." *Die Unterrichtspraxis / Teaching German* 32.1 (1999): 22–31. Print.

Bousquet, Gilles. "A Model for Interdisciplinary Collaboration." *Modern Language Journal* 92.2 (2008): 304–06. Print.

Brockman, Stephen. "A Defense of European Languages." *Inside Higher Ed.* 15 May 2008. Web. 3 Aug 2008.

Byram, Michael. *From Foreign Language Education to Education for Intercultural Citizenship: Essays and Reflections.* Clevedon: Multilingual Matters, 2008. Print.

Byrnes, Heidi, and Hiram H. Maxim, eds. *Advanced Foreign Language Learning: A Challenge to College Programs.* Boston: Heinle, 2004. Print.

Byrnes, Heidi, and Katherine A. Sprang. "Fostering Advanced L2 Literacy: A Genre-Based, Cognitive Approach." Byrnes and Maxim 47–85.

Corral, Will H., and Daphne Patai. "An End to Foreign Language, an End to the Liberal Arts." Editorial. *Chronicle of Higher Education* 6 June 2008: A30. Print.

Eigler, Friederike. "Language and Content Articulation at the College Level: Designing a Third-Year German Course for a Content-Oriented, Task-Based Curriculum." *Die Unterrichtspraxis / Teaching German* 34.2 (2001): 107–18. Print.

Goldberg, David, and Elizabeth B. Welles. "Successful College and University Foreign Language Programs, 1995–99: Part 1." *Profession* (2001): 171–210. Print.

James, Dorothy. "Bypassing the Traditional Leadership: Who's Minding the Store?" *Profession* (1997): 41–53. Print.

Jones, Glen A., Patricia L. McCarney, and Michael L. Skolnik, eds. *Creating Knowledge, Strengthening Nations: The Changing Role of Higher Education.* Toronto: U of Toronto P, 2005. Print.

Kasper, Gabriele. "'A' Stands for Acquisition: A Response to Firth and Wagner." *Modern Language Journal* 81.3 (1997): 307–12. Print.

Katz, Stacey, and Johanna Watzinger-Tharp. "Toward an Understanding of the Role of Applied Linguistics in Foreign Language Departments." *Modern Language Journal* 89.4 (2005): 489–502. Print.

Lafford, Barbara A. "Second Language Acquisition Reconceptualized? The Impact of Firth and Wagner (1997)." *Modern Language Journal* 91.5 (2007): 735–56. Print.

Lally, Carolyn Gascoigne, ed. *Foreign Language Program Articulation: Current Practice and Future Prospects.* Westport: Bergin, 2001. Print.

Liskin-Gasparro, Judith E. "The ACTFL Proficiency Guidelines and the Oral Proficiency Interview: A Brief History and Analysis of their Survival." *Foreign Language Annals* 36.4 (2003): 483–90. Print.

Maxim, Hiram H. "Expanding Visions for Collegiate Advanced Foreign Language Learning." Byrnes and Maxim 178–93.

———. "Integrating Textual Thinking into the Introductory College-Level Foreign Language Classroom." *Modern Language Journal* 90.1 (2006): 19–32. Print.

Mittman, Elizabeth. "In Search of a Coherent Curriculum: Integrating the Third-Year Foreign Language Classroom." *Foreign Language Annals* 32.4 (1999): 480–93. Print.

MLA Ad Hoc Committee on Foreign Languages. "Foreign Languages and Higher Education: New Structures for a Changed World." *Profession* (2007): 234–45. Print.

Pfeiffer, Peter C. "The Discipline of Foreign Language Studies and Reforming Foreign Language Education." *Modern Language Journal* 92.2 (2008): 296–98. Print.

Phipps, Alison, and Michael Gonzales. *Modern Languages: Learning and Teaching in an Intercultural Field.* London: Sage, 2004. Print.

Pratt, Mary Louise, et al. "Transforming College and University Foreign Language Departments." *Modern Language Journal* 92.2 (2008): 287–92. Print.

Rankin, Jamie. "Easy Reader: A Case Study of Embedded Extensive Reading in Intermediate German L2." *Die Unterrichtspraxis / Teaching German* 38.2 (2005): 125–34. Print.

Suárez-Orozco, Marcelo, and Desiree B. Qin-Hilliard, eds. *Globalization: Culture and Education in the New Millennium.* Berkeley: U of California P, 2004. Print.

Trommler, Frank. "Is Literature Central to German Studies?" *German Quarterly* 80.1 (2007): 97–105. Print.

Wellmon, Chad. "Languages, Cultural Studies, and the Futures of Foreign Language Education." *Modern Language Journal* 92.2 (2008): 292–96. Print.

Zimmer-Loew, Helene, ed. *German Language Assessments: A Bibliography.* Cherry Hill: Amer. Assn. of Teachers of German, 2004. Print.

FORUM

OUTCOMES ASSESSMENT AND STANDARDIZATION: A QUEER CRITIQUE

Does it go without saying that queer is not standard? In Gerald Graff's *Profession 2007* essay on what Graff calls "our undemocratic curriculum," it does. Unfortunately, his failure to consider queer (and other) perspectives seriously impairs his argument, as when he mistakes merely "standard" experiences for universal truths. In short, he blames the "extraordinary diversity of texts, ideas, subjects, intellectual perspectives and approaches" now available on college campuses for the achievement gap between "the few who come to college with some already acquired academic socialization" and the "clueless" majority. He argues that this "mixed-message curriculum" functions "to conceal the secrets to academic success," when our mission should be "to make those secrets explicit" (129). In the interest of democratizing higher education, he thus champions transparency, standardization, and, as his Spring 2008 MLA President's Column elaborates, a program of outcomes-assessment measures ("Assessment").

There is much to admire in Graff's commitment to making higher education more democratic. Graff is right to remind us that physical access does not guarantee functional access and to insist that faculty members help all students, especially those most mystified by academic expectations, succeed. He is mistaken, however, in assuming that access to a culture of argumentation constitutes a singularly critical measure of democracy (and in overestimating the extent to which rhetorical proficiency—as opposed to, say, money and power—wins access to the forums in which influential arguments take place). Moreover, if democracy is the goal, he is dangerously misguided in advocating a program of prescribed objectives, quantified outcomes, standardization, transparency, and what passes for public accountability.

When Graff suggests that standardization "might not mean a bad curriculum but a transparent one" (134), he takes the value of transparency to be self-evident, uniform, and universal—that is, transparent. For teachers of queer studies, however, it is not clear that greater transparency about what transpires in the classroom would always "work in our favor." Graff's admonition that transparency must work for us, "if we have nothing to hide," is insulting ("Assessment" 3). As Michael Warner points out, clear expression of an idea, even a good one, does not mean that everyone will like it, as people who have ever been queer-bashed, or careful, or simply strategic in choosing their battles are aware. Graff claims that "outcomes assessment deprivatizes teaching" (3). But teaching is not private in the first place. Classroom speech does not directly address the general public, nor should it, but it is nonetheless a public activity performed by people inhabiting public roles—as any administrator will be quick to remind an instructor who forgets. Graff, however, advances his argument on the basis of the misleading simplification that outside private there is only one public and that this public is the mainstream one of "democratic citizenship" typified by "parents and legislators" (3–4). He reduces a variety of rhetorical contexts to the single distinction of public/private and all possible publics to a generic general public. By this reductive logic, speech that intentionally limits the scope of its address, speech that is subcultural, specialized, or in any way specific in its orientation, can only be seen as secret, elitist, or ashamed.

My students are not the general public; they are people who have signed up to take a queer theory class. I'm sure I've said things in the classroom that might sound odd out of context, but the point is that I didn't say them out of context—I said them *there*, where my rhetorical choices made sense to a group engaged in a common endeavor undertaken in relation to an extensive archive of conversations, texts, and experiences we already shared. By the time we discuss pederasty, fisting, or anal penetration, we have built a context in which these topics are proper to our intellectual project. Graff, however, concurs with David Bartholomae's claim that because faculty members "articulate . . . what it is we value in intellectual work . . . routinely for our students," it "should not be difficult to find the language we need to speak to parents and legislators" ("Assessment" 4). I disagree. What we say to the general public cannot draw on the shared points of reference built up over the course of a semester or more; thus it will be less well suited to convey the complex, challenging, or unfamiliar concepts that are the substance of academic courses. The effort will require not less nuance but more—not because we have something to hide but because we are doing the work for which universities are intended. Advanced education is supposed to advance knowledge, not mirror its current limitations.

That Graff's advocacy of transparency and standardization is bound up with a commitment to outcomes assessment is not surprising: the principle of standardization, however broadly or narrowly applied, is not incidental but integral to the logic of outcomes assessment, as is the related promise of predictability. The transparency associated with predetermined outcomes is presumed to benefit students by providing a set of known quantities from which they can choose. Therefore the products must be standardized: each class in Victorian literature should be the same as every other, no matter who's teaching it or what semester someone takes it in—just as a quarter-pounder is the same in SoHo as in Seattle and a can of Pepsi or a box of Tide is the same in whatever supermarket you patronize. There's a problem with this paradigm: knowledge is not soda pop. The logic of outcomes assessment requires that objectives be standardized and results predictable. But standardization and predictability are not a great foundation for the project of creating new knowledge, nor are they culturally queer values. And for the same reason: they are values that propagate more of the same; they support and sustain the status quo.

If it seems a stretch to compare education to consumer products, consider Graff's claim that "it is no more possible to democratize education without standardization than it would be to democratize affordable clothing, food, transportation, health care, and entertainment without standardization and mass production" ("Our Undemocratic Curriculum" 134). With public funding on the wane, "affordable" would appear the operative word: mass production of instruction saves money. However, it has its costs: the conception of knowledge as already known, prepackaged content subject to delivery by any variety of means is both the condition and the effect of a system in which something called teaching is increasingly accomplished by a disenfranchised cohort of deskilled and deregulated workers rather than by tenured faculty members. In this model, knowledge is not created in the classroom, only at best transmitted there. Meanwhile, the student who encounters something advertised as higher education primarily in the form of taped lectures and podcasts, so-called tutoring services that teach to the test, bundled courseware, and Triple A Notes is conditioned through that experience to see knowledge as an inert commodity and to conceive of education as a process of commodity acquisition, whether it arrives in the form of information, skills, credentials, or cultural capital. Queer possibilities—the idea that the unforeseen might be valuable, for example, or that idiosyncrasy itself might be a virtue—are completely foreclosed.

My gripe with Graff is certainly not that he seeks to make academic success accessible to every student or even—entirely—that he asserts without evidence that a standardized curriculum will accomplish this end. What concerns me are his zeal for outing and then standardizing such secrets and the disregard for difference that informs his whole argument. Graff assumes that the keys to academic success will or should be the same for every discipline and every student and that the basic objectives of higher education will and should be the same in every instance—even though different people bring different needs, values, and purposes to the institution. He assumes that access to a reductive argument culture everywhere and always trumps access to any counterpublic or subculture, though these may offer life-changing and even life-saving ways of thinking and being in the world. He invokes the general public as the appropriate arbiter of academic standards, effectively chaining diverse field-specific judgments to the unitary yoke of popular opinion. He maintains that curricula must be organized to minimize "disjunction" and "contradiction" ("Assessment" 3) and calls this democratic.

Tellingly, Graff defines education as "internalizing the norms of the intellectual community" (3). He also claims that "improving education—and closing the achievement gap—will not be possible until academic institutions get as good at pedagogical simplification as we are at proliferating multiplicity and complication." But simplification has its drawbacks, as his conclusion to this line of argument makes clear: "We cannot make the curriculum more *transparent—that is, more democratic*—until we are willing to be reductive about how academics is played, and this means getting over our protective queasiness about totalizing self-characterizations" ("Our Undemocratic Curriculum" 131; my emphasis). Only a willingness to be reductive could allow this conflation of democracy with transparency— and then subsume both within a normative logic that holds assimilation to be education's highest purpose. It is not elitism that induces queasiness at this point but the ease with which the MLA president arrogates my position, my perspective, my purposes, and those of everyone else with a stake in higher education, to the homogenizing presumption of his self-characterization. It does make me feel queer.

The position Graff assumes at such moments seems possible only for someone who experiences no disjuncture between the public and himself, someone whose private life is fundamentally of a piece with public sentiment and popular opinion. But this is not the case for all our students. It is a position predicated on a sadly enfeebled idea of democracy, here reduced to the formal (but not actual) inclusion of recognized citizens in a closed and self-perpetuating system. A queerer, more open understanding of the democratic project might, in contrast, encompass the extension, expansion, and continual reinvention of currently extant possibilities. It might invite and elaborate practices conducive precisely to "proliferating [the] multiplicity and complication" that Graff derides, because it would recognize what he calls "confusion" to be the condition, ends, and means of a more radically democratic commitment.

Graff is right, nonetheless, that some contexts call for reductive simplification, so I'll give it a shot. If there is a secret to academic life, it is this queer one: intellectual inquiry leads to unexpected places. Outcomes assessment asserts the opposite. Built on prescription and predictability; quantification and comparison; standardization, transparency, and a reductive notion of democratic publics, outcomes assessment offers control and containment in place of open-ended exploration. It conditions students to accept the acquisition of discrete skills and pieces of information in place of genuine intellectual engagement. It relies on anti-queer, anti-intellectual presumptions and procedures to deny students the true key to the academic kingdom: the secret that our future is unknown, that research will reveal surprises, that difference offers a safeguard against narrow-mindedness, that incoherence is a condition of possibility, and that knowledge is neither finite nor fixed. In all these ways, and despite all Graff's good intentions, outcomes assessment and standardization make higher education not more democratic but less.

Kim Emery
University of Florida

WORKS CITED

Graff, Gerald. "Assessment Changes Everything." *MLA Newsletter* 40.1 (2008): 3–4. Print.

———. *Clueless in Academe*. New Haven: Yale UP, 2003. Print.

———. "Our Undemocratic Curriculum." *Profession* (2007): 128–35. Print.

Warner, Michael. *Publics and Counterpublics*. New York: Zone, 2002. Print.

Reply:

1. Contrary to Kim Emery, I don't "blame" the educational achievement gap on "the 'extraordinary diversity of texts, ideas, subjects, intellectual perspectives and approaches' now available on college campuses." In the

essay she quotes, I *defend* this curricular diversity as decidedly "rich" ("Our Undemocratic Curriculum" 129), just as I've defended it against critics for decades as a sign of "the vast superiority of today's university" relative to that of the 1950s (*Beyond the Culture Wars* 4). What I do blame is the failure to *connect* the elements of this admirably diverse curriculum and to give students enough help in making sense of it.

2. Emery turns my qualified defense of educational standardization into the absurd view that "each class in Victorian literature should be the same as every other," like McDonald's quarter-pounders. She also misrepresents me as a supporter of No Child Left Behind–style standardized testing, ignoring my plea to distinguish "between good and bad forms of standardization" and my reference to NCLB tests as examples of a bad form (134).

3. Emery accuses me of overestimating "the extent to which rhetorical proficiency—as opposed to, say, money and power—wins access to the forums in which influential arguments take place." There's no disputing that money and power often get you into those forums, but for those who don't have either, rhetorical proficiency is critical.

4. This in fact is why I stress the need to teach the standard conventions of persuasive argument, a practice that Emery disastrously confuses with supporting the social status quo. Since this confusion is still common, a closer look at Emery's logic is in order.

I do argue, as Emery puts it, that "access to a culture of argumentation constitutes a singularly critical measure" of democratic education and that education involves "internalizing the norms of the intellectual community." But I dispute Emery's assumption that privileging a common "argument culture" means rejecting difference, diversity, "complex, challenging, or unfamiliar concepts," and "a queerer, more open understanding of the democratic project."

On the contrary, far from repressing difference, the norms of argumentation Emery attacks enable difference to emerge and to be perceived *as difference*. This presumably explains why Emery herself operates within these shared norms in her own response: she summarizes views she disagrees with, draws out the logical implications of assumptions, adduces evidence for her claims, and makes other conventional moves.

I concede Emery's point that I do sometimes write as if "the public" is a unitary entity, when in fact, as she rightly says, it contains "counterpublic[s] or subculture[s]." Again, however, Emery can make this point only within a common metalanguage that enables her to compare divergent subcultural perspectives with dominant ones. Again her argument depends as much as mine on a shared discourse as "the appropriate arbiter of academic standards."

In all this, Emery unwittingly illustrates the double bind that Donald Davidson has pointed out in a classic critique of theorists of radical difference like Benjamin Lee Whorf, T. S. Kuhn, and others. Davidson argues that difference already presupposes commonality, or, in his words, "different points of view make sense . . . only if there is a common co-ordinate system on which to plot them." Thus "Whorf, wanting to demonstrate that Hopi incorporates a metaphysics so alien to ours that Hopi and English cannot, as he puts it, 'be calibrated,' uses English to convey the contents of sample Hopi sentences. Kuhn is brilliant at saying what things were like before the revolution using—what else?—our post-revolutionary idiom" (184).

Though Emery believes that the current nonstandard use of *queer* somehow refutes me, it actually illustrates my point that otherness can become intelligible only within what Davidson calls a "common co-ordinate system," which enables the traditional normative meaning of the word to be compared with the subversive one. A struggle currently rages between standard and transgressive usages of *queer*, but this struggle is played out within a shared argument culture even as it stretches that culture's boundaries by opening up new possibilities of what can be said and heard in it. The point is that shared argumentative norms are not a unitary, static monolith that stifles change but are preconditions of change.

It follows that you can't challenge "the norms of the intellectual community" effectively if you haven't learned those norms. This in turn means that socializing students into the public argument culture is not in conflict with helping them become effective critics of that culture but a precondition of it. As Elaine Maimon observes, "Those who would keep students ignorant of the academic landscape in the name of helping them find their own rebellious voices do not understand much about guerilla warfare" (viii). Emery doesn't urge that we "keep students ignorant" of the "norms of the intellectual community," but her linking of those norms with retrograde politics suggests she sees no great need to offer students the kinds of rhetorical power that she herself takes for granted.

Gerald Graff
University of Illinois, Chicago

WORKS CITED

Davidson, Donald. "On the Very Idea of a Conceptual Scheme." *Inquiries into Truth and Interpretation.* Oxford: Clarendon, 1984. 183–98. Print.

Graff, Gerald. *Beyond the Culture Wars: How Teaching the Conflicts Can Revitalize American Education.* New York: Norton, 1992. Print.

———. "Our Undemocratic Curriculum." *Profession* (2007): 128–35. Print.

Maimon, Elaine. Preface. *Writing across the Curriculum: A Guide to Developing Programs.* Ed. Susan H. McLeod and Margot Soven. Newbury Park: Sage, 1992. vii–x. Print.

Cultural Studies and the Dual Requirement of Reading

I am writing with regard to Jane Gallop's paper "The Historicization of Literary Studies and the Fate of Close Reading," published in *Profession 2007.* Gallop premises her bleak outlook on literary studies on a conversation with a job candidate in English a few years back. The candidate's remark on the necessity of archival work in order to get published struck Gallop as an ominous sign for the field's future. When I was entering the job market in French studies, around the same time, I was just as troubled by a question raised in roughly a third of my MLA interviews: What is your view on the teaching of literature and history? Without hesitation, I replied that for me the two were linked; knowledge of a particular historical period could only enrich one's understanding of that period's literary and artistic expression, and vice versa. At the time I suspected that these interviewers were looking to hire a literary specialist, and I knew that my answer betrayed my cultural studies slant. Gallop's paper confirms my suspicion, but it also points to a likely reason behind the question: that cultural studies has drawn literary specialists away from close reading in favor of literary history, making them "amateur" or "second-rate" cultural historians (183, 184).

In the light of Gallop's paper, I would now answer the interviewers' question thus: Close reading is a fundamental practice in my French studies classes. Before calling on my students to analyze a written work or film for its cultural significance or aesthetics, I have them analyze a passage or scene closely. I direct them to consider various elements, including language and voice, setting and narrative detail, the use of cross-cutting and time—in all, the different ways in which an author establishes a theme or characterization, entices the reader to enter the text, or repels the reader. I believe that Gallop and I are in agreement on these fundamental analytic skills in literary studies, and I share her view that "close reading may in fact be the best antidote we have to the timeless and the universal" (185). Close readings draw out the complexities of a text, and regular practice teaches students to read and to become independent critical thinkers.

I saw two general themes running through Gallop's arguments: the arbitrariness of labeling practices in the academy and a reductionist tendency in cultural studies. To these two valid points I reply as a cultural studies practitioner.

In my research—on French literature published in the 1930s and 1940s, Holocaust literature, and other subjects—I have felt compelled to develop both the skills of a historian and those of a literary specialist. Indeed, in highly contested historical junctures such as the Second World War, the distinction between narrative and history is obscured. Particularly in French studies, the century-old heritage of France's *intellectuels* clearly problematizes the distinction between a story and history. Jean-Paul Sartre's stand on the responsibility of authors to engage in their immediate political circumstances asserts that writers and artists are social beings whose influence on the public is inherent to their situation and must weigh into their choices, which have historical ramifications. As the 1945 trial and execution of the French journalist and author Robert Brasillach suggest, words can be equated with actions. Poetic license was revocable in the climate of France's liberation and the purge.[1] The history of the French state's collaboration with the Nazi regime and the intelligentsia's compliance, to varying degrees, with the cultural policy of the new order generated an intense debate over the culpability of practicing writers and artists of the period. This debate over the historical and, more specifically, political role of artists and their works continues today, not least of all in cultural studies.

However, I do not see myself as a historian. It is only one role of cultural studies to aid in the recovery of the personal story and to subject it to critical examination for its historical value. Another task of cultural studies practitioners is the study of representation, which requires close reading. For example, in my recent investigation into author Jean Giono's alleged collaborationism, I found myself forced to look at his 1943 collection of short stories and essays, *L'eau vive*, in order to analyze his position on certain points raised by other critics. How could one explain, for instance, Giono's reference to Adolf Hitler as a "poet in action" in a late-1941 interview, when Giono's active condemnation of Nazism in the years preceding the war only indicated his reprobation?[2] His Occupation diary (1943–44) does not offer clarification, nor do other known comments made by the author during that period. Instead of speculating as to Giono's meaning or choosing among vying interpretations, I looked to the enlightening words Giono wrote between 23 and 28 August 1942, as he composed his short story "Le poète de la famille" ("The Poet of the Family"), which does not support the claim that he admired Hitler. Rather, it reflects his distaste for poetry in action, whose senseless complicity with violence only contributes to the human cataclysm of evil's overpowering good.[3] That he could not withdraw from the cultural scene at a time when no clear choices were to be made only underscores the historical import intrinsic to literature.

This example highlights not only the risks of taking the historical record too literally but also the importance of close reading. My study of Giono's Occupation writing was a hybrid process: a thorough examination of archival documents available to me and a close reading of the author's literary works, especially those that seemed to engage history metaphorically. Yet I do not consider myself a cultural historian. Although my research into French politics has led me to publish on the recent phenomenon of Nicolas Sarkozy's election to the French presidency, I do so as a scholar of French studies. This research serves as a foundation for my literary analysis, since literary works to varying degrees collide or coalesce with the politics of their day.

In the field of artistic and cultural criticism, a number of cultural researchers have dedicated their careers to the task of playing watchdog. This approach has not been without merit. I do share Gallop's reluctance regarding the practice of "understanding literature in a generally cultural and especially political context" (183). What causes me to pause, in particular, is the agility with which some critics imprison one's speech acts in the bonds of another's ideology. I am referring to the risk of excessive, may I say, French-style intellectualism, which can lead to imprudent polemics.[4] Since the Nazi era, charges of literary fascism and ideological collaborationism have labeled artists suspected of complicity with censured political visions. If words are equated with actions, a thorough inquiry into all the available evidence must include the examination of an author's literary production. But it is my position that the interdisciplinary approach of cultural studies is justified only to the degree that it ensures ethical propriety. Cultural studies opened up new research possibilities by its embrace of textuality or, in other words, by its study of the nature of representation in all narrative forms. Yet the cultural study of literary and cinematographic texts is worthy only inasmuch as it remains close to these texts.

In short, cultural studies practitioners must proceed cautiously, avoiding excessive polemics and reductive labels. The terms *Nazi* and *fascist*, for instance, raise a whole series of questions and issues and require historical rigor. This need for caution should come as no surprise to those in cultural studies. The question of labeling is inherently linked to the problematic of identity and otherness, and the relations between self and other are the stuff of cultural studies. This process of labeling has also come under scrutiny as part of the politics of otherness, because it attacks the individual specificity of those it claims to represent. Close examination of the process has shown that boundaries one may valiantly assume—in defense of a cause or in search of a new territory to claim—can prove constricting when they obstruct personal goals or universal, egalitarian goals.

We in cultural studies must be wary of our own labeling tendencies and of political causes that can take precedence over the work of evaluating the unique artistry or sociohistorical aesthetic of a work. Stuart Hall defines the unique contribution of cultural studies in the following way: "[Cultural studies] has to analyse certain things about the constitutive and political nature of representation itself, about its complexities, about the effects of language, about textuality as a site of life and death" (273). Yet, he goes on to say, "I do think there is all the difference in the world between understanding the politics of intellectual work and substituting intellectual work for politics" (275). Clearly, cultural studies should continue to strive to make the academy all-inclusive while at the same time upholding the highest academic standards, both historical integrity and literary perspicacity.

Meaghan Emery
University of Vermont

NOTES

1. Brasillach's written denunciations were judged treasonous and incurred the highest penalty under French law. His inflammatory anti-Semitic discourse, as Alice Kaplan states, could have come under indictment only following the Nuremberg trials, which introduced into legal writ a new punishable offense, crimes against humanity. This legal precedent brought anti-Semitism and racial hate crimes under the state's jurisdiction.

2. Portions of Giono's interview were cited in Alfred Fabre-Luce's 1942 *Journal de la France* (195), and this excerpt is frequently used to indicate Giono's collaborationist bent. See, for instance, Golsan.

3. Giono's self-projection in the story as the observing son rather than the active poet, who is based on his cousin Ludovic Fiorio, further suggests Giono's withdrawal from the vain enterprise of literary engagement.

4. Tony Judt likewise discusses the lack of expertise among French cold-war intellectuals, who, because of their stature, were granted the authority to speak on all matters.

WORKS CITED

Fabre-Luce, Alfred. *Journal de la France*. Vol. 2. Paris: JEP, 1942. Print.

Gallop, Jane. "The Historicization of Literary Studies and the Fate of Close Reading." *Profession* (2007): 181–86. Print.

Giono, Jean. *L'eau vive. Œuvres romanesques complètes*. Ed. Robert Ricatte. Vol. 3. Paris: Gallimard, 1971. 79–452. Print.

Golsan, Richard J. "Myths of Apocalypse and Renewal: Jean Giono and 'Literary' Collaboration." *Substance* 87 (1998): 17–35. Print.

Hall, Stuart. "Cultural Studies and Its Theoretical Legacies." *Stuart Hall: Critical Dialogues in Cultural Studies*. Ed. David Morley and Kuan-Hsing Chen. London: Routledge, 1996. 262–75. Print.

Judt, Tony. *Past Imperfect: French Intellectuals, 1944–1956*. Berkeley: U of California P, 1992. Print.

Kaplan, Alice. *The Collaborator: The Trial and Execution of Robert Brasillach*. Chicago: U of Chicago P, 2000. Print.

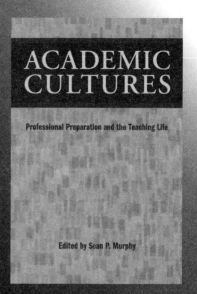

A New Edition of the Leading Research Guide in Literary Studies

Literary Research Guide

An Annotated Listing of Reference Sources in English Literary Studies 5th edition

James L. Harner

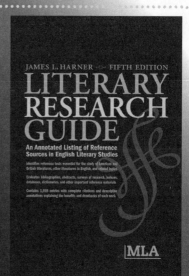

JAMES L. HARNER — FIFTH EDITION

LITERARY RESEARCH GUIDE

An Annotated Listing of Reference Sources in English Literary Studies

Identifies reference tools essential for the study of American and British literatures, other literatures in English, and related topics

Evaluates bibliographies, abstracts, surveys of research, indexes, databases, dictionaries, and other important reference materials

Contains 1,059 entries with complete citations and descriptive annotations explaining the benefits and drawbacks of each work

MLA

J ames L. Harner's *Literary Research Guide*, which *Choice* calls "the standard guide in the field," evaluates important reference materials in English studies. In the new edition Harner has revised nearly half the entries from the fourth edition. There are substantially more electronic resources, particularly reliable sites sponsored by academic institutions and learned societies, including bibliographic databases, text archives, and other online resources. This edition also features a new section on cultural studies.

The annotations for each work
- describe its type, its scope, its major limitations, and its organization
- present parts of a typical entry
- list the type and number of indexes
- evaluate coverage, organization, and accuracy
- explain its uses in research
- cite significant reviews that more fully define the importance or uses of the work or its place in the scholarly tradition
- note related works, including supplementary, complementary, or super-seded ones not accorded separate entries in the *Guide*

The *Guide* concludes with name, title, and subject indexes.

Modern Language Association

MLA

26 Broadway, 3rd floor ▪ New York, NY ▪ 10004-1789
646 576-5161 ▪ (fax) 646 576-5160 ▪ www.mla.org

Recently published

2008. xviii & 826 pp.
Paper ISBN 978-0-87352-808-5
$37.50 (MLA members $30.00)

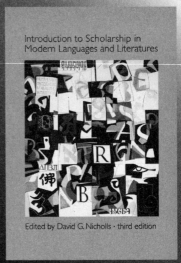